Education and Society

Education and Society

Issues and Explanations in the Sociology of Education

Rob Moore

polity

The right of Rob Moore to be identified as Author of this Work has been asserted in accordance with the UK Copyright, Designs and Patents Act 1988.

First published in 2004 by Polity Press

Polity Press
65 Bridge Street
Cambridge CB2 1UR, UK.

Polity Press
350 Main Street
Malden, MA 02148, USA

ISBN: 0-7456-1708-5
ISBN: 0-7456-1709-3 (pb)

A catalogue record for this book is available from the British Library and has been applied for from the Library of Congress.

Typeset in 10 on 11 pt Sabon
by TechBooks, India
Printed and bound in Great Britain by MPG Books Ltd, Bodmin, Carnwall.

For further information on Polity, visit our website: www.polity.co.uk

With all my love to my wife
Sue Marritt and our daughter Matilda

Contents

Introduction

This book provides an introduction to the sociology of education by focusing upon *issues and explanations*: the things that need explaining and the ways in which they have been explained. In this respect, it adopts perhaps a rather unconventional approach. Its perspective is not straightforwardly historical in the sense of reporting the progression of concerns and approaches as they emerged and succeeded each other; nor is it formally organized around theoretical perspectives. However, it does have a historical sense in that it attempts to present thought in this area in *depth*. It deals with the founding thinkers of sociology in some detail, and tracks backwards and forwards across the field over the past fifty years. It is concerned with the ways in which approaches are conceived of as *being* theoretical, as well as with how different perspectives approach particular issues. Here, there are concerns of different kinds: first, what is entailed in defining an *issue*, and secondly, what is entailed in *explaining* that state of affairs in any particular way. The first has to do with *how* the world is seen to be, and the second with how the world would *have to be* if a particular explanation is to be convincing. If, for instance, education is held to serve the interests of 'capitalism', or 'industrialism', or 'patriarchy', what kinds of things would have to be happening in the world for this to be possible? Is such a world recognizably *our* world? How much, and how convincingly, do explanations account for what we know to be the case? The basic question is, 'How does it work?'

The book does not claim to be a systematically *comprehensive* survey of the sociology of education (though I think it does cover the *key* areas). Bits are missing. This reflects the limits of my knowledge, interests and competence. It is also biased in the sense that it contains the thread of an argument about education and the sociology of education. It is *for* some things and *against* others. Central to this is a view about *knowledge*. The book is a defence of knowledge as the basis for the intelligibility and integrity of education and of the sociology of education as knowledge *about* education. It is for this reason that the final chapter gives considerable attention to fundamental epistemological issues. Although there may be some bits missing in this review, other bits have been added. The book refers to issues about education raised in the areas of stratification and mobility studies, for instance. In an earlier period, sociology of education was strongly aligned with that central programme in sociology. Thirty or so years ago they parted company (at least in the UK). I believe it is time to pay more attention to what is going on elsewhere in sociology that is relevant to education, but that *the* sociology of education is tending to neglect. Also, the final chapter draws extensively upon epistemology and the philosophy of science. These debates, I believe, have a crucial contribution to make to a central area of concern: that of knowledge itself and how it is produced. Such arguments are important because they provide the basis for a *critical realist* counterpoint to constructionism and postmodernism as the major alternatives to positivism – an increasingly sterile opposition that has structured thinking in the field for more than thirty years.

The first chapter begins with the school and educational processes. It reviews the issues associated with educational differentiation, social opportunities and social inequalities. The issues of class, gender, ethnicity and race present a complex and contradictory set of problems for explanatory approaches that take educational processes as their focus. The chapter examines such approaches and concludes that the factors they deal with, processes *internal* to education, are not in themselves sufficient to account for the systematic qualities of educational and social differentiation and the ways in which they change or *fail* to change over time. It focuses upon the striking contrast between the historical stability of class differentials and how gender differences in education underwent a radical change in the last part of the twentieth century. The key issue is the implications of these two facts, the one for the other, and the possibility of explaining *both* within a theoretically consistent, unitary framework – should this be considered possible or desirable.

The next two chapters examine the macro and historical contexts of education by considering economy and class, and state formation and status, in turn. The second chapter notes that neither of the two great rival systems in this areas, Marxist and liberal approaches, can adequately account for the observed facts. As with educational reform and class differentials, so a comparison of education systems reveals that the kinds of things expected to make differences often do not. Societies can vary significantly in educational terms, but remain very similar in terms of mobility rates and economic productivity. Against stereotypical expectations, in comparative terms the earlier English small selective system of higher education stands out for its meritocratic character rather than for its exclusiveness. What kinds of differences do different differences make? The third chapter turns to state formation and nation building. It looks at the distribution of different *types* of education and the way in which one particular form, an education for 'cultivation' associated with the formation of a distinctive *habitus*, serves in itself as a basis for group formation and social stratification. From this point of view, differences *within* classes might, in certain respects, be more significant than those between them.

The first three chapters are concerned with approaches to key areas that all add significant contributions to our understanding, but no one of which can adequately account for all that we know. How might these understandings of educational processes, economy and state, class and status, be brought together in a complementary manner? Chapter 4 returns to the education system and the school, but now located within the evolving structural dynamic of the forces reviewed in the previous chapters. It brings into play those approaches that focus upon schools and pupils *themselves* as active players in the game: the positions and strategies they adopt in the school under the particular conditions in which they and their families find themselves. The structural dynamic models reviewed in this chapter might well provide a framework within which synthesizing accounts could be produced. This requires an examination of theoretical underpinnings and assumptions in explanatory approaches in the sociology of education.

The final two chapters share a concern with deeper theoretical and epistemological issues. Chapter 5 returns to Durkheim, the founding father of the sociology of education. It offers an account of his thinking in terms of the *centrality* of education to his system and one that might also suggest why he should still be placed at the centre of the sociology of education. Central to this is the role that the concept (if not the term) *habitus* plays in Durkheim's thinking about education within the broader framework of his sociologizing of Kant. This presentation also provides a basis for an exposition of the theory of Basil Bernstein, his intellectual successor. The presentation of Bernstein's work attempts to depict what is distinctive about it and the ways in which it stands out within the field. The treatment of these two thinkers raises fundamental questions about how sociology of education is constituted as an intellectual field and about its modes of theoretical inquiry and knowledge production.

The final chapter extends these concerns by focusing upon the question 'What should we teach?' Its interest is not in the curriculum itself as much as in the deeper issues raised by the recognition that knowledge is socially produced – education is crucially the site of the *production* of knowledge as well as its reproduction. The chapter steps back through the sociology of knowledge into epistemology and the philosophy of science in order to explore the ways in which a *critical realist* approach to the social character of knowledge might provide new ways of approaching the old, sterile conflicts between positivism and constructionism and between traditionalism and progressivism.

The book *does* contain within it an *argument* – it takes a position. But it aims in the first instance at an exposition that gives the reader a good sense of the terrain covered by the sociology of education. It aspires above all to be clear and accessible. The examples and references selected have been chosen in the hope that they will be available in most university libraries and clear to readers without a substantial familiarity with the field. Some are there because they are foundational texts, others as exemplars of particular positions, and some because they provide reviews and overviews of the issues under consideration.

To teach, research in, and write about the 'sociology of education' is peculiar in that anyone doing it has *been taught* and *teaches* about being taught, *investigates* teaching and being taught, and, in part, teaches what they themselves *discover* about teaching and being taught! For someone such as myself there is a further complication, in that I spent a fairly long period as a school teacher (a short time in primary and longer in secondary schools as a social education teacher in Inner London), have some experience in Further Education (on Youth Training Scheme courses, for instance), while for some of the time studying sociology of education at Master's and Ph.D. level. I have been (on occasions at one and the same time) the investigated and the investigator (and have reflexively investigated myself!). I meandered from the C stream of my primary school, through a boys' secondary modern school in south-east London, the sixth form of a local grammar school, a London Polytechnic, London University and am now in the Faculty of Education at Cambridge University. I am a teacher, have taught teachers, and many of my current students intend becoming teachers. I put my acknowledgements here because in another way they recapitulate the themes of this book through my own experience in education as pupil, student, teacher and scholar and the many debts acquired on the way.

Acknowledgements

To begin at the beginning: no one forgets a good teacher, and I want to thank Terry Neal my form-master and English teacher at Fossdene Road Secondary Modern School for Boys in Charlton, south-east London – I would not be in the position to write this book were it not for his early encouragement, and having been in the teaching trade for so long myself, I appreciate what he and his colleagues did. Ian Hextall and the late Madan Sarup at Goldsmiths College kept my momentum going in the first part of the 1970s when I was school teaching and also working for the London University Academic Diploma and M.A. (Ed). With Ian I went on to work for my Ph.D., and I owe much to his supervision (much that is included in this book comes from that time). My good friends and colleagues in the sociology team in the Cambridge University Faculty of Education and in Homerton College have provided the very best stimulation and support: thanks to John Ahier (now with the Open University) and to Madeleine Arnot and especially to John Beck who has patiently and unselfishly read each chapter as it emerged and provided me with the benefit of his intellectual clarity and scholarship as well as with instructions as to the proper use of the semicolon. Thanks also to Lynn Jones. I first met Basil Bernstein in 1966 as a sociology undergraduate at Borough Polytechnic (today South Bank University). He remained until his death unstinting in his encouragement, support and intellectual generosity. He was an inspired teacher and mentor, and my debt to him is incalculable. By a strange twist of fate my great good friend Mike Hickox and I (we grew up 'round the corner' from each other in south-east London) started at the same time in the sociology department at Borough Polytechnic – he as my lecturer, me as his student. On a number of occasions since then we have written together. He has provided me from the outset with a model of scholarly integrity and inspirational teaching. Thanks Mike, for everything. Many people have offered encouragement and advice along the way towards the completion of this book: Joe Muller, Parlo Singh, Michael Young, Jonathan Perlmutter, Fazal Ibrahim Ali. My doctoral student Karl Maton was producing his dissertation at the same time as I was writing this book, and we enjoyed the very best of intellectual exchanges in refining our ideas together. I benefited considerably from the advice provided by three anonymous Polity readers: many thanks. Education starts early and lasts long – my parents provided the bedrock: thanks and love to you both.

1

Differentiation, Inequality and the Educational Process

Introduction

The relationship between educational and social inequalities and opportunities is one of the most fundamental issues in the sociology of education, uniting its core theoretical concerns and research interests and its broader uses in public debate and policy making. But education is not simple. It is doing different things in different ways for different groups, and is influenced by a diversity of forces. Inevitably, many of these will be contradictory: e.g. the demand that education promote equality of opportunity may conflict (for some) with the need to preserve standards of academic excellence, or the value placed by liberal educators on developing the 'whole person' with the demand by others that education meet the needs of the economy. This chapter explores a set of problems associated with educational and social differentiation and the various ways in which they have been accounted for across a range of perspectives. The focus is upon factors associated with the education system itself and with educational processes.

There are obvious reasons why sociologists, educators, policy-makers and others should see these things as being of primary concern – it is within schools that the work of education gets done. How we organize the school system determines not only the quality of children's educational lives, but also influences those broader objectives sought through education. Another reason why educational structures and processes are given primacy is that they are open to direct intervention by policy-makers and educationalists. It is harder to affect external relations and factors such as those between education and the labour market or family. However, the conclusion reached in this chapter is that the explanatory scope of school-related factors alone is limited, and that they need to be located within a wider social framework if we are to understand more fully how education works within society. But this carries the possibility that educational change *in itself* might have only limited effect.

Issues of differentiation have become increasingly complex as a result of the multiplication of social differences taken into account with the introduction of gender and ethnicity alongside class. This is associated with a proliferation of explanatory approaches – in the contributions of feminism, for instance (Measor and Sikes 1997). Hence, it is necessary to look at *what* needs explaining and *how* within a variety of approaches applied to different facets of educational and social differentiation. This complexity has been further complicated by post-modern approaches that reject broad categories such as class and gender in favour of more nuanced and multidimensional models of self, identity and difference (Bradley 1996). The purpose of this chapter is to review the complex range of explanatory issues faced by the sociology of education and its various perspectives.

The Problems to be Explained

Historically, sociology of education and educational policy have addressed the differences between *classes*, the *sexes* and *ethnic groups*. As Halsey says, 'Class, gender and ethnicity are now the three giants in the path of aspirations towards equity' (1997: 638). Education is treated as the principle means of creating a more equal society (for some this means equality of opportunity to become unequal, but for others it is achieving greater equity in outcomes). The ideal is that social rewards should be distributed on the basis of merit rather than inherited, and undeserved, social advantages and disadvantages. Class, gender and ethnic inequalities are treated as the obstacles that education has to tackle in order to achieve justice in the distribution of opportunities and rewards. Equality of opportunity in education is seen to be the means of achieving equality in society. However, education itself is also seen by 'critical' theorists as being implicated in the reproduction of social inequalities. Consequently, much of the work of sociology of education has been concerned with identifying such obstructive factors and suggesting progressive alternatives.

To illustrate the issues here, Collins et al. present the view that

> children from different backgrounds achieve different outcomes from
> school *because they do not, in fact, receive the same schooling*... In general,
> they receive a form of schooling that steers them towards the backgrounds
> they come from – be they socio-economically advantaged or disadvantaged.
> Again, while the paths they take may be construed as a matter of choice,
> the systematic dimensions of the outcome point to the strong probability
> that other factors are at work. (C. Collins et al. 2000: 135)

This contains the basic elements and assumptions that tend to underpin approaches to the analysis of schooling and differentiation.

1   Differential educational outcomes are defined in terms of socio-economic *advantages and disadvantages* between groups.
2   There is a judgement concerning the *existential status* of the choices that pupils make relative to these outcomes: for some they are a matter of choice, but for others the result of factors acting upon them.
3   It is suggested that these outcomes are *actively constructed* by different forms of schooling.
4   Consequently, there is an assumption concerning the *effectivity* of educational processes associated with these different forms of schooling ('effectivity' refers to the range of effects a thing has the capacity to produce by virtue of its being the kind of thing it is regardless of which ones actually are produced or how effective they are in any particular circumstance).
5   Then, finally, there is the implicit possibility that changing the forms of schooling will change their effects and, consequently, the outcomes.

There are a number of complex issues associated with each of these propositions and assumptions.

Differences and inequalities, problems and explanations

Although the phenomenon of social differentiation is fundamental to the sociology of education, the notion of 'difference' is not straightforward, and it is necessary to distinguish between various senses of the term. In the first, and, perhaps, most obvious sense, difference can be taken as referring to systematic *mean* differences in outcomes for social groups. However, the term 'difference' has another sense within post-modernist discourse. Here it has to do with the constitutive features of identities and the subjectivities of self, membership and heritage. Underpinning this sense of 'difference' are post-structuralist and deconstructionist semiotic theories of meaning (S. Mills 1997) in which the sense of self is given relationally through contrasts with all those *others* who I am not (e.g. 'maleness' is understood as being *not* female: female is Other). In a general manner, the difference between these two notions of difference is that whereas the first is defined by 'objective' criteria determined by sociologists for their own purposes, the second is more 'subjective' and is constructed discursively through how individuals feel about their identities and how groups want to be recognized by others. How schools respond to and respect these subjective differences are for many researchers a core question. Current post-structuralist approaches follow on from earlier ones grounded in symbolic-interactionism in arguing that differential outcomes reflect the degrees to which different groups feel the school to be relevant to and to value their identity, experience and heritage.

Thirdly, it is important to establish an initial sense of the distinction between a 'difference' and an 'inequality'. It is often the case in the sociology of education that these two are conflated; yet, it cannot be taken for granted that a difference is automatically an inequality – this must be established rather than assumed. This distinction has implications for what is taken to be a 'problem' in the sociology of education.

The underlying value and rationality assumptions involved in defining a difference as an inequality have ramifications for what is defined as a 'problem' (inequality *is* a problem, difference is *not*) and what counts as an explanation (identifying forces acting on people that create inequalities). Basically, the definition of what constitutes a *problem* relies upon a contrast between the actual pattern of social differentiation in education and an assumed ideal pattern that would emerge if negative influences were eliminated – 'the random distribution which would result from the "free play of natural faculties"' (Bourdieu and Passeron 1977: 228). Whatever might be the case philosophically, it is impossible to distinguish between choices and inequalities in any meaningful substantive sense. The existence of enduring systematic differences between groups can be taken as *suggesting* forces at work that constrain people to act in particular ways. The issue of choice has to be located within contextual conditions that may constrain the choices that people can effectively make. We can 'freely' make choices that disadvantage us (see Ogbu 1997: 770)! In part, sociological explanation has to do with making visible the contextual conditions that render apparently irrational choices intelligible – in the way, for instance, that Paul Willis in his classic study *Learning to Labour* (1977) answered the question, 'Why do working class kids get working class jobs?' (see chapter 4).

Difference, explanation and social change

Although, historically, class formed the primary focus of analysis and concern, some argue that we now live in a post-modern world in which class is less significant than other aspects of identity, such as subcultural membership, ethnicity or sexual orientation (Hartley 1997). What kinds of changes in society over the past fifty years might be attenuating the usefulness of the categories traditionally employed in the study of social stratification and educational differentiation (Westergaard 1995: part 3; Brown and Lauder 2001)?

- **Changes in the nature of work:** the effectiveness of class as a concept depended on stable, hierarchical occupational structures with clear divisions between manual and non-manual and administrative and executive strata. This type of 'Fordist' occupational system, based in manufacturing, has largely given way to a 'post-Fordist' system based in service industries and exhibiting a far more fragmented system of 'flexible' working arrangements with widely differing conditions of service, job security and possibilities of career development. Individuals are expected to be multi-skilled rather than specialized and be prepared to regularly change jobs, retrain and update their skills. Different kinds of divisions become significant, such as that between core and peripheral workers, and class loses its salience as an organizing principle in working and social life and in the construction of identity.

- **Changes in family structures:** Fordist production sustained a patriarchal family structure based upon a male bread-winner and a wife and mother who devoted her time to home making and child rearing. This traditional family has now been superseded by a range of family types as a result of increasing divorce rates, changing sexual mores and new attitudes towards states such as single parenthood, cohabitation and homosexuality.
- **Changes in the role of women:** an important aspect of change in the family has been that of the concomitant changes in the roles of women and the impact of feminism. The general trend has been towards the increased independence of women economically and in other areas of their lives. Women experience and expect a much wider range of options than was previously the case (including that of remaining childless – an option being adopted by some 25 per cent).
- **Multiculturalism:** the pluralistic trends described above occurring within indigenous populations are supplemented by other forms of diversity introduced through migration. In the UK, for example, this is represented by the presence of peoples from countries of the old British Empire – mainly from the Caribbean and the Indian subcontinent – and in the USA by the relative decline in the proportion of those of British and Irish origin and the rising numbers of African-Americans and others, especially those of Hispanic descent.

Taken together, these complex patterns of change are interpreted by postmodernists as a decisive shift towards a new social order, radically discontinuous with what went before, one in which the old categories and social models (or 'meta-narratives') in which they are embedded no longer serve. Others see them as less fundamental (Giddens 1990; Alexander 1995), with essential continuities being preserved. However conceived, such patterns of change present problems for educators in terms of what and how to teach, as well as sociologically, problems to do with what needs explaining and how (Hartley 1997).

Class and other differences

Recognizing the multidimensional character of identity and positioning raises the question: Are some dimensions more fundamental than others? (Lopez and Scott 2000: ch. 5) Is class, as Marxists might argue, more fundamental than gender or ethnicity? If so, explanation would adopt a *reductionist* form in which ethnic and gender and status differences would ultimately dissolve into class differences. Feminists adopting a *standpoint* perspective, however, hold that gender requires a distinct body of theory and concepts qualitatively different from those of the 'male' theory of class, and that 'feminist method' is different in kind from 'male' method (Bilton et al. 2002: 461–3). For them, theories and methods are *constitutively* gendered and, hence, radically discontinuous and incommensurable.

In defence of the priority of class, John Westergaard (1995) suggests

> a difference that sets class inequality apart from both gender and ethnic inequality. This is that, in the public sphere and in general principle alike, the latter two operate in large measure through the former. Inequalities between men and women, between blacks/browns and whites – for that matter between Catholics and Protestants in a Protestant dominated society – come to major expression as inequalities of class; but not vice versa. (Westergaard 1995: 145)

As he points out, 'women experience their social subordination especially – though not only – by way of poor placement in the structure of class' (ibid.). And similarly for blacks. To make this point is not to return to class reductionism (class inequalities and modes of discrimination do not *exhaust* those of gender and race), but to note an important asymmetry in the relation between these inequalities so as to view their relationships as interactive and relational rather than as 'conceptually parallel dimensions of inequality' (ibid. 147) associated with paradigmatic differences in theory and method.

Within the American context, Ogbu (1997) has made a similar observation about the class/race relation, but makes a different point in order to explain the persistence of racial inequalities in education. Ogbu constructs a set of careful distinctions to define the specificity of 'racial stratification' as separate from class. He argues that although social inequality is universal, social stratification is not. Stratification occurs when *groups* are defined by certain criteria (e.g. colour, sex), then ranked relative to each other, and individuals are treated according to group membership. He defines stratification in this way:

> A stratified society is a society in which there is a differential relationship between members of its constituent groups and the society's fundamental resources, so that *some people (e.g. white Americans), by virtue of their membership in particular social groups, have almost unimpaired access to the strategic resources*, while *some other people (e.g. black Americans), by virtue of their own membership in other social groups, have various impediments in their access to the same strategic or fundamental resources*. In addition, the different social groups in the hierarchy are separated by cultural and invidious distinctions that serve to maintain social distance between them. In a stratified society there is usually an overarching ideology, a folk

or/and scientific 'theory' embodying the dominant group's rationalisations or explanations of the hierarchical ordering of the groups. Subordinated groups do not necessarily accept the rationalisation of the system; however, they are not entirely free from its influence. (Ogbu 1997: 766–7)

Stratification can occur without class (e.g. in pre-industrial societies), and class does not necessarily entail stratification (as distinct from social inequality). Individuals can change class, but in a racially stratified society cannot change their colour and what that entails. Strata membership is assigned on the basis of *ascribed* (assumed intrinsic) characteristics, whereas class membership is *achieved* and is marked by external characteristics (such as socio-economic status). Strata contain classes (e.g. middle-class black Americans), but those of the inferior strata are not continuous with the same class in the dominant group. A black American, Ogbu argues, can achieve a high class status, but still suffer the consequences of racial stratification and be segregated from whites of the same class and disadvantaged relative to them.

Following Ogbu's analysis, a full understanding of the position of black pupils in white-dominated racially stratified society requires engagement with the *specific* dynamics of stratification conceptualized as distinct from class, but interacting with and working through it. That dynamic might also involve calling upon concepts developed within feminism concerning gender and sexuality. Sociological accounts would draw upon a range of theories and concepts that complement and 'talk' to each other, as distinct from either a reductionism that treats everything as simply an effect of one fundamental category or a standpoint approach that posits an array of paradigmatically incommensurable perspectives reflecting different interests. The key question is: Can sociology of education produce synthesizing explanations of increasing complexity at increasingly higher levels of abstraction? Hence, the ways in which we go about understanding education and society also relate to how we understand sociology itself as an explanatory discipline.

These complexities in defining educational inequalities in terms of relative advantages and disadvantages are discussed by C. Collins et al. (2000) in a report on gender differences in education in Australia.

There are several paradoxes and problems with this approach to educational equity. These are best represented through a series of questions. Firstly, if one gender were to be out-performing and out-participating the other at the top of the range, does this constitute under-performance and participation by the other gender at the top? Does this constitute disadvantage? If this is understood as disadvantage, then how does that compare with those males and females at other levels of performance? Who is disadvantaged, the gender being out-performed at the top or the gender out-performing others at lower levels of the performance hierarchy? Or the gender being out-performed at each level? Are they all disadvantaged equally? Or, are both genders at the bottom particularly disadvantaged in comparison with those further up? If this is the case, then how should the 'what about the boys?' issue be redefined? . . . Educational disadvantage is often understood as poor performance in all school learning areas, and particularly in certain 'key' school learning areas. But perhaps it is also best understood as being unable to convert one's schooling into further training, education or secure work or indeed into other aspects of a meaningful life. It is difficult to discuss educational disadvantage without reference to what students can do now and later with the capital they accrue through education – be it human, cultural or social capital. Indeed, one might argue that a student's cultural and social capital needs to be as well developed through schooling as their human capital and that anyone who is only developed in one area is disadvantaged. (C. Collins et al. 2000: 60–1)

Collins et al. point to the *cumulative* effects of educational advantages over time, when children have left school. Education is an investment in 'human, social and cultural capital' that can be 'converted' into further education, training and work. It is important that these cumulative effects are given proper explanatory weight, because they may influence pupil expectations concerning their futures *after* school in ways that affect their behaviour while *at* school: boys may not do so well as girls because they *don't have to*, given the advantages that males enjoy in the labour market! An implication of this is that if boys did achieve educational parity with girls, then females would be *even more* disadvantaged in the world of work. Increasing equality between the sexes within education would increase inequalities outside it. Educational advantages do not translate straightforwardly into social and economic advantages, and pupils are aware of this.

Collins et al. point out that while girls out-perform boys in education, they also adopt a more expressive approach, selecting subjects they find interesting, but which might not attract the greatest returns in the labour market. Boys study more instrumentally useful 'packages' of subjects, but may miss out on the development of personality attributes that girls gain, and may increase their alienation by studying what they feel they 'have to' rather than what they want to. Some boys might do better in 'feminine' subjects. The authors observe that:

> it is clear that current performance and knowledge hierarchies seriously disadvantage some groups of boys, encouraging them to avoid 'feminine' subjects and to over-enrol in mathematics and 'hard' science and hence to under-perform. The real curriculum challenge is to teach both males and females to see more clearly how gender and power relations impinge upon and constrain their life options. As a consequence, they would then be in the position to make *informed, rather than socially constructed, decisions* about what they want to learn and achieve. (C. Collins et al. 2000: 89, my emphasis)

But is boys' instrumentalism *intrinsically* a 'better' choice? From a liberal educational perspective, the *girls* might be seen as making the better choice – they may gain less in economic terms but gain more as people. Distinguishing between an 'informed' versus a 'socially constructed' decision inevitably involves value judgements.

The dimensions of difference

The significant dimensions of the social differences associated with education can be summarized as follows:

Class: the case of class differentials in education presents a peculiar problem for sociology. The evidence shows that, in the UK and elsewhere (Erikson and Goldthorpe 1993), the pattern of *relative* difference remained virtually unchanged throughout the twentieth century, *despite* all the reforms aimed at reducing it. The *absolute* level of education in society has risen consistently, but in a proportionate way between classes. Hence class differences were reduced successively at *lower* levels, but the overall pattern of difference has remained the same. Why have class differentials persisted despite all the changes that have taken place in education, including that in *absolute* levels of attainment? Why have working-class pupils raised their average level but not changed their *relative* position?

Gender: here, the situation is the opposite. The outstanding phenomenon over the past twenty years has been that of girls and young women steadily overtaking male achievement at every level: in higher education as well as in school, a 'gender revolution' (Arnot et al. 1999). This has two aspects: first, that of achievement levels *per se*, and secondly the spread of that success into areas traditionally considered 'male' such as mathematics and the sciences. Females have succeeded in doing precisely that which lower classes did not – they have changed not only their absolute but also their *relative* position. Significantly, whereas class was the major focus of educational policy and reform in the second half of the twentieth century, gender reform was, in most cases, at best fragmentary and at worst treated with official hostility!

Ethnicity: here, *no* overall generalization can safely be made. The point about the performance of ethnic minorities relative to the majority population in the UK, for instance, is that some have higher than average levels of attainment and others have lower levels, and these positions change over time and even vary from one part of the country to another (Heath and McMahon 1997; Gillborn and Mirza 2000). The majority groups of indigenous white English, Welsh, Scots and Irish, in aggregate, score slightly below the national mean. In the case of ethnic group data it is important to be sensitive to the categories employed: 'Indian/Pakistani/Bangladeshi', for example, are sometimes combined, yet there are considerable educational and cultural differences between (and within) these groups. The situations in different countries need to be considered individually, taking into account patterns of settlement and migration, the presence of colonized indigenous people, etc.

This complex pattern of differences, change and stasis presents a major explanatory challenge. How, at one and the same time, can we adequately account for both the gender revolution *and* the stability of class differentials *together* with the complexities of ethnicity? The problem is to maintain consistency. If it is claimed that the gender revolution is the result of education itself being made more 'girl-friendly', then why should reforms of a similar kind (applied in a more systematic and extensive manner) not have worked for working-class pupils? If racist stereotyping accounts for the disadvantaged position of black African-Caribbean boys, how do we account for the relative success of their female peers or of black African boys or of some Asian groups, but not others? The basic explanatory issues are to do with the types of effectivity being attributed to different aspects of the education system and its structures and processes and the underlying models of social causality and the person.

The order of difference

The educational differences associated with class, gender and ethnicity are of different *orders*. Gillborn and Mirza (2000) show that in England and Wales in 1997 45 per cent of *all* pupils attained five or more higher grades in the GCSE examination (mostly taken at age 16). This comprised 51 per cent of girls (6 per cent above the mean) and 42 per cent of boys (3 per cent below the mean). However, the difference between white pupils and Afro-Caribbean pupils was *twice* that (it must be remembered that some ethnic minorities have superior levels of attainment to whites – the differences between top- and bottom-scoring ethnic minority groups is *greater* than the difference between blacks and whites alone), and the class difference much greater still with children of managerials/professionals just over 20 per cent above the mean and those of unskilled manuals around 25 per cent below (Gillborn and Mirza 2000: 22–3). It should also be noted that if the professionals were treated separately from managerials, the class gap would be even greater, because there is a significant educational difference between these two class fractions (Savage et al. 1992, Power et al. 2003). In explanatory terms, differences *within* groups (e.g. between sections of the middle class) are every bit as important as differences *between* groups.

Differences within groups

We cannot successfully account for why *some* members of certain categories underachieve in relative terms without at the same time (i.e. in the same theoretical language) explaining why others of the same category do not. Differences between groups are based on averages, but there is always a significant amount of variance around the mean, and this variance is of considerable importance. Differences *between* the categories are associated with changes *within* them. Hence, the combination of class stability and gender change means that the preservation of differences between the classes is associated with changes between the sexes within each class. This can affect the choice of partners, for instance – people tend to choose partners of a similar educational level. The interactions between different dimensions of difference (and between stability and change) can have significant implications for different groups, depending upon where they are starting from and the kinds of thresholds they might reach and pass (Savage and Edgerton 1997). Gillborn and Mirza report that:

> By 1995 a pattern was established with a gender gap of similar proportions within each ethnic group (with girls in each group about ten percentage points ahead of boys)...however, throughout this period there have also been consistent and significant inequalities of attainment between ethnic groups *regardless* of pupils' gender. Since 1991 white girls and Indian girls have attained five higher passes in roughly similar proportions with a considerable gap between them and Pakistani/Bangladeshi and African-Caribbean girls.... Here the girls attain rather higher than their male peers but the gender gap within their groups is insufficient to close the pronounced inequality of attainment associated with their ethnic group as a whole. (Gillborn and Mirza 2000: 24)

Consequently, the gender gap (though of a similar proportion) has different consequences for different groups. This relates to class differences between ethnic groups and the ways in which their positions interact with educational and social opportunity structures – how they relate to various educational and occupational thresholds and ceilings. The *dynamic* aspect of these relationships also has to be taken into account. Mean attainment levels and differentials change *over time*, and this is in itself significant in that the circumstances of each generation have been changed by the performance of its predecessors.

Social differences in education associated with class, ethnicity and gender interact, but each has an effect specific to itself. Gillborn and Mirza summarize their findings for England and Wales as follows:

> Comparing pupils of the same gender and social class background there are five groups for whom we have a value for each ethnic group in the research: in four of these cases Indian pupils did best, followed by white, Pakistani/Bangladeshi and Black pupils respectively...the available evidence points to the following:
>
> • no group has been completely excluded from the improvement in GCSE attainments during the late 1980s and 1990s;
> • by 1995 the gender gap was present within each ethnic group regardless of social class background;

- ethnic inequalities persist even when simultaneously controlling for gender and class;
- when comparing like with like, in terms of gender, class and ethnic origin, consistent and significant ethnic inequalities of attainment remain clear.

(Ibid. 26)

These complex interactions between class, ethnicity and gender underline the importance of the point stressed by Arnot et al. (1999: 28): we must always ask the question, 'which girls and which boys?' rather than deal in broad generalizations. Dichotomies such as male/female, black/white, middle class/working class can obscure the ways in which *some* members of each opposed category can be more like each other than they are like the majority of their own group.

The three major dimensions of social difference – class, gender and ethnicity – present very different educational profiles and diverse problems for the sociology of education. Although each dimension above can be considered separately, they are interactive. Each of us has a class membership, a sex and an ethnic identity. For purposes of analysis, we can take them apart. The problem is to put them back together!

Explaining the Problems

Reviewing the range of explanatory approaches entails identifying *what*, for each, is picked out as educationally significant. An initial distinction can be made between 'external' accounts that focus upon the child's social background or presumed genetic constitution (e.g. cultural deprivation, identity and self-image or IQ) and 'internal' accounts that look at features of educational *organization* (e.g. the tripartite system, streaming and setting) or educational *processes* (e.g. teacher expectations and stereotypes). Essentially, the former are concerned with how different groups relate to the school, the latter with the way in which the school relates to different social groups. Internalist approaches concerned with educational differentiation form the main focus of this chapter. These two perspectives have identified the following kinds of factors generating social differences in and through education.

Externalist approaches

The principal concern of externalist approaches has been with 'educability'. Educability is understood as referring to those aspects of an individual's 'socially determined capacity to respond to the demands of the particular educational arrangements to which he is exposed' (Floud and Halsey: 183, quoted in P. Brown 1987: 13). The education system is treated as unproblematic. What *is* held to be the problem is the failure or incapacity of *certain kinds of families* to adequately equip their children to fully benefit from school. Hence, the following kinds of things are identified as causing social differences in education:

- presumed innate differences between groups in terms of IQ or cognitive capacities,
- material deprivation,
- cultural deprivation such as a general lack of literacy in families and of the social and/or linguistic skills and knowledge required to effectively deal with schools,
- social differences in degrees of educational motivation and social aspiration,
- differences in 'cultural capital'.

Externalist accounts, then, are associated with *deprivation* theories and *compensatory education*, where schools attempt to make up for assumed deficiencies in the home and community, classic examples being Project Headstart in the USA and the Educational Priority Areas established following the Plowden Report in the UK in the 1960s. A similar response can be seen more recently in the UK in the New Labour government's Educational Action Zones policy linked to the concept of 'social exclusion' (Jordan 1996). Although at one level approaches of this kind have a strong element of common-sense reasonableness – surely some communities *are* suffering multiple deprivations that affect children's education – they have been criticized on the grounds of imposing unexamined normative assumptions upon groups that do not conform to standard white middle-class values in the home and school (they *pathologize* groups by treating their values as deficient rather than as simply *different*).

Internalist approaches

Internalist accounts focus upon 'educational differentiation', and more specifically upon those processes *associated with the school* that categorize, select and order pupils in terms of academic and other criteria. The focus is upon the school itself in terms of features such as:

- the organization of the educational system in such a way that it may reflect and reproduce class and other divisions,
- social biases in the formal curriculum such as the stereotypical representation of traditional gender roles or of white superiority or the assumption of middle-class cultural values,

- the covert transmission of such assumptions through the 'hidden curriculum' and teacher expectations resulting in a 'self-fulfilling prophecy' of success for some groups and failure by others,
- the failure of schools to acknowledge and include certain kinds of cultural identities, especially in respect to ethnicity and sexuality.

Internalist accounts look to education as the main cause of differentiation. In the 1960s and 1970s they developed as a critique of externalist accounts that were seen as 'blaming the victim' by pathologizing certain groups and simply taking for granted the socially neutral and benevolent character of the school. At that time this approach drew upon qualitative, interpretative sociology: the 'New Sociology of Education', the central focus of which was the critical analysis of 'the social construction of reality' in school knowledge and educational processes. To say that something is a 'construct' is to say that a term or concept does not refer to something outside itself in the world that is independently *real*. The construct *constructs* a reality that appears to confirm that what it *says* is real really *is*! Hence, intelligence tests do not refer to and objectively measure a real attribute of people, but act selectively to legitimate differences constructed on social grounds and reflecting power relations and interests.

This type of analysis advocates transforming educational processes in ways that (a) take critical (or 'reflexive') account of previously unexamined assumptions and their links to power, and (b) positively develop new kinds of inclusive 'radical pedagogies' that challenge those assumptions and contest existing power relations (see Giroux 1997). Although applauded for their sensitivity to what happens in the classroom itself, constructionist approaches are criticized for being overly idealist and subjectivist and for neglecting (or even rejecting the very idea of) structural factors and constraints.

A deeper sense of the complexities of the interactions between the factors associated with externalist and internalist approaches and the manner in which they are contextualized within broader processes of social change can be developed by considering the gender revolution in education and the extent to which it is explicable in terms of changes *within* the education system itself. This must be set against the background of the peculiar *stability* in class differentials in the twentieth century.

Closing the Gender Gap: Women and the 'Educational Revolution'

The outstanding feature of educational change in the second half of the twentieth century was the gender revolution (Arnot 2002). This is one aspect of the more general complex of changes in gender relations in modern societies, involving family structures, economic participation and the impact of feminism. Madeleine Arnot describes the situation as follows:

> As part of a counter-hegemonic movement, feminist teachers challenged the ways in which gender categories were constructed, reproduced and transmitted through schooling. They challenged the principles of social order – the gendered principles for the distribution of power and social control – and the framing of a unitary social identity 'woman'. Feminism had essentially destabilised the category of femininity for a generation of young women by making the process of problematisation critical to identity formation. Being female became associated not with a static class-based categorisation but with a dynamic process of 'becoming'. Women, therefore, were encouraged to become actors within a set of social relations that were described as arbitrary not given. (Arnot 2002: 191)

Feminist initiatives in education opened spaces within which wider social changes could be interpolated in the form of a critical questioning of the role of the school in reproducing gender relations. As Arnot says, for pupils (and teachers also) this activity was directly related to identity formation through the ways in which girls could come to question things such as subject and career choice.

It is important to stress that there is not just one 'feminism' or just one kind of educational feminism (Arnot and Dillabough 1999). In both cases, feminism presents a plurality of positions and perspectives, drawing upon a range of other traditions (Marxist, psychoanalytic, existentialist, etc.) as well as developments internal to feminism itself. Writers in the area typically prefer to use the plural *feminisms* (Bilton et al. 2002: 487–93, 527–9; Measor and Sikes 1997; Weiner 1994). The variety of feminisms represents both the range of issues that can be addressed and the range of approaches through which they might be addressed.

The varieties of feminism

Arnot et al. (1999: ch. 5) make a broad distinction between 'liberal' and 'critical' educational feminisms. The former are primarily concerned with issues of equality of access, experience and opportunity. The latter are more concerned with fundamental issues concerning the androcentric and ethnocentric nature of school knowledge and its relationship to white male domination in society. The critical feminisms include Marxist, black, lesbian, radical and post-structuralist approaches, amongst others. With the exception of post-structuralists, the critical approaches view sexism in education as the product of underlying patriarchal structures in society, and hence see it as deeply entrenched and endemic.

For Marxist feminists, patriarchy and capitalism are intertwined – the solution to the problems of the one entails (but does not necessarily guarantee) solutions to the problems of the other. On this basis, feminism is in alliance with other movements seeking fundamental social change. Radical feminism sees patriarchy as an autonomous system of oppression of women by men that operates independently of capitalism and other economic formations. Hence, transcending capitalism would not automatically solve the problem of patriarchy, because the labour movement and socialism are *not* necessarily non-patriarchal. Consequently, women must recognize their own separate struggle and seek their own solutions independent of other issues. Aligned with the radical feminists are lesbian theorists who are concerned with the way in which patriarchy controls female sexuality and imposes 'compulsory heterosexuality'. Lesbian feminists argue that mainstream feminism has also assumed a heterosexual perspective that marginalizes the situation and experiences of homosexual women and prescriptively positions heterosexuality as normal.

By contrast, liberal approaches view sexism as a residual cultural hangover from the past, which can be eliminated by progressive reforms and changes in consciousness. The basic problem is that of 'ignorance', which can be 'cured' through appropriate education. Post-structuralists see sexism as the 'normalizing' activity of dominant 'regulative discourses' and, hence, less amenable to change, but, in so far as they are self-consistent, they share with liberals the rejection of the macro-structural theories of the other critical approaches and the 'grand narratives' in which they are embedded.

Weiner (1994: ch. 4) has summarized this range of perspectives in feminism and in feminist educational research. Drawing upon her account (Weiner 1994: 71–3), the grid shown in table 1.1 can be constructed to illustrate the range of main educational feminisms and their particular concerns and research interests (though, as she herself admits, even this is not exhaustive – see also Measor and Sikes 1997). Weiner points out that these approaches differ in how they see education itself as being able to contribute to change of a fundamental kind. Whereas liberal feminism assumes a reformist approach within existing social arrangements, Marxist and radical feminists believe that far more fundamental changes must occur in the very nature of society, and that education's capacity to produce change is limited.

Summary

The first part of this chapter has raised a set of issues of different kinds in order to illustrate the complexity of the field of the sociology of education. This set of issues can be summarized as follows:

The problems of educational differentiation and social inequalities: these have to do with the body of facts that need addressing and

Table 1.1 The major educational feminist perspectives

Perspective	Major concern	Research questions	Key terms
Liberal	focus on girls' underachievement in the schooling system and education more generally in order to campaign for change	the causes of differential attainment patterns between the sexes in certain subject areas (particularly in maths, science and technology); sex stereotyping in optional subject areas and in careers advice; bias in the way examinations and tests are constructed and marked; sex differences in school staffing patterns	access, choice, disadvantage, under-representation, underachievement
Radical	criticisms of the male domination of society and the nature of school knowledge	role played by sexuality in the oppression of girls and women in the classroom and staffroom, and in the schooling process more generally; the role for the single-sex school in the creation of an autonomous female learning culture	patriarchal relations, domination and subordination, oppression and empowerment, woman- and girl-centredness
Marxist	the degree to which education and schooling have been effective in producing sexual inequality compared to the reproduction of class inequality	how gender and power relations are continually reproduced in schooling; the formation of gendered class groupings in the schooling context; the relationship between the family, schooling and the labour market in maintaining dominant class and gender relationships	capitalism, production, reproduction, class, gender, patriarchal relations, correspondence theory
Black	criticizing the endemic nature of both racism and sexism	the actual experience of black girls and young women in British schooling and in higher education; the sexism and racism of teachers; the construction of women and black students as a problem for, and within, education	anti-sexism, anti-racism, black disadvantage, institutional racism, stereotyping, lack of expectation
Post-structuralist	the ways in which sex and gender are constituted through discursive practices	the 'regime of truth' of the progressive primary classroom; 'praxis' and 'self-reflexivity' of the feminist researcher	gendered identities, regulative discourses, subjectivity, power–knowledge, reflexivity

the patterns and trends that need to be accounted for. Attention was drawn to (a) the stability in class differentials, (b) the gender revolution, and (c) the wide variety of differences between ethnic communities. It was stressed that it is important to take account of the ways in which these relationships change over time and the significance of variance *within* groups as well as differences between them.

The problems of distinguishing between differences and inequalities: at one level this problem is beyond solution – how could we ever demonstrate definitively that one person's choice is freely made and another's determined? However, it can be reasonably argued that a major concern for sociology is to account for enduring structures of aggregate social differences in light of the view that some conditions of life are humanely preferable to others and that attempts should be made to ameliorate the circumstances of those less fortunate and to improve the lot of people in general. It is important to be sensitive, though, to the fact that the definition of what constitutes a problem in sociology cannot be disentangled from value judgements that in part reflect assumptions about the existential status of people's choices – why *shouldn't* working-class kids get working-class jobs? What is wrong with being working-class? What is wrong with being a good wife and mother? These more philosophical concerns are of direct significance for teachers, in that within the Western liberal tradition the aim of education is precisely to develop in individuals the capacity to be autonomous or authentic decision-makers (Bonnett and Cuypers 2001), and this, in turn, links with the view that the education system should be promoting social opportunity, mobility and change. These secular humanist values can be fiercely contested by religious believers in traditional faith communities and by politically conservative traditionalists.

The problems of explanation: the issue here is not just that there is a wide variety of explanatory perspectives in sociology, but that they operate in different modes (e.g. some attempt to reduce all explanation to one primary dimension, some assume a multiplicity of standpoint-specific perspectives, some aspire to integrative general theory). In addition, with reference to the range of things that require explaining, it is important that consistency is maintained across areas. If certain kinds of factors are invoked in order to account for the gender revolution, then it should be assumed that such factors would be equally effective in the class and ethnicity areas. Is the method of explanation adopted in one area consistent with what is observed in others? How does an explanation of the mean condition for any group accommodate the fact of variance? Essentially, this has to do with the types of *effectivity* being attributed to particular aspects of education by different explanatory perspectives. Related to this is the key issue: How much can the educational process itself explain about educational differences, and how much difference does education make? These concerns will be the focus of the next section.

The Ethos of Masculinity and the Limitations of Internalist Explanation

As Weiner et al. point out, the major public response to the gender educational revolution (at least in the media) has been a moral panic over the 'underachievement' of boys: 'It appears as if female success is viewed as a corollary to male failure. Rather than celebrating girls' achievements and aspirations, we have now a discourse of male disadvantage' (1997: 620). It is as if the success of girls is in some way at the expense of boys. However, as Collins et al. argue, defining educational advantages and disadvantages is by no means straightforward; furthermore, as both sets of writers emphasize, female 'advantage' in education does not automatically translate into economic and social advantages. Weiner et al. explore how the 'boy problem' is described in different ways according to class and colour. Although educational processes might be described in certain ways as 'masculine', there is not just *one* masculinity, and masculinities are not all treated equally in schools.

The masculinity issue has been thrown into sharp focus by the case of the over-representation of black boys amongst those pupils excluded from school for disciplinary reasons in the UK. A study of this problem by Wright et al. (1998) explores the dynamic whereby the behaviour of certain black boys in a school is mediated by teachers' stereotypes of black masculinity (Mac an Gaill 1988; Sewell 1997; Youdell 2003). They say:

> This does not deny that Black males may act in ways which require school sanctions, but it does suggest that their experiences within education should not differ from White peers and other Black females who also behave in similar ways. It is important to note that Black male perception of differential teacher responses to them and their schooling identities informs their subsequent relations with school staff. (Wright et al. 1998: 84)

Debates around these issues amongst researchers have been fierce and sometimes bitter. At one level the question is: Does the over-representation of black boys amongst excluded pupils imply that more black boys *actually* behave in ways that would lead to the exclusion of *any* pupil, or is it that teachers are more likely to construe the behaviour of black boys as problematic in ways that result in disproportionate exclusion? In sociological terms, this relates to a long-running methodological debate about the relationship between objectivity and the interpretative problems raised by constructionist approaches (Foster et al. 1996). In earlier times symbolic-interactionist perspectives such as labelling theory described 'deviant' behaviour in the classroom (and elsewhere) as socially produced through the arbitrary imposition of 'labels' upon certain categories of pupils who depart from the teacher's unconsciously held model of 'the ideal pupil'. For labelling theorists a further stage of this process is when it begins to shape (through internalization) the self-image of those being labelled in such a way that they *become* the type of person the label stereotypically represented – a self-fulfilling prophecy in which pupils come to confirm teacher expectations about pupils of their 'kind' (Becker 1971; Keddie 1971). This process radically reverses the common-sense view that disruptive pupils simply are 'in fact' disruptive. It argues that disruptive pupils are constructed as such by these complex processes of formal and informal educational differentiation acting upon pupil self-image.

Analyses of this type are significant because of the way in which they attribute a certain kind of *effectivity* to internal processes of educational differentiation. What is at issue is indicated by Weiner et al.'s observation concerning discourse theory and the ideas of Michel Foucault: 'Discourses are structuring mechanisms for social institutions (such as schools), modes of thought, and individual subjectivities: they are "practices that systematically form the objects of which they speak"' (Weiner et al. 1997: 621–2). The quote from Foucault indicates the force of the effectivity being attributed to educational discursive processes: they *form* the objects (in this case 'pupils') of which they speak. The attribution, in this way, of *strong* effects to internal processes of educational differentiation is the core issue of this chapter.

Wright et al. stress that there is a range of 'schooling masculinities' ranked hierarchically. The dominant (or 'hegemonic') model is white and middle-class, and is associated with academic success. Others, such as that associated with sporting prowess, are acceptable but of lower status. Still others are unacceptable and illegitimate. These masculinities and access to them are regulated by class and colour. Certain types of black masculinity are especially problematic, and 'lead Black males to be positioned by teachers, White male peers and themselves, as highly aggressive and sexualised' (Wright et al. 1998: 78). Hence, although the dominant ethos of the school is 'masculine', some male pupils can be 'too' masculine, and others, presumably, not masculine enough or masculine in less valued ways. This gendered and sexualized system of educational differentiation generates a position system within which categories of pupils are distributed by colour, class and sex.

The writers say that 'Working-class and Black male pupils fall foul of these dominant definitions of schooling masculinity through their representation as academic failures. They then take up different expressions of masculinity in order to find other forms of power' (Wright et al. 1998: 78). The notion of a hierarchy of legitimate and illegitimate 'masculinities' functions here in the same way as features of school organization such as streaming in earlier accounts of class differentiation within schools (e.g. Hargreaves 1967; Keddie 1971). Despite the Foucauldian resonances of this more recent study, the logic of explanation is continuous with classic differentiation/polarization studies of anti-school subculture formation (see chapter 4).

The problem of black male exclusion is located by Wright et al. within a broader feminist problematic. Under the heading 'An Ethos of Masculinity' (ibid. 77), the writers provide a thorough example of the educational differentiation model as grounded in radical feminism (see below). However, it is important to underline that the concern here is *not* feminism *per se*, but *internalist* theories of educational differentiation in general, of which this is a topical instance – there is no intrinsic reason why feminist approaches to education should adopt this particular form, and there would be no difficulty in selecting a similar piece from an earlier time on the 'middle-class ethos of the school' written within a symbolic-interactionist, phenomenological or labelling theory perspective.

> Feminist researchers on the reproduction of gender divisions within education have focused on the implicit and explicit forms of masculinity which exist within schools. The ways in which specific 'disciplined knowledge' has, in the past, been constructed as gendered is not the only way that gender is reproduced within this sphere, as this aspect of researching gender often focused more on the need to integrate girls into technical and science subjects, than on the way boys take up masculine identities. However, feminist research did reveal an ethos within education which promoted qualities of individualism, competitiveness and differentiation, and this ethos has been theorised as masculine. If young females are conceptualised as oriented towards personal relationships and males towards structures and role differentiation, then the basic principles of education (and practices) within schools are at odds with the social orientation of girls, favouring instead the ways that boys in general are socialised. Additionally, the processes by which achievement is measured through the comparison of one child with another foster forms of competitiveness, often aggressive, which coincide not only with young male orientation, but also the 'technical-limited rationality' seen to dominate the market place. The important work of feminist researchers in education has highlighted (and in many ways helped to address) the educational performances of young women in schools, such that increasing educational achievements of girls in comparison to boys can be seen as evidence of this. (Wright et al. 1998: 77–8, original references omitted)

The general principles of internalist approaches towards the effectivity of differentiation, represented here, can be summarized as follows:

1   Research reveals that both formally and informally gender relations are *reproduced* in education around a dominant 'masculine' model.
2   Specifically, this 'masculine' model is expressed in an inescapable *ethos* of individualism, competitiveness and differentiation.
3   Schooling contributes to the *formation* of a range of male identities.

4   Not all such identities are *equally* valued.
5   The basic *principles* of education are in line with the ways in which boys are socialised but at odds with the social orientation of girls.
6   Feminist research has had an *impact* upon these arrangements in such a way that the educational performance of girls relative to boys has improved.

There are three basic difficulties common to constructionist-type educational differentiation theories: problems of *description*, problems of *effectivity*, and problems of *validity* (see also Foster et al. 1996).

Problems of description

In the first instance, the education system, its schools, their structures and processes, have to be described via an all-embracing categorization: as 'middle-class', 'masculine', 'white' or whatever. The problem is: *what* exactly is it that defines 'middle-classness', etc., and how are these qualities to be identified within the school? Ideally, these features should be theorized independently; it would then need to be *demonstrated* that the relevant features of the school are indeed instances of these things. Unfortunately, this is rarely done in a rigorous fashion (upon inspection, such attempts frequently turn out to be simply tautological). The feminist problematic typically defines 'masculinity' in terms of 'individualism, competitiveness and differentiation'. But *why* should these particular qualities be 'masculine'? In what sense are they this, and how do we know it?

The root problem is that it is difficult to isolate specific characteristics that are *so* specific that they can be unproblematically identified as definitive (or constitutive) of any one particular group or category. In social populations it is almost invariably the case that *mean* differences between categories are relatively insignificant compared to the variation around any characteristic *within* categories. There is no measurable feature of difference *between* the sexes that exceeds the variation *within* each sex on that count. Hence, if we contend that mathematics is 'masculine', what this means is that, of that small minority of the population who are mathematicians, more are men than are women; but the great majority of men and women are more like each other in *not* being mathematical. The same applies to the group of 'aggressively competitive individualists'. More may be men, but a significant number will be women (as anyone who watches professional tennis tournaments will know!), and the majority of both sexes will be more alike in *not* being aggressively competitive individualists.

The implication of this is that such descriptions are only ever partial (are, indeed, 'constructs'!). The relative distribution of any set of characteristics between categories may be disproportionate; but it is always so far from absolute that in any binary set of classifications (male/female, black/white, middle-class/working-class) there will always be a significant minority of one category that has *more* of the defining characteristic of its opposite than the majority of members of the opposite group (if maths is held to be 'masculine', it will still be the case that *some* women are more mathematical than the *majority* of men). It is precisely this propensity of populations that historically enabled significant numbers of working-class people to be *more* educationally successful than the average middle-class person. In modern, pluralistic liberal democracies it is extremely difficult for any group to appropriate a characteristic with *such* a degree of exclusiveness that it is significantly unavailable to other groups.

Problems of effectivity

The issue of effectivity is central to differentiation theory because this is where the 'work' gets done – where processes of educational differentiation are held to have determinate effects upon pupils in ways that they generate socially differentiated educational outcomes. From symbolic-interactionism, through labelling theory and the phenomenology of the New Sociology of Education, to discourse theory today, the differentiation paradigm has attributed *strong* effects to educational processes acting on pupil subjectivities. Constructs such as stereotypes and labels *construct* pupil identities, influencing both how teachers come to see and treat pupils and how, consequently, pupils may come to see themselves. The problem of description works itself out in practice through analyses of education that purport to reveal how the defining social characteristics are expressed there. The masculine character of education is identified in the content of curriculum knowledge and teaching methods, etc. These things both position and supposedly affect different categories of pupils in different ways. Girls are not only disadvantaged by the masculine ethos of the school, but are also socialized into the gendered divisions associated with it.

What conditions would have to be met in order for processes of educational differentiation to generate the effects attributed to them (Jones and Moore 1996)? Ideally, the situation in schools would be one where, (a) educational processes and bodies of knowledge have given, unitary forms that, (b) pupils receive in a predictable manner that, (c) produces determinate effects. (Teachers might be inclined to say, 'If only ... !') In reality, the educational process and the transmission of knowledge are fragmented, unpredictable, provisional and contested. Pupils not only *fail* to learn things or get things wrong, they discount things, reject things or reinterpret them in their own particular ways. Significantly, pupils invariably have access to other sources of knowledge and authority. Reality is so far removed from this ideal, and educational processes so unpredictable and indeterminate, that the effectivity of differentiation must be severely limited, making such internal mechanisms implausible as *primary* reproducers of structures of social inequality.

The black sociologist Maureen Stone, in a classic critique of this type of approach (1981), pointed out that the negative self-image model of the black pupil depended upon the assumption that black people depended upon white people for their view of themselves – white racism, rather than making black people feel inferior, might make them think how stupid white people are. It can make them very angry! This approach also disadvantaged them by encouraging teachers to adopt a progressive 'therapeutic' approach rather than providing the rigorous academic education that they and their families wanted and that would bring them the real advantages of good qualifications. This leads to a further point about how pupils *themselves* relate to the educational process. Symbolic-interactionist accounts depend upon the idea of 'significant others' through whom individuals build up a self-image. However, teachers need not *be* significant (either positively or negatively) for pupils. As will be discussed later (chapter 4), the *majority* of pupils adopt an attitude of indifferent instrumentalism towards school – it doesn't bother them that much one way or the other. Certainly for *some* pupils, the school and its teachers may matter a great deal and have a significant positive impact upon their identity and development. Others, such as the black boys discussed by Wright, may get boxed into a particularly unpleasant corner that also profoundly affects them. Some may actively set out to 'resist'.

There are two points here. The first is that rather than working with a general presumption about the effectivity of educational differentiation, effects need to be established in *particular* cases. The second is that pupils are not only positioned by the system of educational differentiation – they also position *themselves* in relation to it. We have to take account of how pupils position themselves within education, as well as of how discursive processes define positions for them. What is striking about the pattern of positions that pupils themselves generate through their educational outcomes is not how closely it corresponds to the internal differentiation system, but how much it *does not*. This leads on to the 'validity' problem and also raises the issue of pupil 'strategies', to be discussed in chapter 4.

Problems of validity

The effects of the system of educational differentiation are attenuated for the reasons given above. If this is so, then how valid is the view that the levels of educational attainment, the relative positions of different groups, and their changes over time are driven by conditions and changes *within* the educational system and its processes of differentiation? Is it the case, for example, as Wright et al. suggest, that the gender revolution in education is *evidence* that changes in educational processes inspired by feminist research brought about the improvement in the relative position of girls?

The following observations can be made about this particular case that are relevant to a more general evaluation of the explanatory capacity of internalist approaches (see Arnot 2002: 190–1 for a contrary view, responding to Moore 1996).

- The improving relative position of females in education was a well-established, long-term trend throughout the second half (and accelerating in the final quarter) of the twentieth century. Its consistent features do not obviously correlate with identifiable episodes or periods of change *within* education.
- The impact of Equal Opportunity (EO) programmes in education promoting anti-sexist or multicultural and anti-racist education was (according to feminist researchers, see Weiner 1994) unevenly distributed, fragmentary and often met with official hostility. Such initiatives were not implemented extensively enough, and for long enough, to generate the systematic features of the long-term trend of relative improvement in girls' levels of attainment.
- It is difficult to see any straightforward correlation between those areas of the education system where such policies were implemented and particular advantages to the girls educated there. The *most* successful girls in the UK have been those in traditional, single-sex selective schools (least likely to have been committed to EO positive image initiatives and most influenced by 'masculinist' forms of organization, knowledge and teaching style), and the least successful girls were typically represented in mixed-sex, metropolitan comprehensives where such policies *were* most often implemented.
- At the same time, changes tended to occur most often at the lower levels of the system (e.g. in upper secondary schools, associated with the GCSEs), but this did not prevent girls extending their success to the 'A' (Advanced) level and degree level, where changes have been less pronounced. Female improvement has been as successful at the higher, more traditional ('masculinist') levels as at the more progressive ('feminized') lower ones.

In short, the requisite changes in educational processes were not extensive enough or sustained enough to validly be seen as generating the long-term, systematic features of the gender revolution in education. On the other hand, the second half of the twentieth century did witness sustained, systematic attempts of the *same kind* to reduce class differentials in education (the move away from selection and streaming towards comprehensive schools, mixed ability teaching, reforms of curriculum and teaching methods, etc.). These, however, had no significant impact on class differentials. But does this imply that what goes on in schools makes *no* difference?

Does School Make a Difference?

In 1972 an American researcher, Christopher Jencks (building upon the Coleman Report into education in the USA, with which he had been associated) published a book entitled *Inequality*. It had an explosive effect upon public discussions of education. Jencks's conclusion appeared to pull out the rug from under the reformist optimism that had supported educational expansion in the previous two post-war decades. The essence of his critique was that, as far as any *individual* is concerned, luck is more significant in shaping life chances than education. What Halsey et al. (1997: 34) term 'Jencks' pessimism' encouraged a research programme on the effects of the school in order to address the issues: *Does* it make a difference? How *much*, and *how* (though not all researchers in this field would classify themselves as sociologists or cede its achievements to the sociology of education)?

Essentially, the issue for educational research was: Are some schools more effective than others, and, if so, *why*? The significant difference between this approach and that of Jencks is that it investigates differences between *schools*. Today, this research programme is known as 'school effectiveness', but it started life by focusing upon what Neville Bennett (1976), in a seminal investigation, called 'teaching styles': basically, the 'traditional' versus 'progressive' distinction. A leading UK contributor to this field of research, Peter Mortimore (1997), says:

> Had Coleman and Jencks had access to more micro-level variables, such as school climate, staff behaviour, pupil attitudes, and institutional relationships they could have tested their conclusions against these more detailed factors. It is this shift in focus from macro- to micro-variables – from the system to the individual school – that has inspired a number of researchers to consider the effects of individual schools on the learning outcomes of their own students. (Mortimore 1997: 476–7)

In this respect, school effectiveness research shares a common focus with educational differentiation analysis. It differs, however, in that its methodology has been more quantitative than qualitative (the development of statistical techniques such as multi-level analysis has been central), and it is more concerned with organizational features of schooling than with discursive processes.

The basic idea of this approach (see, for instance, a pioneering study by Rutter et al. 1979) is to attempt to match schools, as far as possible, in social terms (socio-economic background, gender, age, ethnicity, etc.), so that those factors are held constant, and then to see whether there are significant differences in outputs such as attainment levels, forms of behaviour, etc. If there are, then it is fair to assume that these are the result of differences between the *schools* themselves – some are more 'effective' than others. The second stage, obviously, is to then identify those differences in how schools are organized and run. Research established that there are indeed significant differences between schools in these terms. Mortimore's review of research findings suggests that around 10 per cent of the 'variance between students is accounted for by the school once background factors have been taken into account' (1997: 478–9). To put this into perspective, he says:

> In terms of the English examination system used by secondary schools, 10 per cent is the equivalent of over 14 points (GCSE points scale). This can be roughly translated into the difference between being awarded seven E grades and seven C grades. Obtaining C grades in seven subjects will permit the student to move on to A level work and open up the possibility of working in the more prestigious occupations. In contrast, obtaining even seven subjects at E grade is seen in England as evidence of fairly low achievement. (Mortimore 1997: 479)

Hence, although 10 per cent may not seem a massive amount, it nevertheless translates into significant differences in opportunities for pupils in relation to the thresholds it enables them to cross (see also Mirza 1992: ch. 3). The key question is: What is it that makes the difference between schools? Mortimore provides the following summary derived from a set of case studies by the National Commission on Education (in Britain):

> A leadership stance that builds on and develops a team approach; a vision of success which includes a view of how the school can improve and which, once it has improved, is replaced by a pride in its achievement; school policies and practices which encourage the planning and setting up of targets; the improvement of the physical environment; common expectations about pupil behaviour and success; and an investment in good relations with parents and the community. (Ibid. 481)

This list should not be considered definitive. Researchers in this area invariably urge caution – not least because policy-makers are inclined to pounce with joy upon such findings as presenting 'kwik-fix' solutions for 'school improvement'.

School effectiveness research indicates that schools *do* make a difference. Pupils who attend more effective schools gain benefits over those who attend less effective ones. However, the literature in this area offers a number of provisos:

- As far as *educational inequalities* are concerned, it is important to stress that more effective schools are more effective for *all* pupils (e.g. Smith and Tomlinson 1989). Making all schools more effective would improve the attainments of all pupils *pro rata*. Hence, group differentials would remain the same.
- Increasing the effectiveness of schools is an intrinsic good, but doing so would not necessarily improve the position of the most socially disadvantaged. Consequently, school effectiveness does not automatically translate into a policy for improving equality of *social opportunities*.

Mortimore and other key researchers have stressed the limitations of school improvement in this respect.

- Best estimates seem to suggest that the school attended explains around 10 per cent of the differences between pupil attainments. As Mortimore shows, this is not insignificant. However, it does mean that the more significant factors explaining that variance are to be found elsewhere. However, in an educational market-place where differing capacities to make effective choices are important, there might be a relationship between these other factors and the likelihood of a pupil attending a more effective school (see chapters 3 and 4).

Contrary to 'Jencks' pessimism', schools *do* make a difference. Stepping back a pace from the finer detail, it appears that the general principle to be abstracted from this research is that of *coherence*. Effective schools are those that at a number of levels cohere around commonly held understandings, objectives, expectations and aims that are *collectively* generated and enforced. Rutter et al. (1979) glossed this quality by the term 'ethos'. An important implication of this is that the specific *ideological* form that this takes is not relevant to effectiveness. What counts is that the school is a *community* of shared values, aims and expectations consistently applied. From an educational point of view, this is important. In key respects this research *defuses* false ideological divisions in educational debates. It shows that all schools (a) should have high *academic* expectations of *all* pupils, and that (b) they should have the flexibility to adapt teaching styles to the particular needs of particular groups of pupils. The approach to teaching method is pragmatic rather than ideological. Having asked the question, 'Which boys, which girls?', we then ask which method within our repertoire of teaching methods works best, and provide teachers with sufficient autonomy to apply their professional judgement *in situ* (Pollard 1994). Taken together, both differentiation analysis in the sociology of education and school effectiveness studies by educational researchers point to a number of ways in which different aspects of school organization and educational processes *might*, under various circumstances and in different ways, have varying effects, both positive and negative, upon different categories of pupils. But the extent to which this is so must be settled pragmatically for particular cases, rather than assumed wholesale on the basis of broad dichotomies such as middle-class/working-class, male/female, black/white.

The relationship between social differences and educational differentiation is complex, and it would be unrealistic to imagine that there is a simple answer to any of the problems encountered in this area. From a common-sense point of view, it would be reasonable to believe that *all* of the kinds of things covered contribute *something* to the situation at some time for some groups, but none by itself or even such things in combination can reasonably be seen as endogenously generating the complexities and contradictions within the systematic qualities of trend data as they evolve over time.

Conclusion

This chapter has outlined the complexities in the pattern of relationships between educational and social differences and the variety of ways in which the sociology of education has attempted to account for them. It has distinguished between approaches that stress factors external to the school, the concern with 'educability', and those that stress factors internal to education, the concern with 'differentiation'. These latter perspectives attribute *strong* effects to internal factors and see them as the primary drivers of educational reproduction and change (e.g. by arguing that traditional education reproduced gender differences and that anti-sexist initiatives in schools *caused* the gender revolution). Two kinds of sceptical objections were raised to this view. The first concerned the assumptions being made about how educational processes and pupils interact and the conditions that would have to be met in order for such processes to have such strong determinate effects. The second objections were to do with the complexities presented by the changing patterns of differences between the dimensions of class, gender and ethnicity and the problems of accounting for how it is that the types of things that apparently (for strong internalists) worked for gender failed in the case of class and are inconsistent in the case of ethnicity.

In terms of the changes that occurred in the period after the 1944 Education Act, the educational system in England and Wales constitutes a virtual historical laboratory of educational reform, but class differentials nevertheless remained stubbornly intractable. As far as gender is concerned, too much change has occurred relative to educational change, and as far as class is concerned, far too little! The position of women in education suggests that educational relations need to be located within more general structures of social and economic change – the education system and its processes represent a mezzanine level between the micro-dynamics of the classroom and macro-structures and movements. The next two chapters will examine the broader themes of economy and class and state and status. Chapter 4 will consider ways in which these levels can be pulled together through *structural-dynamic* models of educational change.

2

Education, Economy and Class

Introduction

The purpose of this chapter is to review approaches that attempt to account for the modern education system primarily with reference to *economic* factors and class relations. As Halsey et al. state, 'No sophisticated theory of education can ignore its contribution to economic development. Indeed, throughout the twentieth century the relationship between education and the economy has constantly assumed ever greater significance' (1997: 156). They link this to the influence of *human capital theory* (Karabel and Halsey 1977: sec. 3; Woodhall 1997; Brown and Lauder 2001). This approach was developed in the 1960s, and its basic point is that education should be viewed as an *investment* rather than as individual consumption. The reason for this is that education develops the productivity of human labour, and labour is increasingly the most significant factor in economic productivity and competitiveness. Investing in education as human *capital* is the best way of improving economic performance. On this basis governments in the industrial world have made substantial investments in education, and through organizations such as the World Bank have encouraged developing countries to do likewise. This thinking is still with us today, although the economic context has changed significantly with globalization and the growth of 'post-Fordist' forms of production.

The relationship between education and the economy raises a wide set of issues to be explored in this chapter and the next. First, there is the question of the rise of the modern education system itself. Clearly mass education systems emerge alongside modern industrial economies, and in many respects they can be seen as an exemplification of the progressive spirit of the modern, post-Enlightenment world. However, as will be seen, the linkage is not as straightforward as might be supposed. Secondly, the contribution of mass education systems is not only economic. It is also assumed that education operates as a civilizing influence producing the informed, tolerant, reasoning citizens of liberal democracies. Third, education systems are treated as the major instrument for promoting social justice through equality of opportunity, meritocracy and social mobility. Much is expected of the education system in modern society, but, precisely because of that, a great deal of blame can also be attributed to it if expectations are not met. In the second half of the twentieth century, around the pivotal decade of the 1970s, the view of education crucially shifted from optimism to disenchantment – education began as the solution, and ended as the problem. From a sociological point of view the issue is that of causality and effectivity: what *is* the character of the linkage between education, the economy and those other dimensions of society to which education is meant to contribute so much? Can education really do all the things expected of it? Can it fairly be blamed for so much that goes wrong? Is it actually the case, as Basil Bernstein famously said, that 'education cannot compensate for society' (Bernstein 1977: ch. 7)? It is important, then, to be clear about the kinds of assumptions underpinning accounts of the relationship between education and society.

In order to have a sense of what is involved here, it is well to begin with some fundamental problems.

1   The development of modern education systems and economies is not clear-cut. The historical emergence of modern national education systems does not straightforwardly reflect the sequencing of industrialization. The most obvious anomaly is England: the first country to industrialize, but very late in developing a mass education system. These issues will be addressed in the next chapter with reference to state formation.

2   In the post-war period of social-democratic optimism, the promise of education was taken as its capacity to promote social justice through equality of opportunity, ensuring social mobility through meritocratic selection. As was shown in the last chapter, despite all the educational reforms aimed at reducing class differences in education, differentials remained largely unchanged. Sociologically, this is a key issue – especially when set against the 'gender revolution'. In this crucial respect, education significantly *failed* to do what was expected of it.

3   The logic of human capital theory depends upon a direct correlation between levels of economic development and forms of educational provision. Again, this connection is by no means clear-cut. As with all questions of correlation, the issue is to demonstrate a *causal* link between factors. It might be that richer societies have more developed education systems because they are richer, rather than their being richer because they have more developed education systems. The evidence is not sufficiently unambiguous for the answer to be stated with confidence. Societies of similar levels of economic development are much more alike in terms of features such as rates of social mobility

than they are in terms of levels of education or the forms of their education systems. Putting that the other way around, the degree of variation in the character of national education systems does not correspond to a similar range of variation in economic growth rates, productivity or social mobility.

Unfortunately, the basic conclusion in this central area of concern regarding how education works in modern society must be that competing theories are 'underdetermined' by the facts, which are such that contradictory theories are equally well supported by the evidence. The pot is either half empty or half full depending on how you choose to look at it. For instance, the amount of social mobility in modern societies is too great to be reasonably described, in Marxist terms, as a simple reproduction of class inequality, but not enough to represent the open meritocracy of liberal theory. As Goldthorpe argues (see below), *both* the Marxist 'logic of capitalism' and the liberal 'logic of industrialism' fail to fully describe and account for the character of modern, advanced industrial societies and their education systems.

Marxist and Liberal Logics of Development

The question of education systems has been approached through two theoretically contrasting 'logics' defining modern society and its development (Goldthorpe 2000: ch. 8). In the Marxist case there is the 'logic of capitalism', and in the liberal case 'the logic of industrialism'. These, in turn, are associated with contrasting problematics and research programmes. The Marxist tradition, according to Goldthorpe, is concerned primarily with *class formation* and 'with explaining the incidence and forms of collective class action'.

> Such action was, of course, of key importance in Marx's overarching theory of history: all history was 'the history of class struggle', and was periodised by the revolutionary outcomes of such struggle. But all history was also the history of the development of forces of production and of the contradictions thus created with established relations of production. For Marx, and for his followers, therefore, a crucial problem was that of how exactly these two lines of argument should be integrated – especially as they were applied to capitalist society. The abiding theoretical task was to explain just what were the processes through which intensifying internal contradictions would actually generate the degree of class consciousness and of class conflict necessary for the working class to act out its historically appointed role as the 'gravedigger' of capitalism. (Goldthorpe 2000: 162)

Within the Marxist theories of the 1960s and 1970s, education usually figures as an agency for the *reproduction* of capitalist social and economic relations. Such 'reproduction' theories explicate educational processes in terms of how they

- reproduce the privileges and dominance of the ruling class (e.g. through access to educational advantages leading to elite jobs and social positions);
- secure the legitimacy of capitalist social relations through the inculcation of the dominant ideology;
- block the development of a counter-hegemonic working-class consciousness that could effectively challenge capitalism;
- systematically prepare pupils for their differentiated future positions within the capitalist economy and social structure.

The following extract from the Introduction to an influential collection of papers entitled *Schooling and Capitalism* (Dale et al. 1976), illustrates these key ideas and also makes use of the Marxist distinction between 'base' and 'superstructure':

> Increasing interest in Marxism, both within this country [UK] and abroad, has given central importance to the problem of relating both the institutions and ideologies of the superstructure to the economic base. The cultural and educational apparatuses, together with their ideological assumptions, are presented as part of a theory of social control. From the premise that social being determines consciousness, the intermediary intervention of educational and intellectual structures has become a major concern for analysis. We have now a range of analyses of the superstructure with theories of cultural production, reproduction and transmission. (Dale et al. 1976: 2)

Sociology of education informed by this theoretical framework is primarily concerned with processes of 'cultural production, reproduction and transmission'; with explicating the links between economic relations and social and cultural forms and 'recovering' them from within the processes of education. The most influential version of a Marxist sociology of education of this type was the 'correspondence theory' of the American writers Bowles and Gintis (1976), examined in detail below.

The liberal theory, by contrast, approaches modern society as being 'industrial' rather than 'capitalist', and on this basis its analysis is primarily concerned with class *decomposition*. In direct opposition to the Marxist model, liberal theory promotes the idea that the central tendency of the logic of industrialism is to steadily *dissolve* class as a primary dimension of modern society. Whereas Marxist theory predicts the increasing significance of class, liberal theory predicts its gradual withering away.

> What liberal theory aims primarily to explain is how, in the course of development of industrial societies, class formation gives way to class decomposition as mobility between classes increases and as class-linked inequalities of opportunity are steadily reduced. These tendencies, it seeks to show, follow most importantly from the demand imposed by the logic of industrialism

for an ever more efficient utilisation of human resources – as reflected in the expansion of educational provision, the egalitarian reform of educational institutions, and the progressive replacement of criteria of ascription by criteria of achievement in all processes of social selection.... Thus, it may be shown how, within an increasingly 'open' and 'meritocratic' form of society, conditions are created which at a political level first of all facilitate the 'democratic translation of the class struggle' – the abandonment by national working classes of revolutionary for civic, electoral politics – and then further undermine the connection between class membership and political action even in the individualised form of voting behaviour. (Goldthorpe 2000: 162)

Education plays a key role in the liberal approach as one of the major engines of progressive social change. It responds to the needs of industrial society and its developmental logic by

- producing the 'human capital' required by an increasingly high-skill, science-based economy;
- promoting the 'civic' values and behaviour appropriate to advanced liberal democracy;
- developing a 'meritocratic' selection system whereby people can achieve social status by virtue of their actual abilities and contributions rather than having it merely 'ascribed' by the accident of birth;
- facilitating an 'open' society characterized by high levels of social mobility reflecting the relationship between ability and opportunity.

These things are achieved through a process of educational reform in which educational institutions and methods assume the forms appropriate to 'advanced industrial society' (see below) and, in doing so, generate broader, progressive social change. Educational reform leads to social reform. Where Marxists see education as a mainly passive 'reproducer' of class relations, liberals see it as an 'interrupter', breaking intergenerational links of inherited class position through the promotion of equality of opportunity expressed through education-linked social mobility (the move from 'ascribed' to 'achieved' status).

The key point of disagreement between the approaches is what they see as most salient in the economic organization of modern industrial society. Marxists define it in class terms (i.e. the economy is organized around the *interests* of capital and the capitalist class), whereas liberals see it in mainly *technical* terms as politically neutral. For liberals, capitalism (through the mechanism of the market) seeks to organize production at levels of *optimum* efficiency in order to promote profits. Marxists, however, argue that the drive for profit *limits* the effective use of production to meet the *real* needs of the majority of people. The economy could be *more* effectively organized to meet human need under socialist forms of ownership and control. In these terms, liberalism in general, and liberal educational philosophies in particular, are viewed as *ideologies* operating on behalf of capital – they prevent people from seeing through the smoke-screen of the bourgeois economic system to its 'real' class base.

Goldthorpe points out that there is a further theoretical issue at stake. This has to do with what Marxist and liberal approaches have *in common*. Both theories operate with 'logics of development' (of capitalism and of industrialism). These provide basic principles from which other things are deduced. Characterizations of education and accounts of what it does (or could do) are derived from the logics of development and their functional exigencies. In this manner, both theories operate with a particular kind of social causality in which it can be argued: 'because of *this* in society, then *that* in education', or, alternatively, 'change education *thus*, and *these* things will follow in society'. By virtue of this, both the theories are predictive and testable – and this is highly commendable. However, in these terms, Goldthorpe argues, *both* crucially fail! The failure of Marxism is well known: due, first, to the failure of the working class in advanced modern society to develop a revolutionary consciousness and politics, and, second, to the collapse of the Soviet Union and its 'Communist' empire in Eastern Europe. However, he more controversially contends that the liberal model has also failed to deliver. This failure is central to a key goal of the sociology of education: that of attempting to understand how education 'works' in society.

> In the decades following the Second World War – during which liberal theory achieved its fullest expression – the economic development of industrial societies went ahead at a quite unprecedented rate. It would therefore seem reasonable to suppose that, over this period, any logic of industrialism with the potential to undermine the prevailing force of class within these societies should have initiated well-defined trends of change indicative of this potential. But such trends have proved remarkably hard to establish. Indeed, to have shown that, in a number of key respects, they have simply not occurred might be regarded as the main achievement of class analysis as a research programme.
>
> Thus . . . the available evidence from investigations into both educational attainment and social mobility is scarcely supportive of the idea of a generalised, long term movement towards greater equality of life chances for individuals of differing class origins. Rather, class inequalities in these respects appear typically to display marked temporal stability, extending over decades and including those of the 'long boom'. (Goldthorpe 2000: 163)

Although modern societies have not developed as Marx expected, they have not developed as the liberal paradigm predicted either! It is important to be clear about the significance of this as far as sociology of education is concerned. In the post-war period, not only did industrial societies expand in the way that Goldthorpe describes, but their education systems underwent significant reforms of the type supported by the liberal argument (Brown and Lauder 2001). But, despite these substantial reforms, overall class inequalities in education remained remarkably stable. The outstanding feature of the period of liberal social change was precisely

the *lack* of change in the structure of class inequality and relative opportunity. Indeed, with the geo-political triumph of neo-liberal capitalism,
social inequality and absolute poverty have increased in both the USA
and the UK! The issues here are complex, and they form a core problematic for the sociology of education around which many other things
revolve.

Goldthorpe argues that, in contrast to Marxist and liberal approaches
that gave priority to class *dynamics* (class formation and class decomposition), the key focus should be the *stability* over time of major 'Macrosocial
regularities, expressing salient features of the class stratification of modern societies' (ibid. 484). The puzzle is that these regularities have endured while other things have *changed*: for example, class differences in
educational attainment persist *despite* significant egalitarian educational
reform. On this basis, Goldthorpe and various collaborators argue that
what requires explanation is (a) the *stability* of social mobility rates over
time, and (b) the *commonality* of mobility rates between societies (Erikson
and Goldthorpe 1993).

Descriptions and explanations

Two different kinds of questions can be asked about social theories: first,
how do they *describe* society: e.g. in Marxist, liberal or 'post-modernist'
terms; from a feminist perspective as 'patriarchal'; or as racist? What is the
more specific set of problems, issues and concerns which they address –
e.g. class and gender inequalities, equal opportunities, etc.? And secondly,
how, within the frameworks of those descriptions, do they *explain* the
kinds of relationships and processes with which they are concerned?

More specifically, in relation to education, such 'structural' theories
operate in the following way:

- Under the heading of a *general* description of society, they produce
  particular accounts of education. The description of society provides
  a means for depicting the education system, its structure and processes
  in a particular way.
- The relationship between the general and the particular is a *causal*
  one in the sense that (a) the wider social order shapes the education
  system and (b) the education system sustains key features of the social
  system and (c) facilitates (with varying degrees of efficiency) its further
  'logic of normal development', but may also (d) contain the potential to
  initiate radical changes (e.g. in class inequalities or in gender relations).
- These causal relations between education and society require the specification of effective mechanisms. *How* does society 'tell' education
  what to do? (Does this happen transparently through the political system and policy making, or is there a hidden hand such as 'capital' or

'patriarchy' guiding events?) What are the key features of the education system producing the effects attributed to it? Is it its institutional
structure, the curriculum (*what* is taught), pedagogy (*how* things are
taught) or some complex combination of such things?

- The assumptions about interaction and mutual causality or 'overdeter-
  mination' (i.e. the effects of parts upon each other and on the whole,
  and the effects of the whole on the parts) and the specification of effective mechanisms provide a guide to reform and possible change:
  change *these* things in education, and *this* will follow in society as a
  consequence, or vice versa.

In that these theories are to do with social *change*, they also entail (a)
a historical schema involving (b) a principle of periodization and (c) a
characterization of the contemporary situation and its immanent future.

Advanced Industrial Society and the Logic
of Industrialism

The extract below is from the Introduction by Jean Floud and A. H. Halsey
to the influential and representative collection of essays that they, together
with C. A. Anderson, edited in 1961, entitled *Education, Economy and
Society*. Although contemporary descriptions of society and its emerging
economic imperatives differ in key respects from Floud's and Halsey's
earlier one, they argue in the same kind of way from a general description
of society and of economic change to the education system.

> Education is a crucial type of investment for the exploitation of modern
> technology. This fact underlines recent educational development in all the
> major industrial societies. Despite idiosyncrasies of national history, politi-
> cal structure, and social tradition, in every case the development of educa-
> tion bears the stamp of a dominant pattern imposed by the new and often
> conflicting pressures of technological and economic change.... In an ad-
> vanced industrial society, it is inevitable that the educational system should
> come into very close relationship with the economy. Modern industrial tech-
> nology, based on the substitution of electrical and atomic for other forms
> of power and introducing new and more intricate forms of the division of
> labour, transforms the scale of production, the economic setting of enter-
> prise, and the productive and social role of labour. It is dependent to an
> unprecedented extent on the results of scientific research, on the supply
> of skilled and responsible manpower, and consequently on the efficiency
> of the educational system.... Education attains unprecedented economic
> importance as a source of technological innovation, and the educational
> system is bent increasingly to the service of the labour force, acting as a
> vast apparatus of occupational recruitment and training. Social selection is
> added to its traditional function of social differentiation: it must promote

new, as well as maintain old, elites. Furthermore, it must cater to the new educational needs of the mass of population, deriving from the changed status of labour in modern processes of mass production. (Halsey et al. 1961: 1–2)

This view can be associated with a cluster of ideas that, in combination, provided a 'self-image' for Western societies in the 1950s and 1960s and defined a central role for education. They were as follows:

1   **Technological convergence:** this was the view that, by virtue of technological developments underpinning economic growth, advanced industrial societies were converging towards a common model. This model would override the differences between the capitalist West and the Communist East and also provide the template for the newly emerging nations of the Third World. The new form of industrialism entailed the transformation of *both* capitalism and state socialism, rendering obsolete the ideological differences that divided those systems in the past. This 'technicist' model of the logic of industrialism treated the technical forms of production as politically neutral.

2   **The managerial revolution:** an important feature of the technicist logic of advanced industrial society was the emergence of a new breed of professional managers in industry, supplanting both the old-style Western capitalists and Soviet bureaucrats. These managers would be highly trained specialists whose concern would be with the efficient management of resources rather than with simply a drive for profit maximization or imposition of the party line. As salaried professionals, they would operate with different, and more socially responsive, purposes than either capitalists or party officials. As the new managerial elites of both West and East, they would present a common set of interests and concerns, in contrast to the conflictual ideologies of their predecessors.

3   **The end of ideology:** this logic of development would inevitably lead to the eroding of ideology and ideologically motivated politics. The neutrality of technology and the means of optimizing its efficiency would leave no space for ideological divisions – both problems and solutions are *technical* in character and can be addressed for the general good by managerial experts with no special vested interests of their own. A new era of *pragmatic* politics would ensue.

4   **The affluent society:** technologically driven economic expansion could provide steadily rising incomes for everyone, removing the sources of social division and resentment that had fuelled the spread of fascism and communism in the pre-war period. In combination with Keynsian economic management and the Welfare State, the productivity of advanced industrial societies could sustain full employment and provide a decent and improving quality of life for all its citizens.

5   **Embourgeoisement:** this is the view that we are all (or are fast becoming) middle-class now. Essentially, this argument claims that as a result of affluence and the changing occupational structure, the great majority of citizens see themselves as and in fact *are* middle-class.
6   **Meritocracy:** because such societies depend upon (increasingly) highly skilled forms of labour at all levels, they cannot afford to waste talent – human capital is their primary resource. Consequently, through their education systems, they will select, develop and allocate talent from whatever social background. All citizens will have equal opportunity to achieve according to *merit* (talent + effort). In this respect, advanced industrial society will retain significant inequalities of rewards but nevertheless engender a sense of social justice amongst its members – again, removing the sources of resentment that feed extremism.
7   **The 'tightening bond':** the meritocratic imperative entails that an individual's achieved social status will come to depend more and more upon their level of education. Educational credentials (indexing the development of individual productive capacity) will become the major criterion for occupational placement. Consequently, as this logic inexorably drives status allocation from 'ascription' to 'achievement', social mobility will increase, and society will become 'open' as individuals circulate to find their 'natural' (and deserved) position in the social hierarchy.

The model of 'advanced industrial society' provided a template and a logic of *normal* development against which actual societies could be compared and ranked. Generally, the USA was seen as exemplifying the model and its developmental logic, and in this respect America was 'advanced'. Britain, by contrast, was commonly seen as exemplifying not 'difference' but 'lag', and was therefore 'backward'. The American case provided the examples of appropriate institutional forms to which less advanced countries should aspire and towards which (in any case) the logic of normal development was propelling them. In addition to the United States providing the material instance of advanced industrial society, the *theory* itself had a significant input from American sociology – perhaps not surprisingly!

At every point, education is central to this vision, in the ways described above in relation to Goldthorpe's liberal model. It is, of course, the *failure* of this 'modernist' project to be fully realized that Goldthorpe identifies as the failure of the liberal 'logic of industrialism'. Certainly *some* changes of the kind described above did occur, but others did not, and certain key regularities, as Goldthorpe argues, have remained peculiarly intractable. Given the centrality of education to the project, it is easy for education to be held accountable for this failure, and, indeed, to some degree this happened in the 1970s when its social-democratic politics fell to the radical critique of the New Right (see below). However, this kind of explanation – and attribution of blame – presupposes that the basic logic of the thesis is valid; failure (in the English case) comes from elsewhere: anti-modern cultural and educational values, a backward-looking social elite, unreformed institutions, etc. As Goldthorpe implies, the alternative stance is to question the logic (or the very idea of a 'logic') itself. Perhaps, the entire project was fundamentally mistaken in the first place, and other factors are at work that require quite different types of explanation.

Advanced industrial society and functionalism

The 'logic of industrialism' model in the sociology of education has its origins in Durkheim's ideas about organic solidarity as refracted through the 'functionalist' school of American sociology exemplified by Talcott Parsons. In the post-war period, one reason why this model was attractive was because it presented an alternative to Marxism. The major point of contrast was that, for Marx, conflict was an endemic feature of capitalist society, reflecting the inevitably antagonistic relationship between capital and labour. The 'advanced industrial society' perspective, by contrast, postulated that class conflict would wither away with increasing prosperity and the 'end of ideology' associated with a new pragmatic politics of instrumental consensus. Marxist analyses of capitalism could thus be consigned to the dustbin of history, on the grounds that they reflected only the particular conditions of an early phase of industrial capitalism and had no relevance to the advanced stage.

The classic statement of the functionalist model is Davis and Moore's 1945 paper 'Some principles of stratification'. Davis and Moore explain 'the functional necessity of stratification' as follows:

> [T]he main functional necessity explaining the universal presence of stratification is precisely the requirement faced by any society of placing and motivating individuals in the social structure. As a functioning mechanism a society must somehow distribute its members in social positions and induce them to perform the duties of those positions. (Davis and Moore 1953: 47)

According to Davis and Moore, the basic problem in meeting this necessity is that positions vary (a) in functional importance, (b) in how 'agreeable' they are, and (c) in how much training they require. Furthermore, people vary in their capacities; hence there is the need to get the right people, with the right abilities and motivations, into the appropriate positions. Society distributes material rewards and status unequally, and in such a way as to regulate the efficient distribution of its personnel across the system of positions. In the classic formulation of functionalist stratification theory, Davis and Moore say that 'Social inequality is thus an unconsciously evolved device by which societies insure that the most important positions are conscientiously filled by the most qualified persons' (ibid. 48).

On this basis, then, social inequality is both inevitable and *rational*, and not a problem *per se*. It is a matter of arriving at the historically appropriate structure of differentiation and reward. Clearly, this theory can serve as a major rebuttal of the Marxist view that treats class inequality in capitalist society as intrinsically problematic. It also provides an alternative central concept by replacing 'class' by '*status*' (Scott 1996: ch. 4). The approach had political appeal in the post-war/cold war period (especially in the USA) because it legitimated and normalized those aspects of capitalism that Marxism saw as leading to its downfall.

The education system is given priority as the agency that performs the key functions required by stratification in advanced societies. Parsons (1965) identified the school (and more specifically, the classroom) as doing two things. First, it socialized the child: 'it is an agency through which individual personalities are trained to be motivationally and technically adequate to the performance of adult roles' (p. 434). Secondly, it is 'an agency of 'manpower' allocation' (p. 435). These two (interrelated) processes have both a general and a specific purpose. On the one hand, they involve commitment to the 'broad *values* of society' and, on the other, relate to the performance of a 'specific type of role within the *structure* of society' (ibid.). As a socializing agency, the school stands between the family and wider institutions. It detaches the child from the circumscribed experiences and values of the home and prepares him or her for entry into society at large. The need for a specialized institution of this type in advanced society reflects the fact that as a result of society's increased complexity and the rapidity of social change, individuals cannot acquire the attributes that society needs them to have from within the family or local community alone. Individuals need to be detached from local contexts and integrated into systems of societal or 'universal' scope. According to Parsons, the school progressively realigns the child's system of attachments, reordering the relationship to parents and other adults and to peers and members of the opposite sex. Essentially, the child moves from a situation in which his or her status is *ascribed* by biological criteria, and he or she is specifically the *parents'* child, to one where status is *achieved* against the criteria of school assessment, and the child is simply one amongst many in the class but, at the same time, treated as an *individual* in their own right.

> The family is a collectivity within which the basic status-structure is ascribed in terms of biological position, that is, by generation, sex, and age. There are inevitably differences of performance relative to these, and they are rewarded and punished in ways that contribute to differential character formation. But these differences are not given the sanction of institutionalised social status. The school is the first socialising agency in the child's experience which institutionalises a differentiation of status on non-biological bases. Moreover, this is not an ascribed but an achieved status; it is the status 'earned' by differential performance of the tasks set by the teacher, who is acting as an agent of the community's school system. (Ibid. 437)

Although the functionalist model has fallen into general disrepute, there are themes in it that have persisted into current debates – in particular, the issues of 'individuation' and the detachment of the individual from the family and local context (see Scott 1996: 100–10). For present purposes, it is Parsons's comment on the difference between 'ascribed' and 'achieved' status that is interesting. In a general sense, this difference is often presented as one of the main markers for distinguishing modern from traditional societies. In the latter, an individual's status is generally ascribed by traditional norms, whereas in the former it is increasingly something achieved. The education system is pre-eminently the sphere in which the person becomes an *individual* – that is, detached from the ascribed status positions and identities of family and locality, achieving alternative possibilities upon the basis of his or her own efforts within a universalistic system of abstract criteria.

The Logic of Capitalism

There are certain problems with the Marxist position in the sociology of education, mainly because Marx (unlike Durkheim and Weber) said very little about education. There is no canonical 'Marxist sociology of education'. Also, there is no *one* Marxism (Sarup 1977). In effect, what counts as the 'Marxist sociology of education' must be settled pragmatically by asking what it was that was generally acknowledged as such within the field. The answer to this is a book by two American economists, Samuel Bowles and Herbert Gintis, *Schooling in Capitalist America* (1976; see also Cole 1988). The authors describe their book as a 'substantive excursion into economics' (p. 53). Bowles and Gintis seek to reveal the gap between official representations of life in capitalist democracies and the realities. These lacunae are not (as the theorists of 'advanced industrial society' assumed) technical problems inherited from the past and passing away with time, but intrinsic to the system by virtue of its capitalist form. They begin with the major contradiction between the formal democracy of the political system and the totalitarian character of the economic system.

> Our critique of the capitalist economy is simple enough: the people production process – in the workplace and in schools – is dominated by the imperatives of profit and domination rather than by human need. The unavoidable necessity of growing up and getting a job in the United States forces us all to become less than we could be: less free, less secure, in short less happy. The US economy is a formally totalitarian system in which the actions of the vast majority (workers) are controlled by a small minority (owners and managers). Yet this totalitarian system is embedded in a formally democratic political system which promotes the norms – if not the practice – of equality, justice and reciprocity. (Bowles and Gintis 1976: 53–4)

Hence, their starting point is the recognition that the democratic character of the political system is absent from the economic system – the bourgeois revolutions of the eighteenth and nineteenth centuries established political but not economic democracy. In this sense, socialism completes the revolutionary transformation of modern society by extending democratic principles to economic relations. This contradiction between the two systems creates a major problem of legitimation. How are people reconciled to massive inequalities of economic power and wealth when the official ideology of society is democratic and egalitarian? This is the task of the school system. It is accomplished through the manner in which the development of the technical skills required in the economy is achieved within a particular *ideological* form that legitimizes educational differences as reflecting natural differences in ability. In essence, the problem is the social management of aspirations, expectations, mobility and social inequality.

Bowles and Gintis see the functionalist, 'advanced industrial society' model as an ideological defence of capitalist inequality. They see the economic sphere as organized by the class relations of capitalism and, by its very nature, embodying the inequalities and vested interests that this entails. Production is organized, in the *first place*, by class principles, and the technical aspects of production are mobilized in support of those class relations and interests. Hence, the *social* relations of production are *intrinsically* political, and their defence ideological. It is interesting to note, however, that in certain respects there are strong parallels between the two models in terms of how they see education as relating to the economy. Indeed, the Bowles and Gintis model has been described as a kind of 'Marxist functionalism'. Education functions on behalf of *capitalist* society rather than *industrial* society. The two approaches differ fundamentally on the question of whether the 'social relations of production' are technically neutral or in fact embody a political principle working to the benefit of the capitalist class. The obvious implication of the latter claim is that things could be *better* organized for the benefit of *all* under a socialist system. Bowles and Gintis develop this point in the final section of their book, where they discuss social, economic and educational alternatives. In the classic Marxist fashion, they define the problems of production under capitalism in terms of the contradiction between the 'forces of production' (i.e. society's *potential* for production) and the 'social relations of production' (i.e. its actual limitation by capitalist class relations) (see p. 277).

The education system under capitalism 'functions' to prepare a socially differentiated work-force both *technically* and *ideologically*. The ideological dimension has two aspects. First, individuals must be prepared for (and reconciled to) the particular circumstances of their destined work – its disciplines, routines, authority structures, etc. Secondly, it must prepare them to accept social inequality in general (there are obvious parallels here with the Parsonian functionalist account described earlier). In other words, the technical preparation of the work-force must occur in a particular ideological form (a similar argument is to be found in Althusser's influential essay 'Ideology and the ideological state apparatus'; 1972).

The education system produces its ideological effect by making social and economic inequalities appear 'natural' and, therefore, reasonable and just, by *individualizing* achievement and failure. Educational processes are officially presented as *fair* in the sense that formally the system is open to all and provides equality of opportunity. This is not only the official political and professional ideology, but the entire educational apparatus is bolstered by techniques (e.g. IQ tests) that are presented as neutral and objective. The meritocratic ideology of education is supported by (what is claimed to be) a scientifically objective battery of techniques. Educational psychology underpins the official meritocratic ideology. Therefore, if an individual 'fails', it must be their own fault – they either did not try hard enough, or they lack ability (merit can be defined as 'ability + effort'; Goldthorpe 1997). The system naturalizes and individualizes social inequality, making it appear both reasonable and just – 'blaming the victim'.

The correspondence principle

Although Bowles and Gintis's theory concerns the relationship between the education and economic *systems*, it nevertheless has direct implications for the analysis of the school and the classroom. This results from the manner in which they see education as performing its function on behalf of capitalist production. It does so on the basis of a 'correspondence' between the social relations of production and the social relations of schooling.

> The educational system helps integrate youth into the economic system, we believe, through a structural correspondence between its social relations and those of production. The structure of social relations in education not only inures the student to the discipline of the workplace, but develops the types of personal demeanour, modes of self-presentation, self-image, and social-class identification which are the crucial ingredients of job adequacy. Specifically, the social relations of education – the relationships between administrators and teachers, teachers and students, students and students, and students and their work – replicate the hierarchical division of labour. (Bowles and Gintis 1976: 131)

This approach is, consequently, often referred to as 'correspondence theory'. The school system reproduces the organization of social relations within capitalist production (Bowles 1979). This is expressed in 'differential socialization patterns of schools attended by students of different social classes' (Bowles and Gintis 1976: 132).

> Thus blacks and other minorities are concentrated in schools whose repressive, arbitrary, generally chaotic internal order, coercive authority structures, and minimal possibilities for advancement mirror the characteristics of inferior job situations. Similarly, predominantly working class schools tend to emphasise behavioural control and rule-following, while schools in well-to-do suburbs employ relatively open systems that favour greater student participation, less direct supervision, more student electives, and, in general, a values system stressing internalised standards of control. (Ibid. 132)

Hence, the relationship of correspondence provides a way of analysing educational processes as well as describing structural relations between education and the economy. This approach focuses *not* upon the *content* of educational knowledge (as would be the case in ideology analysis) but on the structuring of the *social relations* of schooling. An implication of this is that changes in school knowledge alone do not necessarily constitute a radical change in the nature of education if the social relations remain the same. It is *pedagogy* and its institutional stratification, rather than the curriculum, that becomes the key site, because it is the 'how' rather than the 'what' of education that is of key significance. This supported the dominant view in the 1970s (especially in Britain) that progressive education represented the 'radical' model for educational change on the basis that its (supposedly) egalitarian, child-centred pedagogy challenged and subverted the hierarchical social relations of 'traditional' education. The effective mechanism of radical educational and social change would be the development of 'radical pedagogy' (Apple 1997; Giroux 1997).

Although in certain respects Bowles's and Gintis's study can be seen as a 'conventional' Marxist analysis, in that it operates with a base/superstructure model, in other respects it marked some innovative changes. First, it directed attention away from the social relations of *distribution* (inequalities of wealth and power) in capitalist society to relations of *production*. In this respect it was more radical than earlier kinds of leftist analyses of education (such as those of the Fabian 'political arithmetic' tradition) – it required changes not just in how wealth is distributed but in how it is produced. Bowles and Gintis argued that the inequalities of distribution are reproduced *through* the reproduction of the social relations of production. Secondly, although their study was primarily at the macro level, through the 'correspondence principle' it had direct implications for the study of the school and the classroom. As Karabel and Halsey point out (1977), within what I have termed the 'advanced industrial society' paradigm, little or no attention was paid to the school itself – it was, in effect, a 'black box'. Bowles's and Gintis's approach allowed the macro and micro levels of analysis to be brought together. What went on in schools could be understood in terms of the relationship of correspondence between education and production. This was probably a major reason for the success of their study and its influence, especially because it resonated with the interests of the New Sociology of Education.

Criticisms

Inevitably, the book and the correspondence principle have been subjected to a considerable amount of critical debate (Hickox 1982; Arnot and Whitty 1982; Cole 1988; Rikowski 1996) including an interesting retrospective review by Gintis and Bowles themselves (1988). Thus, *Schooling in Capitalist America* has been a fruitful contribution to the sociology of education, as it provided the focus around which a number of important issues have been defined and developed. It is probably not going too far to say that its critical legacy is in how it encouraged the development of more complex and advanced understandings than were present in the text itself.

The key problems can be grouped under three headings that are of more general relevance – to the 'logic of industrialism' as much as to the 'logic of capital'. The *first* set of problems will be addressed in the next chapter: namely, the lack of a strong *historical* synchronization between the development of economic and educational systems. Green (1990: 47) concludes that nation by nation, educational responses to economic development 'bear no close correlation with the chronology of industrial advance'.

The *second* set of problems is to do with *limitations* in the original formulation of the argument. These are fruitfully developed by the debates that *Schooling* initiated (as remarked above, Gintis and Bowles themselves contributed to these developments). They can be usefully listed in more detail because they have general significance.

- Problems of *omission*: the narrow focus upon class ignored other major forms of social inequality in society, especially those related to gender relations, the family and race. Gintis and Bowles address these issues in their later work (1988). In addition, they also paid little attention to the role of the state. Their later model attempts to systematically incorporate these missing dimensions whilst preserving the centrality of the correspondence principle.
- The problem of *relative autonomy*: as a consequence of the base/superstructure approach that they adopted, they tended to treat education (as part of the social superstructure) as simply 'reflecting' the economic base and lacking autonomy in its own right. Specifically, the 'relative autonomy' of the education system could be expressed in terms of (a) its own institutional structures and the interests, aspirations and conflicts of its personnel; (b) educational concerns with

the production and distribution of knowledge that are not simply reducible to the needs of the economy (it must be remembered that the education system is *itself* a site of production: of *knowledge* – see chapter 6); and (c) the experiences, knowledge, interests and aspirations brought into the system by pupils and students which could be in conflict with official educational knowledge and aims.

- The problems of *contradiction* and *contestation*: the simplifications produced by the previous two sets of omissions suggested a too direct and unmediated relationship between the educational system and production. Including these other factors has the effect of 'expanding' the model in which correspondence operates in such a way that it is possible for contradictions to develop between sites within education and production, politics and the family, and for these contradictions to provide the spaces whereby official education and capitalist relations of production can be challenged. This possibility is essential for achieving the political aspirations that the book proclaims. As it stood, the determinism of the base/superstructure model made it difficult to see how political change or the development of alternative 'radical pedagogies' could occur.

Expanding the model in this fashion produces a necessary and valuable sense of complexity, but also leaves *one* crucial issue unresolved: how does it *work*? If the education system is serving the needs and interests of capitalism in the way that Bowles and Gintis suggest, what are the *mechanisms* by which the needs of capital are identified, transmitted into the education system, and, further, translated into an educationally effective form? These considerable problems are intensified by the fact that all that is going on is going on within the fog of ideology.

The *third* type of problem is theoretical and has to do with the manner in which the argument is located within Marxism. The point here, however, is different. It relates to the use that they make of the key theoretical concept 'social relations of production'. This central concept of Marx's theory is pivotal in Bowles and Gintis's account. It is precisely the *correspondence* between the social relations of education and those of production that provides the explanatory core of the theory. It is through this idea that the theory permits a close focus upon the *way* in which education may serve the interests of capitalism. But there is a major problem here. Do Bowles and Gintis mean by 'the social relations of production' what Marx meant by the term? Bowles and Gintis are referring, in their analysis, to social relations *in* production: i.e. to the immediate social relationships between members of different classes articulated *within* the occupational system, in work itself. But this is *not* what Marx means by the concept 'social relations of production'.

For Marx, capitalist social relations are the consequence of specific historical conditions establishing commodity exchange relations (including the commodification of labour power) (Marx 1976: ch. 6; Moore 1988). These relations *precede*, and are the constitutive principle of, classes and their relationships. For Marx, 'capitalist social relations of production' are not equivalent to the relationships between classes in capitalist society in much the same way that the 'interest of capital' is not the same thing as the 'interests of capitalists'. This point is fundamental for two reasons: first, because it raises questions about the *explanatory* power of Bowles's and Gintis's analysis (the theoretical authority implied by the term 'social relations of production' is, perhaps, not warranted), and secondly, because it points to different ways of seeing how Marx's theory might contribute to the sociology of education (Rikowski 1996; Cole 2003).

Schooling in Capitalist America initiated a significant programme of theoretical development in which the appreciation and conceptualization of complexity was considerably expanded. However, it must be noted that this 'expanded' correspondence theory retained the basic thesis as its central tenet. The programme brought about an increase in *complexity*, but left the principle intact, and in this respect, it can be argued, did not produce qualitative *theoretical* advance (Moore 1988). This has further implications for how we might construct a 'Marxist sociology of education'. The major problem today, after the fall of the Soviet empire and the apparent triumph of neo-liberal capitalism, is to decide exactly what constitutes a Marxist approach under the new conditions of globalization and post-Fordism.

Education Systems and Social Opportunity

Social opportunity and mobility are central to the liberal model and its view of the role of education in advanced industrial society. Educational reforms were inaugurated on the basis that they would facilitate the progressive development of such societies. As has been mentioned, there is a long-standing view that English education is especially backward-looking with its commitment to forms of liberal-humanist education that stress (in *both* traditional and progressive cases) the moral and spiritual development of the 'whole child' rather than adopting more instrumental vocational and technical approaches (Hickox 1995). This position is referred to as 'declinism', and it attributes Britain's long-term relative economic decline to these peculiarities of its education system (Barnett 1986; Mathieson and Bernbaum 1991; Edgerton 1996 provides a critique of this argument). In the case of the New Right in the 1980s, economic declinism was supplemented by arguments concerning moral and social decline attributed to progressive education and to developments such as anti-sexist and anti-racist education (Beck 1998).

In discussing an influential contribution to the declinist position by the American historian Martin Wiener, John Ahier points out that:

> There are not only some shortcomings in the social history upon which the Wiener thesis is based, but the model of the social and historical explanation used is very dubious, especially in the way it understands the place of educational institutions in social change. Like some of the other explanations of Britain's economic decline...Wiener's approach tends to assume that an industrial society should proceed along an unswerving path of economic growth. The space for the construction of his 'anti-industrial culture' is given by the comparison of an unexamined notion of the *normal* stages of national economic development with the actual industrial progress of Britain. Thus functionalist concepts like 'lag' and 'residue' are used to explain why this particular national economy has moved at a different pace from others. (Ahier 1991: 126–7)

As Ahier argues, the case of British decline becomes 'a problem' only on the basis of some model of 'normal' development from which it is assumed to have deviated; Britain should and *could* have developed otherwise. The 'pathology' model of British education presupposes a 'healthy' alternative that can be constructed from the logic of 'normal' development and which provides a template for progressive reform. The major, ongoing debate concerns what form the education system should adopt in order to become appropriate to modern Britain at any particular time.

Sponsored and contest mobility

An influential way of viewing these issues in sociology was provided by Ralph Turner's seminal paper, 'Modes of social ascent through education: sponsored and contest mobility' (first published in 1961 and still of considerable interest). Its concern is with describing differences between the education systems of societies of a similar type. Turner begins by distinguishing between the *extent* of mobility and the *mode* of mobility, and argues that a preoccupation with the former has distracted attention from the latter. The 'extent of mobility' has to do with attempts to estimate the amount of social mobility in society promoted by education. The 'mode of mobility' has to do with the institutional structure and organization of the education system and, most crucially, with 'the organising folk norm that defines the accepted mode of upward mobility' (R. Turner 1961: 121). He develops this argument by constructing two contrasting 'ideal types' termed 'contest' and 'sponsored' mobility, based upon the American and English education systems. He summarizes their principles as follows:

> *Contest* mobility is a system in which elite status is the prize in an open contest and is taken by the aspirants' own efforts. While the 'contest' is governed by some rules of fair play, the contestants have wide latitude in the strategies they may employ. Since the 'prize' of successful upward

mobility is not in the hands of the established elite to give out, the latter are
not in a position to determine who should attain it and who should not.
Under *sponsored* mobility, elite recruits are chosen by the established elite
or their agents, and elite status is *given* on the basis of some criterion of
supposed merit and cannot be taken by any amount of effort or strategy.
Upward mobility is like entry into a private club, where each candidate
must be 'sponsored' by one or more of the members. (Ibid. 122)

In contrast to the gentleman's club image of the English-type sponsored
mobility, American-style contest mobility is more like a race in which all
the contestants start on an equal footing and run as far as they can. In
formal terms, these differences relate to methods of selection. In contest
mobility the system is relatively 'open', with selection being delayed as
long as possible and with opportunities to try again. In the sponsored
system, rigorous selection starts early (e.g. in England, with the 11+ examination) and continues through stages whereby the numbers involved
are successively reduced by a ruthless culling by attainment, producing a
highly selected, small university cohort. Crucially, the sponsored system
involves assimilation to the values and norms of the culture of the social elite, and education is, at least in the English case, strongly identified
with a particular 'form of life' represented by a liberal-humanist education based on the Oxbridge model. By contrast, the contest model is more
vocational and technical, and neither the education system nor the ruling
elite presents a distinctive and *exclusive* common culture (marked, for
instance, by a standard accent or common life-style).

Turner relates these differences to historical differences in social structure and class systems between the two countries.

English society has been described as the juxtaposition of two systems of
stratification, the urban-industrial class system and the surviving aristo-
cratic system. While the sponsored mobility pattern reflects the logic of
the latter, our impression is that it pervades popular thinking rather than
merely coexisting with the logic of industrial stratification. Students of cultural change note that patterns imported into an established culture tend
to be reshaped into coherence with the established culture as they are as-
similated. Thus, it may be that the changes in stratification attendant upon
industrialisation have led to many alterations in the rates, the specific means,
and the rules of mobility, but that these changes have taken place within
the unchallenged organising norm of sponsored mobility. (Ibid. 125)

The theory provides contrasting models that link the organization of the
education system and its culture to broader historical issues of stratification and class formation. These differences are seen as alternative
solutions to the general problem that all societies have of 'maintaining
loyalty to its social system'. The differences between the two are essentially different ways in which society can address the issue of maintaining
the loyalty of the majority who are *not* members of the social elite. Although in a common-sense way, the 'contest' system appears more open,

democratic and progressive, and the 'sponsored' more closed and con-servative, Turner points out that research of the time in England 'reveals surprisingly little bias against the child from a manual-labouring family in the selection for grammar school, when related to measured intelli-gence. It is altogether possible that adequate comparative research would show a closer correlation of school success with measured intelligence and a lesser correlation between school success and family background in England than in the United States' (ibid. 129). This is an important ob-servation, because it warns against making too hasty a judgement about the social consequences of *differences* between education systems and the *effects* of their characteristics. The English system, though elitist, was not, in comparative terms, noticeably more biased in terms of its class distri-bution of opportunities – indeed, later evidence proves it to be amongst the most meritocratic (Müller and Karle 1996).

The key issue raised by Turner's distinction between the 'extent' of mobility and the 'mode' is how the latter might affect the former. In their 1956 account of 'English secondary education and the supply of labour', Jean Floud and A. H. Halsey (1961) conclude their discussion of the re-lationship between the English education system and economy by saying:

> The most radical inference is that English secondary education should be re-organised along comprehensive lines. There is indeed something to be said for the view that the *common secondary school is best suited to the needs of a technological society* – least likely to stand in the way of free vo-cational choice and movement, most likely to produce the maximum supply of skilled and responsible individuals particularly in the middle ranges of the occupational structure. But these advantages could be reaped from such a reorganisation only if the spirit as well as the form of English secondary education were changed. (Floud and Halsey 1961: 89, my emphasis)

In Turner's terms, the writers are describing a move from the established sponsored mode of ascent towards something closer to contest mobility (see Halsey 1971: 271). Floud and Halsey stress what they see as the need to dismantle the English system of early selection and postpone selection to the *post*-secondary school phase. Part of the justification of this is that (a) in the middle range of 11+ selection, there was a great deal of imprecision and misallocation between grammar schools and secondary moderns, and (b) early selection prematurely dampened the aspirations of lower-class pupils. The move towards a contest system represented by the comprehensive school is one towards an apparently more 'open' system encouraging both greater meritocracy and technical efficiency in meeting economic needs. Basil Bernstein has noted that:

> Their basic view was that education was contained by the rigidities of an out-moded class structure which deeply penetrated its organisational forms. *It is important to realise that Floud and Halsey used a manpower and equality argument as a double-barrelled weapon to bring about change in the procedures of selection and the organisational structure of schools.* (Bernstein 1977: 165)

They combined human capital objectives with those of social justice – expediency and principle. The reform of English education was seen as the means of reforming English society more generally – in particular, as a way of breaking the hegemony of the elite culture of the 'establishment' described by Turner in his model of sponsored mobility. These ideas and concerns are reflected in major educational policy documents of the time. However, all the major education reports of the period (from Crowther in 1959 to Dainton in 1968) were caught between what seemed to be the *conflicting* objectives of social and economic instrumentalism and the humanist values of liberal education. Crowther, for instance, acknowledged education's crucial economic role, and immediately added what came to be the standard qualification. 'But children are not the "supply" that meets any "demand" however urgent. They are individual human beings, and the primary concern of the schools should not be with the living they will earn but with the life they will lead' (quoted in Hough 1987: 9–10). The distinction between education for earning a good living and education for living a good life was a recurring mantra reflecting a taken-for-granted assumption that the first objective necessarily compromised the second, and higher, one (Moore 1987). For many, this reflects an inherent educational conservatism that has habitually inhibited proper reform of the system in England (Mathieson and Bernbaum 1991).

However, although it tends to be taken for granted that the 'contest' system is progressive and modern, and the 'sponsored' system backward and conservative, Turner himself does not make that kind of point. Indeed, in a number of places he stresses the *efficiency* of the sponsorship mode of mobility and suggests (as we have seen) that the English system might be *more* meritocratic than the American. Turner is primarily concerned with the manner in which societies, through their education systems, *manage* social mobility (and non-mobility), rather than with how different *types* of education system *facilitate* mobility to varying degrees. Earl Hopper, in an 'expanded typology' derived from Turner's original two types, calls this the 'warming-up/cooling-out' dilemma (Hopper 1971: appendix; Hopper 1977): how upward mobility is encouraged for some, and how those who remain stationary are reconciled to their position. His expanded typology demonstrates that there can be a number of ways in which education systems can be conceptualized in these terms and identified empirically (Hopper 1971: 101). That is, assuming that education systems *do* function for this purpose (among other things), they can do the same thing in a number of different ways. But, crucially, as Turner intimated, these differences in the *management* of mobility are not necessarily associated with differences in *facilitating* mobility. Indeed despite the fact that the English system *did* move significantly towards an 'open' style contest model in the years after Turner wrote his paper (he notes the beginnings of this process), as Goldthorpe stresses over thirty years on, the kinds of changes expected to follow have *not* occurred (Moore 1996). Again, we come back to the key issue: what kinds of differences do different differences make?

The *really* interesting implication of Turner's paper, borne out by the evidence, is that the kinds of changes promoted by the modernist project of educational reform do not actually make much difference in the areas where they were expected to count for most. Contrary to the apparent expectations of the Floud and Halsey type criticism of the English education system, the more 'open' contest form of mobility might not be associated with any more *actual* mobility than the 'closed' sponsored type. This, in turn, raises issues of social causality and explanation and about claims made for proposals for educational reform. Turner's arguments remain relevant today as the UK moves towards a mass system of higher education.

In the forty years since Turner's imaginative paper was first presented, there has been an accumulation of evidence concerning mobility and opportunity structures that, as Goldthorpe argues, call into question the logics of both the liberal and the Marxist accounts that propose a *strong* link between education and the economy, opportunity and stratification. Chapter 4 will address these problems again, with reference to the model developed by Raymond Boudon.

From euphoria to disenchantment

The progressive optimism of the liberal approach assumed that there was an internal dynamic of change driving society towards an increasingly equal and meritocratic form on the crest of rising prosperity with education at its centre. From the 1960s to the 1970s there was, however, a quite remarkable turn-around from optimism to pessimism. Torsten Husén described this as 'euphoria' giving way to 'disenchantment'.

> But at the very peak of its dazzling success, in the almost euphoric moment of being conceived as the prime instrument of individual self-realisation, social progress, and economic prosperity, education began to be beset by doubts about what schools were achieving and serious criticisms were launched. The school as an institution came under severe attack and in some quarters there was talk of 'crisis', even a worldwide one. (Husén 1979: 9)

This crisis was the confluence of a number of tendencies that converged upon the conclusion that the faith placed in the reforming power of education was misplaced. Modern society in its advanced industrial form was *not* progressing according to plan. This required a re-theorization of society, and this occurred with varying degrees of radicalism. Husén summarizes the situation as follows:

> The most evident symptom of changed attitudes towards education is the wave of criticisms from both left and right that swept many countries in the late 1960s. The former consensus about the benefits of traditional schooling and the conviction that education always represented an intrinsic good were

gone. So was the belief that education was the main instrument for bringing about a better society. The conservatives blamed the school for its low academic standards, its lack of discipline, and for neglecting the talented students. The radical left accused the schools of being joyless, oppressive and autocratic. A new breed of Marxist educators perceived schools as instruments of capitalist society. Schools were there to produce a work force that would fit the hierarchical and oppressive working life in that type of society. (Ibid. 11)

The title of Husén's book was *The School in Question*. The most pessimistic form that disenchantment took was the view that rather than making all the difference, education perhaps made none at all!

In general, the criticisms of education in the period of disenchantment took two broad forms: those that questioned the functioning of *education* within society (reformists) and those that questioned the *society* within which education functioned (radicals). For radicals, the failings of education were only to be expected given the society. There were (and are) left- and right-wing variants of both positions. The problem for left radicals was that advanced industrial society *is* capitalist, but for the New Right it wasn't capitalist *enough*. Although the cracks appeared slightly earlier – most clearly in the student revolt of the late 1960s – it was the oil crisis of the early seventies that set in train the significant economic and cultural changes that have shaped contemporary education. As Phillip Brown and Hugh Lauder say:

> Since the first oil shock of the early 1970s western societies have experienced a social, political, and economic transformation that is yet to reach its conclusion. At its epicentre is the creation of a global economy that has led to an intensification of economic competition between firms, regions, and nation states. The globalisation of economic activity has called into question the future role of the nation state and how it can secure economic growth and shared prosperity. (Brown and Lauder 1997: 172)

In the light of these events it is possible, retrospectively, to see that the advanced industrial society model recorded a specific historical context in the West, when industrial societies enjoyed a high degree of 'organization' by virtue of the coinciding or superimposition of their economic, political, territorial and cultural spheres – the condition that Halsey et al. (1997) call 'economic nationalism' (see also Brown and Lauder 2001: part 1). Globalization is in one sense a response to the effects of the oil crisis, in that corporations, in order to cut costs, shifted production from high- to low-wage economies; but in another, it was the product of a broader set of emerging conditions and possibilities: those associated with new technologies and trade regimes that facilitated instantaneous, global flows of capital. Corporations burst through national boundaries, significantly reducing the capacities of nation-states to effectively steer their economies. These effects also provided the context for the politics of the New Right, announcing a new configuration of state and market, nation and economy (Jessop 1993). For education the most significant effect of this was the 'marketization' of schooling. In the UK, the 1988 Education Reform Act (Floud and Hammer 1990) marked the culmination of a Thatcherite New Right educational reform programme that radically restructured the education system.

This restructuring of relations contained apparently contradictory tendencies. On the one hand there was a considerable strengthening of control by the central state (exemplified in the National Curriculum), but on the other there was the development of quasi-market mechanisms which attempted to make schools behave much more like businesses in a market (Whitty 1991, 1997; Apple 2000). Schools were put into the position of having to compete with each other for pupils. These mechanisms included open enrolment, whereby parents could (at least in theory) send their children to the school of their choice, the devolving of education funding directly to schools themselves and away from Local Education Authorities (LEAs), and changing the membership of school governing bodies so that they more directly reflected the views and interests of 'consumers' (parents, that is, not children).

The major losers in this new order were teachers and the LEAs. The LEAs lost most of their previous powers and responsibilities. The teachers lost their historic control over the curriculum. Essentially, from their point of view, there was a movement from a position of high professional autonomy to one of low autonomy. Teachers' work became much more highly regulated by mechanisms such as the National Curriculum and SATS (periodic standardized national tests). More fundamentally, this reform programme was also one of culture change, attempting to replace the liberal-humanist model of English education with one based on enterprise values (Grace 1997). The restructuring of the teacher's role reflected the New Right view that education itself (through its commitment to progressive values and its hostility to the world of work) was the problem.

The basic principle that the various elements of this programme share is that of *commodification* whereby, as Michael Apple puts it, 'The world, in essence, becomes a vast supermarket' (Apple 1997: 597). For critics such as Apple the logic of commodification in education works against the values of democracy, equity and social justice, and serves the interests of dominant social groups (Apple 2000). Where schools are having to compete with each other, and where some parents are better placed to make and exercise choice, there will be increasing social segregation and inequalities of outcome (Ranson 1990; Whitty 1991, 1997; Ball et al. 1997). For supporters of such reforms (e.g. Chubb and Moe 1997), however, the shift towards market forms of education increases autonomy, efficiency and responsiveness. Teachers have to satisfy parents' demands and expectations.

Education and Globalization

In a number of ways, education's place within (and contribution to) the 'disorganized' conditions of a globalized, post-Fordist world is harder to define than in 'advanced industrial society'. What is the 'logic' of this new condition? There is no simple consensus as to its form, and some – post-modernists – reject the very idea of 'logics' (or 'grand narratives') in any case. A fundamental issue concerns the relationship between the market-based, New Right programmes of reform and the deeper movements of socio-economic change. Are the former the 'natural' expression of the latter? What freedom of manoeuvre is there under these conditions? What is the range of political options?

Although there is general agreement that things have changed in the last decades of the twentieth century, there is less agreement as to the *depth* of the change. The basic question is: Are we living through a *transformation* of modernity in which continuities with the modernism of 'advanced industrial society' remain (we are in a condition of 'late' or 'neo'-modernity; Giddens 1990; Alexander 1995; Hartley 1997)? Or are we experiencing a radical break with the past such that we are now in a *post* modern age? The issues posed by philosophical post-modernism will be discussed in chapter 6. For the moment, it is necessary to have a sense of the general contours of change and their complexities (Brown and Lauder 2001: part 2). These can be summarized in terms of the following factors:

Economic: (a) Post-Fordism, marking the move away from the large, hierarchical, bureaucratic forms of mass production towards flatter and 'leaner', networked organizations where individuals are 'multi-skilled' and ready to assume 'flexible' ways of working, and more open, less secure conditions of service (part-time or fixed-term contracts, etc.). (b) The decline of 'old' heavy manufacturing industries and their replacement by new hi-tech industries and service sectors (in finance, computing, entertainment, etc.). (c) Globalization involving the dominance of transnational corporations, global movements of capital, and the promotion of 'free trade' through international deregulation. (d) The decline of economic nationalism.

Social and cultural: (a) The impact of the above are associated with an emphasis upon consumption rather than production. This is reflected in the move away from standardized mass production to increasingly differentiated forms of 'niche marketing' where products are produced not in bulk but are specialized with a view to particular groups of consumers. (b) This situation produces a 'post-modern' culture promoting and celebrating difference and diversity. (c) These processes of individuation are associated with a deepening of 'reflexivity' on the part of individuals and a sense of the self

as decentred and fragmented rather than as given – a sense rein-
forced by the experience of space–time compression associated with
the World-Wide Web. (d) Politically, these forces encourage a movement away from the old politics of class and economics towards a
new 'identity' politics of recognition grounded in issues of gender,
ethnicity and sexuality.

A major difference between these 'late' or 'post' modern accounts and
the earlier 'advanced industrial society' one is that the notion of 'convergence' has been largely abandoned. Rather than there being one route to
modernity (exemplified by the USA), it is now more often argued that
there are many. Especially in view of the rise and success of Pacific rim
economies (the 'Asian tigers', etc.), different regions and civilization areas
can be seen as progressing along their own routes to modernity, drawing
upon their own cultural legacies (Confucian values, for instance). This
development is important, because it calls into question the link between
modernization and *Westernization*.

These changes present problems and challenges for education (Hartley
1997). In particular, *what* to teach becomes more problematic. In the
first instance, this reflects the processes of individuation, diversity and
multiculturalism and the lack of a sure sense of core values or a particular
'national' way of life. This is not only to do with multiculturalism and
ethnicity, but with complex changes in family structures and radically
changing attitudes to gender and sexuality. Transitions – for example,
from school to work, from dependency to adulthood – are less predictable
and certain than they once were (Ahier and Moore 1999). Beyond the
social and the cultural, in epistemological form, the question of what
to teach is radically contested by post-modernism's relativizing, sceptical
challenge to the very idea of rationally objective knowledge (see chapter
6). The changing nature of work and the rapidity of technological advance
make skills and knowledge quickly obsolete. Though knowledge is central
to the 'learning society', its fragility under such conditions requires the
individual to develop a particular type of *capacity* for learning – to become
a 'lifelong learner' (Ahier et al. 2003: ch. 3) – rather than just a particular
body of knowledge and skills.

Typically, the rhetoric of government educational reforms suggests that
those reforms are imperative responses to social change – that there is no
alternative. That this might not be the case is indicated in Roger Dale's
discussion of 'the state and the governance of education'. The difference
between 'government' and 'governance' is that the former refers to the
institutions of government and state, whereas the latter refers to the *range*
of means whereby desired outcomes might be attained – for examples,
through privatization, private/public combinations, contracting out, etc.

> Much recent work on the economics and politics of the welfare state has dis-
> tinguished three forms of what is usually referred to as 'state intervention'.
> These relate to three distinct and separable *activities* involved in welfare

policy: how it *is funded,* how it is *provided* (or delivered), and how it is *regulated* (or controlled). It is argued that it is not necessary for the state to carry out all of these activities, while remaining in overall control of education. These activities have to be co-ordinated, and in line with the hollowing-out thesis it has become common for three major *institutions of social coordination* to be distinguished. Several versions of these distinctions appear, but common to them all is the identification of the state and the market as two of the three key institutions of social co-ordination. The third, community, is always a residual category to the state and market and is conceptualised differently (though usually implicitly) according to the conception of state and market taken. Once again, it should be noted that the 'traditional' assumption has been that all the activities involved in the co-ordination of education were carried out by the state. However, a moment's thought shows us that the state has never done all these things alone; the market and especially the community have been indispensable to the operation of the education systems. The difference now is that the areas of their involvement have been greatly expanded and formalized as the area of direct state involvement has contracted. Combining these two sets of variables into a three-by-three table, then, sheds some new light on the governance of education. (Dale 1997: 274–5)

By employing the concept of 'governance' in this way, Dale is able to demonstrate a number of different solutions to the way in which the key activities of 'funding', 'regulation' and 'provision/delivery' can be distributed between the state, the market and the community, as given in the permutations of those categories. The same ends can be achieved in a variety of ways by a variety of agencies.

Hence, it is not a matter of a simple choice between state or market systems of educational provision. Rather, there are complex reconfigurations of relationships and a range of possibilities. Furthermore, Dale argues, these things also involve redistributions between *supranational* and *sub-national* bodies (e.g. for the UK between the European Union and devolved bodies such as the Scottish Parliament) and, globally, these complexities make possible different types of *regional* solutions and models (Dale and Robertson 2002).

Brown and Lauder (1997) describe two 'ideal typical' responses to globalization: neo-Fordist and post-Fordist routes to economic development, which have profoundly different educational implications' (p. 173 and table 10.1 on p. 175):

Neo-Fordism can be characterised as creating greater market flexibility through a reduction in social overheads and the power of trade unions; as encouraging the privatisation of public utilities and the welfare state; and as celebrating competitive individualism. Alternatively post-Fordism can be defined in terms of the development of the state as a 'strategic trader', shaping the direction of the national economy through investment in key economic sectors and in the development of human capital. Post-Fordism is therefore based on a shift to 'high value' customised production and services using multi-skilled workers. (Brown and Lauder 1997: 176)

They identify neo-Fordism with the USA and the UK, and post-Fordism with countries such as Germany, Japan and Singapore. Essentially the difference between the two is that neo-Fordism attempts to compete in the global market by weakening the bargaining power of workers and trade unions, encouraging labour market flexibility and inviting inward investment through deregulation and low-tax regimes favourable to multi-national corporations. By contrast, post-Fordism competes on the basis of *quality* of goods and services. It seeks to preserve a basic floor of protective rights and entitlements for the work-force (e.g. a minimum wage, job security). In relation to education, Brown and Lauder argue that the neo-Fordist market model combined with employer short-termism has an inbuilt tendency towards social polarization and inadequate long-term investment in quality training and education. The post-Fordist approach sees government as making a much stronger intervention, both to promote social justice in education and to underpin the sustained development of high-quality human capital.

For Brown and Lauder, 'There is no hidden hand or post-industrial logic which will lead nations to respond to the global economy in the same way' (ibid. 175). By exploring a range of responses to globalization, they, like Dale, point to the fact that the recognition of complexity entails the acknowledgement of possibility – that there *are* alternatives, and that collective judgements can be made as to which paths to follow.

Conclusion

Reviewing models of the relationship between education and economy produced over the last fifty years reveals two main features: (a) each in itself is to some significant degree incomplete, and (b) that incompleteness is associated with some state of affairs that is counter-intuitive given the assumptions of the guiding 'logic'. Goldthorpe provides a key statement of the issues. First, he points to the relative failures of both the liberal and the Marxist logics of industrialism and capitalism. Secondly, he points to the strange case of the stability of class differentials in educational attainment over the twentieth century. In addition, it can also be noted that between nations of similar levels of industrial development there can be significant differences in their educational systems (in levels of participation, organizational forms, cultures) which are not associated with theoretically anticipated differences in factors such as rates of social mobility.

What is being called into question by these explanatory shortfalls and anomalies is the nature of the link between education and economy, and the effects of education upon society of its capacity to facilitate certain kinds of changes as regards the distribution of social opportunities between social groups. The stability of class differentials is made even more striking by the change that took place in the relationship between the sexes in education. In the main, the thrust of educational reform in the post-war period was fuelled by the view that existing educational arrangements were getting things wrong. The fault lay within education itself. The alternative, however, might be to question the assumptions of the various logics of normal development that underpin and contextualize reform programmes. From a sociological point of view, it is the question of linkage and effectivity that is central.

More recent analyses of education, post-industrialism and globalization, in contrast to the earlier logic of advanced industrial society, highlight complexity and the range of possibilities. The awareness that there are many roads to modernity, as opposed to a single model of normal development towards which we are converging, questions the very idea of 'logics' (or 'grand narratives' to the sceptics), and certainly the view that there is a vanguard exemplary society (the USA) which provides a template for those coming along behind. These ideas are an important counterweight to neo-liberal 'end of history' triumphalism. In which case, the critical investigation of linkage and the loci of effects become more urgent. Economy tells only half the story. The next chapter concerns state formation and status – not as alternatives to economy and class, but as complementary to them.

3

Education, the State and Status

Introduction

The previous chapter was concerned with approaches that link education to the economy by producing general accounts of society and their forms of production and relate the education system to associated 'logics of development'. But the problem with prioritizing the economy is that it does not explain *enough* about what we know to be the case. This chapter takes as its starting point *state* formation. The relationship between education and the economy directs attention to class and the technical and ideological characteristics of production. The relationship to state formation directs attention to *status*, and introduces a new dimension: the manner in which education (in certain forms) can confer honour upon the individual, and how this quality can be an 'asset' or form of 'cultural capital' valued and of value in its own right. These two perspectives, economy and state, are not exclusive, however, but inextricably linked. This chapter will cover the relationships between education and

- state formation and bureaucracy;
- the role of the credential and the formation of a 'middle class of education';
- the 'cultural capital' associated with cultivation, distinction and status;
- status groups and social closure;
- *habitus*.

It concludes with the ideas of Pierre Bourdieu and his attempt to bring the concepts of class and status together in a unitary model.

There are two broad areas to be considered. The first is the formation of the modern nation-state and the development of education systems. Here, the emphasis will be upon the kinds of factors associated with *differences* in state formation, and how they appear to be associated with differences in the emergence and the forms of national education systems. The second is to look more deeply at *what it is* that the state requires of education. This has two aspects: (a) the association between bureaucracy, rationalization and what Weber terms an education of 'cultivation' (or *Bildung* in the German tradition), and (b) how this is associated with group formation, stratification and 'status'.

Whereas considerations of class directed attention to *vertical* differences between groups, 'status' directs attention to the significance of a *horizontal* difference *within* the middle class between those, mainly professional, groups that acquire the education of 'cultivation' and those, mainly industrial and commercial, who do not (Power et al. 2003). Hence, we will be looking at the distribution of different *types* of education, and not simply at the different 'amounts' of it that various groups acquire.

State Formation

The advantage of beginning from the state is that the historical emergence of national education systems fits better with state formation than with the development of industrial economies: e.g. the early development of a modern education system in Prussia with its strong central state compared with Britain with its long tradition of decentralization. As Andy Green describes it in his major study of this topic:

> The classic form of the public education system, with state financed and regulated schools and an elaborate administrative bureaucracy, occurred first on the Continent, notably in the German States, in France, Holland and Switzerland. All these countries had established the basic form of their public systems by the 1830s, although in France universal attendance was not achieved until some 50 years later. The northern states of the USA followed, developing public education systems, according to their own more decentralised design, in the period between 1830 and the Civil War. Britain, the Southern European States, and the American South, lagged considerably behind, in England's case delaying the full establishment of an integrated system until the following century. (Green 1990: 3)

Green suggests that, in addition to the economy, historians have linked the development of education systems to factors such as urbanization and changes in family structures and social stratification (ibid. 26–7), but have neglected the relations between these phenomena. Sociologists have sought such links, but tend to lack a good grounding in the relevant history. He attempts to bring the two together in an account that is both historically informed and theoretically grounded.

Green insists that any adequate account of the development of the modern education system should be non-reductive – we should not seek a single cause, but grasp the complex interactions between the kinds of factors just mentioned. First, the state has to be historically located and placed within a broader social context, and secondly, the interconnections within that context have to be fully appreciated. A complex set of factors is articulated within configurations that provide the conditions of emergence, development and differentiation of education systems. There is a pattern of similarities and differences revealed by a comparative analysis of cases (Green selects England, France and the USA). It is in this patterning that the significance of the state is revealed.

If education systems differ as states differ, in what educationally significant ways are states different? Green's study suggests that the key factor is the degree of *centralization*. The general tendency is for centralized states to have developed education systems earlier than decentralized ones. If we take the historical procession of education systems, the successive ordering of countries is also an approximate rank order from high to low centralization. Centralization, in turn, is linked with the speed and intensity of key episodes of nation building (Green 1990: 310–11). Green relates this to three kinds of historical factors:

- external military threats and territorial conflicts that lead 'victim nations' to strengthen their military and state machines;
- internal transformations such as the French Revolution that resulted in the need to establish a new sense of social order and identity;
- relative economic underdevelopment, leading states to develop growth and competitiveness.

The degree of centralization affects both *when* education systems emerged and the *form* they adopted. The English system, even at the end of the twentieth century and after the introduction of a National Curriculum in 1988, still remains a hybrid system involving a wide range of schools with varying degrees of independence from the state and, of course, a strongly entrenched, elite private sector of 'public schools'.

The State and Bureaucracy

Implicit in the centralization/decentralization dimension is the way in which different societies resolve the problem of the relationship between central and provincial power. This problem is not specific to the modern Western nation-state in its formative period. Weber indicates the general issue when he tells us that the 'literati' (i.e. the classically educated administrative class) of imperial China

> created the concept of 'office', above all, the ethos of 'official duty' and of the 'public weal'. If one may trust the Annals, the literati, being adherents of the bureaucratic organisation of the state as a compulsory institution, were opponents of feudalism from the very beginning. This is quite understandable because, from the standpoint of their interests, the administrators should

be only men who were personally qualified by a literary education. On the other hand, they claimed *for themselves* to have shown the princes the way towards autonomous administration, towards government manufacture of arms and construction of fortifications, ways and means by which the princes became 'masters of their lands'. (Weber 1967: 111)

This points to three things: the importance of the office-holders within the state bureaucracy, the tension between the bureaucratic principle and that of feudalism, and the manner in which that tension was associated, politically, with that between the central authority and local power. Crucially, the bureaucracy enabled the princes to be the 'masters of their lands' – that is, to impose central power.

Weiss and Hobson refer to this aspect of the state as its 'infrastructural/penetrative power': the extent to which the state is able to establish a societal structure of sufficient scope and efficiency to secure its aims such as collecting taxes itself rather than being reliant upon local powers to do it for them. They say that:

> Bureaucracy is the handmaiden of infrastructural/penetrative power, through which the state is able to interact with society independently of the nobility's provincial autonomy. Sometimes this led to head-on conflicts between the state and nobility . . . But the creation of a central bureaucracy, as with the royal court, allowed the state to suck the nobility into the centre, thus breaking down the spatial distanciation which had previously limited state power. Bureaucratisation was, above all, a strategy implemented by rulers to accumulate centripetal power in what was essentially the principal mode of noble pacification. (Weiss and Hobson 1995: 35)

In the Prussian case, for instance, the bureaucracy was of a 'fiscal-military' character. The Prussian state evolved from the manner in which the Great Elector of Brandenburg-Prussia, Frederick William (1640–88), undercut the power of the Junker landed nobility by developing a bureaucratic structure that, through its independent tax-gathering powers, relieved the central state of reliance upon them (ibid. 35–8). The historian T. C. W. Blanning (2002) describes how the Great Elector 'determined not to fall back under the sway of the provincial Junkers . . . sought assistance from socially neutral technocrats' (pp. 198–9). He outlines the situation of this 'estate of bureaucrats' in Weberian terms:

> In Max Weber's classic analysis, a bureaucrat has five essential characteristics: he is governed by an abstract concept of duty, not personal fealty to an individual; he owes his appointment to his technical qualifications, not to purchase or nepotism; he has a tenured position and can be dismissed only with good cause; he is paid a regular salary and is not dependent on fees; and he enjoys a career structure based on promotion by merit and/or seniority. In Prussia its origins are to be found in the exclusion from central government of the noble Estates by Frederick William, the Great Elector after the Thirty Years War. (Blanning 2002: 198)

Following this development on into the eighteenth century we see the introduction of examinations for entry into the upper reaches of the administration – eighty-five years before similar reforms in Britain. Blanning draws attention to two important aspects of this situation. First, the universities that produced the mandarins became the 'main conduits through which the Enlightenment found its way into public life' (p. 199), thereby spreading progressive ideas (see also Israel 2001); secondly, this led to the 'formation of an intelligentsia' (Blanning 2002: 201). He says of the influential philosopher Christian Wolff that, as 'the son of an artisan, he rose simply by dint of his talent.... It can be assumed with some confidence that had he been born an Englishman he would not have gained access to Oxford or Cambridge' (pp. 201–2). In this respect, the education system and the bureaucracy brought into being a new class: a middle class of education. It is not just that the middle class *became* educated; rather, that this class was *constituted* through education and absorbed people from a variety of backgrounds.

Centralization, then, is associated with the development of bureaucracy as a means whereby the central authority can transcend local nobility power and allow the state to 'interact with society independently of the nobility's provincial autonomy' (Weiss and Hobson 1995: 35). Crucially, these developments entail the following:

- shifting key powers from localities to a central apparatus that covers the whole society (nation-state);
- replacing the noble, linked through heredity to the land, by the salaried official who is separated from the office in the sense that he does not 'own' it, profit directly from it, or have the right to pass it on to his successors (though it is only in the modern bureaucracy that these ideal-typical conditions are fully met);
- systematically replacing traditional, local and dynastic principles of authority and social organization by others that are technical and legal-rational in character.

Together, these things construct a common interest between central power and a class (of literati, intelligentsia, or a middle class of education) of administrators and functionaries, defined through their education, that runs the bureaucratic apparatus. It is education that provides this class with both its expertise and its distinctive ethos: an 'ideology of cultivation' (*Bildung*). The extent and form of this class relate to the degree and manner in which the development of the state is part of a campaign of 'nobility pacification' whereby the central power attempts to bypass local, landed powers and develop its own means of interacting with society (including the facilitation of economic change).

Weiss and Hobson argue that the crucial factor in successful state formation is the balance between coercion and concession. The English state in the eighteenth century was successful, they suggest, because state power was wielded 'not against but through key societal actors' (p. 48). 'Despotism in the eighteenth century proved to be far less empowering for states than the so-called concessional strategy of negotiating access to resources. Despotic coercion was a sign of weakness, not strength' (ibid.). Hence, decentralized states are not necessarily *weak*, and centralized states are not necessarily *strong*. It is important to take into account the *particular* infra-structural features of the state and its 'penetrative' and 'extractive' capacities – its 'relative political capacity' or RPC. In this respect, Weiss and Hobson argue, the British state was highly successful because of

> its ability to penetrate society and collect taxes; its ability to achieve consensus; and the commercial nature of the economy as well as the existence of key financial institutions – the Bank of England and the City of London. In essence, by co-operating with the land-owning and capitalist classes, and developing a strong centralised fiscal bureaucracy, the British state enjoyed major benefits over its various continental rivals. The couplet of an infra-structurally strong state alongside a growing capitalist economy led the way in the experience of European state- and economy-formation. (Weiss and Hobson 1995: 47)

In one crucial respect the British state *was* centralized: in the area that really counted, the capacity to collect taxes efficiently! This itself reflected the political accommodation between parliament and monarch, and central and local power, worked out between the Civil War and the Glorious Revolution, and also that between the gentry and the emerging bourgeoisie in the late eighteenth and early nineteenth centuries. Because of its efficient but *restricted* centralization, the British state did not require an *extensive* central bureaucracy as part of a campaign of 'nobility pacification'. Because the bit that counted most worked best, it was not necessary to extend state bureaucratic power into other areas, as happens when the local nobility retains key fiscal (and other, especially military) powers. It would appear that it was precisely the *success* of the British state in this key area that resulted in its comparative *weakness* (or restricted scope, or 'penetration') in others, such as *education*. Paradoxically, the late arrival of a national education system in Britain reflected the *particular* manner in which (fiscal) state centralization was successful, rather than a chronic weakness and absence of centralization *per se*.

Bildung and the German Mandarins

The development of the education system in modern Europe entailed *class or status group formation* that brought into being that section of the middle class that owes its social position *to* education. In the Prussian case it occurred in a pronounced form that highlights a distinctive effect of education associated with the concept of *habitus*, which will be discussed further below. Bryan Turner describes this group in Germany as 'a special status group (the *Bildungsbürgertum*) which, in association with the state and the church, attempted to develop a *new type of personality*, namely a person whose emotions were *regulated by the discipline of education*' (B. Turner 1993: 10, my emphases).

> It was this bureaucratic state structure which generated the social context for the development of the ideals of *Bildung*, that is the ideals of the educated cultivated state employee of the middle classes. This moral world view of the *Bildungsbürgertum* which developed a criticism of the aristocracy, whose cultural lifestyle was based on sport, heavy drinking and sexual immorality, and against the lower classes who where thought to be in any case socially and politically dangerous. (Ibid.)

Turner associates the manner in which state formation occurs with different models of citizenship, relating to differing relationships between the individual and the state. This, in turn, is associated with a fundamental ambiguity within the concept of citizenship: 'social citizenship is both a condition of social integration by providing normative institutional means of social membership, which are based upon legal and other forms of entitlement, and citizenship is also a set of conditions that promotes social conflict and social struggle where the social entitlements are not fulfilled' (ibid. 11–12).

A *direct* link with state bureaucracy (as distinct from licensed or delegated authority (Freidson 1994)) is not necessarily a universal characteristic of educational status groups. In the US and UK cases the liberal professions are significantly *autonomous vis-à-vis* the state – indeed, autonomy (albeit relative) is precisely one of their marks of 'distinction'. Hence, this 'middle class of education' can be found across modern societies, but its relationship to the state can vary in terms of relative autonomy. It is necessary to look more deeply into state formation in order to understand why this should be, and at the kinds of factors that, on the one hand, bring the 'middle class of education' into being, but, on the other, create variations in its relationship to the state.

The German middle class of education, like its French counterpart, was strongly integrated into the state. But, unlike the Germans, the French (or at least a significant section of the intelligentsia) defined themselves with reference to a foundational event – the Revolution. They remained a *critical* intelligentsia that, though integrated in the sense of being state employees, nevertheless, from Voltaire through Durkheim to Sartre, maintained a tradition of intellectual distance that monitored the state's delivery of the 'entitlements' of citizenship. In the German context, according to Turner, the incorporation of the middle class of education within the state involved commitment to 'order and stability against both dissent and external opposition' (1993: 10). In the US and UK cases, where the lesser degree of centralization involved less extensive incorporation into the state, the intelligentsia has been less cohesive (indeed, whether these countries can be said to have an *intelligentsia* in the Continental sense is debatable; Hickox 1986), and has been particularly concerned to keep its 'infrastructural/penetrative power' within limits (consider, here, the differing situations of the medical profession in the UK and the USA).

Educational stratification

There are further reasons why the development of education systems and the modern state should be linked. The modern bureaucratic state requires educated functionaries in society at large, and not just amongst its elite. As Ringer says:

> Governments needed not only trained lawyers, but also health officials, postal clerks, chemistry teachers, railroad engineers, and other white-collar specialists. Moreover, the authorities were naturally interested in maintaining standards in such fields as pharmacy and construction. As a result, there was hardly an area or discipline for which some sort of examination was not eventually devised. In an economic environment in which opportunities for the self-made man without formal training were relatively scarce, the diploma offered a certain security. Thus the free and learned professions absorbed much of the available middle-class talent, and a species of private officials grew up side by side with the regular civil service. One is tempted to speak of a 'social fusion' in which the administrative and higher professional classes were drawn together. The officials contributed aristocratic and bureaucratic values, but it was the academic ideology of 'cultivation' which provided the most important bond between the various elements of the alliance. (Ringer 1977: 540)

Education provided the particular types of skills required by the state, especially those of literacy, but also technical expertise. Educational credentials were an asset in the German society described by Ringer, (a) because they got people jobs, and (b) because, for some, they conferred *status*: an advantage in its own right – an *intrinsic* return through 'honour'. In the middle of the nineteenth century, Ringer tells us, 'to be certified as highly learned... was to be accorded a great deal of formal respect.... The proud wife of an impoverished university instructor was still a *Frau Doktor*, and this meant something' (ibid. 537).

Ringer is describing a major source of stratification within German society that is generated by a crucial division *within* education: a 'sharp demarcation' (ibid. 537) separated primary school teachers from those in high schools and the universities. The education system itself was 'divided into two almost unrelated compartments' (ibid.). Despite the early development of the education system in the Germanic states, it remained the case that the great majority of children experienced only eight years of primary education, and that it was virtually impossible for them to reach a fully accredited secondary school or university. Indeed, even their teachers came from 'preparatory institutions' rather than 'the regular institutions of higher learning': 'the separation of popular and practical education from cultivation was quite complete' (ibid. 538). Ringer argues that 'the persistent emphasis upon personal "cultivation" (*Bildung*) in the German intellectual heritage was itself an agent of social stratification. Study of the classics was held to be particularly productive of cultivation, and disinterested learning was thought to affect the whole person, not just the intellect, of the learner' (ibid. 537).

The 'ideology of cultivation' in the German system served as a major source of social differentiation. Indeed, Ringer argues that the vertical division was 'less significant in some respects than the lines which separated industrial and commercial from professional and bureaucratic elements within the upper as well as within the middle and lower classes' (ibid. 541). Even as the social composition of the academic elite changed over time, the newcomers, he notes, tended to come from the 'non-economic' or 'non-industrial' sectors of German society. Ringer says that 'the highly educated in late nineteenth Germany thought and acted as a unique social group and developed their own characteristic set of values' (ibid. 543). Weber was himself a product of this group, and his experience of this educational division in German society clearly informs his typology of educational types:

> Historically, the two polar opposites in the field of educational ends are: to awaken charisma, that is, heroic qualities or magical gifts; and to impart specialised expert training. The first type corresponds to the charismatic structure of domination; the later type corresponds to the *rational* and bureaucratic (modern) structure of domination . . . . Between them are found all those types which aim at cultivating the pupil for a *conduct of life*, whether it is of a mundane or of a religious character. In either case, the life conduct is the conduct of a status group. The charismatic procedure of ancient magical asceticism and the hero trails, which sorcerers and warrior heroes have applied to boys, tried to aid the novice to acquire a 'new soul', in the animist sense, and hence, to be reborn. Expressed in our language, this means that they merely wished to *awaken* and to test a capacity which was considered a purely personal gift of grace. For one can neither teach nor train for charisma. Either it exists *in nuce*, or it is infiltrated through a miracle of magical rebirth – otherwise it cannot be attained.
>
> Specialised and expert schooling attempts to *train* the pupil for practical usefulness for administrative purposes – in the organisation of public authorities, business offices, workshops, scientific or industrial laboratories, disciplined armies. In principle, this can be accomplished with anybody, though to varying extent. The pedagogy of cultivation, finally, attempts to *educate* a cultivated type of man, whose nature depends on the decisive stratum's respective ideal of cultivation. And this means to educate a man for a certain internal and external deportment of life. In principle this can be done with everybody, only the goal differs . . . . In reality, none of these types ever occurs in pure form. (Weber 1967: 119–21)

Weber's description of 'The pedagogy of cultivation [that] attempts to *educate* a cultivated type of man . . . to educate a man for a certain internal and external deportment of life' points towards a deeper level of concern: that of the concept of *habitus*.

Habitus and 'The Pedagogy of Souls'

Weber was especially sensitive to these qualities of 'cultivation' and treated them in a manner reflecting his cultural tradition. Turner points out that it is

> important to keep in mind that Weber's own answers were the cultural product of the *Bildungsbürgertum* tradition. This tradition assumed that a cultivated person should attempt to adhere to a number of civilised criteria of personal existence that included inner loneliness, personal cultivation, responsibility and loyalty. These values were the values of the old German educational elite, but these values were under attack from new social forces and conditions that were broadly associated with urban capitalism. In particular, Weber was only too conscious that the processes of specialisation with the rationalisation of society made the achievement of personal integrity and wholeness extremely difficult to achieve. This anxiety was the basis of Weber's pessimistic comments in the conclusion of *The Protestant Ethic and the Spirit of Capitalism* about hedonists with no heart and vocational men without a soul. Specialisation negated the whole tradition of the cultivated personality with broad interests and a general education, namely the Enlightenment values of the age of Goethe. (B. Turner 1999: 64)

These observations provide a sense of the particular cultural background that influenced Weber's thinking, but also point to some more general issues. The first is the tension between the liberal-humanist educational ideal of a broad education with a moral and civilizing purpose and the increasingly specialized and utilitarian demands of the economy for types of technically skilled labour, and the second has to do with the legacy of this German tradition within social theory – especially that pessimistic strain (represented in the twentieth century, for instance, in the work of Horkheimer and Adorno 1979) that sees the Enlightenment as turning from a project of emancipation to one of oppression (and influencing contemporary post modernism – see chapter 6).

Although assuming a heightened and distinctive form in the German tradition (Ringer 1969), the effects of the educational 'ideology of cultivation' are general in the Western tradition and more widely (as Weber illustrates in his study of the Confucian 'literati' in China). The distinctive quality it bestows – status or 'distinction' in Bourdieu's terms (see below) – can, for some, be more important than wealth, the pursuit of which is perceived as vulgar.

The Chinese literati

Weber's (1967) study of the Chinese literati is seminal. The key to the literati's power was their classical literary education. This was economically significant because of the extreme importance in China of sustaining the harvest through the regulation of the waterways and the irrigation system, associated in turn with knowledge of the calendars and stars, with horoscopes and the ritually correct ordering of events (Weber suggests that the literati may have evolved from the court astrologers). Essentially, the literati can be seen as mediating the earthly relationship between the sacred and the profane – between events below and their symbolic representation in portents and events above: 'Only the adept of scriptures and of tradition has been considered competent for correctly ordering the internal administration and the charismatically correct life conduct of the prince, ritually and politically' (Weber 1967: 110). The literati, by virtue of their education, possessed an indispensable, but also *esoteric*, expertise. In political terms, the bureaucracy, staffed by the literati, was the means whereby the princes could extend their power, and underwrite their control of society, relative to that of provincially based feudal nobility. Hence, the particular expertise possessed by the literati was exercised through the bureaucracy of the imperial state, and that itself was extended as part of the strategy to keep in check the power of the feudal lords.

Essentially, there are two different principles at work against each other here. That of the bureaucracy is rationalistic: it emphasizes correct procedures both ritualistically and administratively. By contrast, that of the feudal lords was charismatic and hereditary. The earliest documents, Weber declares, describe 'a very schematic state organisation under the rational leadership of officials. It was based upon bureaucratically controlled irrigation, special crop cultivation (silk), draft registers for the army, statistics and magazines [i.e. arsenals]' (ibid. 37). At the personal level, the qualities of the literati, exemplified by 'the Master', Confucius, are '[c]ontrolled ease and correct composure, grace and dignity in the sense of a ceremonially ordered court-salon' (ibid. 156). Weber grounds his typology of education historically within religion and religious transformations of the self.

Sanctification, cultivation and *habitus*

The religious dimension of Weber's approach is important, because it introduces a theme that was central also to Durkheim (below and chapter 5): the social formation and transformation of the self. In *The Sociology of Religion* (1966), Weber employs the term *habitus* when discussing what he calls 'methodologies of sanctification' (see especially chapter 10). Essentially, sanctification is concerned with salvation and with the religious transformation of the self (rebirth or the acquisition of a new soul). Weber makes a contrast between those forms of transformation induced by ecstatic means (e.g. through drugs, orgy, music and dance; see also Durkheim 1995), which break down 'organic inhibitions' (p. 157), and those which result from following 'systematic procedures' or what we might aptly in this context call 'disciplines'. The crucial distinction is that the former type, though frequently extreme in its effects, is short-lived: 'these acute ecstasies are transitory in their nature and apt to leave but few positive traces on everyday behaviour' (p. 158). By contrast, the transformations of the self created by systematic methodologies of sanctification are enduring:

> As the process of rationalisation went forward, the goal of methodically planned religious sanctification increasingly transformed the acute intoxication induced by orgy into a milder but more permanent *habitus*, and moreover one that was consciously possessed.... The ultimate purpose to be served by the planned procedure of sanctification remained everywhere the same purpose which was served in an acute way by the orgy, namely the incarnation within man of a supernatural being, and therefore presently a god. Stated differently, the goal was self-deification. Only now this incarnation had to become a continuous personality pattern, so far as possible. (Weber 1966: 158)

It is not the specifically religious historical detail that is significant here, but the general character of *habitus* that Weber is describing: the relationship between the 'internal and external deportment of life'. Such developed 'methodologies of sanctification' may take the form of 'a systematic regulation of the ethics of everyday living' associated with an 'ethic of "good works"' (ibid. 154). This systematization 'treats individual actions as symptoms and expressions of an underlying ethical *total personality*' (ibid. 155, my emphasis).

> It is instructive to recall the attitude of some of the more rigorous Spartans towards one of their comrades who has fallen in battle after having sought such a death as a purification measure which would atone for an earlier manifestation of cowardice. They did not regard him as having rehabilitated his ethical status, since he had acted bravely for a specific reason and not 'out of the totality of his personality', as we would term it. In the religious sphere too, formal sanctification by the good works shown in external actions is supplanted by the value of the total personality pattern, which in the Spartan example would be an *habitual temper* of heroism. A similar principle applies to social actions of *all sorts*. If they demonstrate 'love for one's fellow man', then ethical systematisation of this kind requires that the actor possess the charisma of 'goodness'. It is of ultimate importance that the *specific action be really symptomatic of the total character* and that no significance be attached to it when it is a result of accident. (Weber 1966: 155–6, my emphases)

Hence, although religion provides the exemplary case, the phenomenon to which Weber refers is not exclusive to it. The discipline of the warrior may well rank a close second, but Weber tells us that 'a similar principle applies to social actions of all sorts', and he immediately provides a modern, secular example. The act is a symptom, or 'case', that reveals the existence of an underlying 'patterning' of the personality – of a *habitus*. It is the formation of these enduring dispositions that is the aim of 'the pedagogy of cultivation'. It is interesting that both Weber and Durkheim in the same period, quite independently (as far as I am aware), produced theories of the relationship between religious ritual, *habitus* and education that are, except for certain details, virtually identical!

Durkheim employs the term *habitus* with reference to what he sees as a radical historical change associated with the emergence of Christianity (see also Bernstein 2000: ch. 5; Beck 1999). The distinctive feature of Christianity, he argues, is that it requires the creation within the individual of a 'general disposition of the mind and the will which will make him see things in general in a particular light' (1977: 29).

> Christianity consists essentially in a certain attitude of the soul, in a certain *habitus* of our moral being. To nurture this attitude in the child will henceforth be the essential aim of education. This is what explains the emergence of an idea which was totally unknown in the ancient world and which by contrast played a substantial role in Christianity: the idea of conversion. A conversion, as Christianity understands it, is not really a question of adhering to a particular set of beliefs and specific articles of faith. True conversion involves a profound movement as a result of which the soul in its entirety, by turning in a quite different direction, changes its position, its stance, and as a result modifies its whole outlook on the world. (Ibid. 29)

In a commentary on Durkheim and Foucault, William Ramp (1999: 85) describes this as 'schooling as formation of the subject and mastery of the soul', as a 'totalizing pedagogy of souls'. The crucial point is that the concern with the mind as a whole required a unified and totalizing pedagogy. Durkheim argued that for the ancients, knowledge was acquired in an *ad hoc* fashion from different teachers with no overarching framework. The concern in Christianity was an awareness that, 'underlying the particular condition of our intelligence and sensibility there is in each one of us a more profound condition which determines the others and gives them their unity; and it is this more profound condition which we must get at if we are truly to do our job as educators and have an effect which will be durable' (Durkheim 1977: 28). For this to happen, knowledge must be underpinned by its own structure and exhibit a unity directed at shaping the whole child. This structuring of knowledge is reflected in the school, which must provide a 'morally cohesive environment which closely envelops the child and which acts upon his nature as a whole' (ibid. 30). It was in the European Middle Ages that this 'great and important innovation' (ibid. 31) occurred, and it is in this form that the school still functions, in a secular manner, in modern society – the principle aim is to 'imbue in [the child] some deep and internal state of mind, a kind of orientation of the soul, which points it in a definite direction, not only during childhood but throughout life' (ibid. 30). In chapter 5, Durkheim's concept of *habitus* will be related to the role that education plays in his general project of sociologizing Kant's philosophy.

It is not difficult to see why there should be a link, in Weber, between the enduring dispositions produced by the pedagogy of cultivation and the kind of trust accorded to the mandarins and which was their principal social asset. As Weber says, 'the specific action is symptomatic of the *total character*' (my emphasis). The individual's actions have an *integrity* that is located within the very nature of the self – the 'second nature' (as Bourdieu would say) that accompanies the self transformed (reborn) by the kind of pedagogy that Weber describes as a 'planned methodology of sanctification (Weber 1966: 157). In the modern world it is primarily within the professions that these pedagogies prevail, though we can also identify their principle at work within the craft traditions and the military – the 'warrior's code' (Ignatieff 1998). Similarly, the pedagogy of cultivation links also with 'status group', in that the shared 'style of life', its members' 'tastes', are the collective expression of *habitus* or the manner in which the 'internal deportment' formed by the pedagogy exhibits itself in everyday life.

The concept of 'character' or 'personality' is especially significant in Weber's theory. Turner says:

> [B]y 'personality', Weber does not have in mind a psychological construct. Rather 'personality' refers to a life-plan or a structure within which the chaotic events of the life-cycle can be located. A 'personality' is an organisation of life-events which permits an individual to mature and develop. In this respect, Weber's 'personality' may have much in common with the ideal of the educated and civilised person of the educated middle classes of Germany (*Bildungsbürgertum*) and can also be seen as the sociological legacy of Goethe's *Bildungsroman*. Weber's view is that authenticity consists in 'facing up to reality' and in making a conscious choice about a life-style which can be rationally defended. Authentic personality involves a certain degree of isolation and separation in order to bring up a reflexive ordering of one's personal and social reality. (B. Turner 1999: 63)

Turner stresses two problematic aspects of the condition that Weber describes, as far as modern societies are concerned. The first, already mentioned, is that the kind of general, liberal-humanist education associated with the formation of this kind of personality is threatened by technical rationality and instrumental specialization (Ringer 1969). The second is to do with how 'making a conscious choice about a life-style which can be rationally defended' involves an *existential commitment*. As a 'social action' theorist, Weber is more aware than is Durkheim (or, at least makes more explicit) the manner in which the generative properties of *habitus* require a *reflexive* act by the individual in order to be realized as a social practice. It is in this manner that *habitus* is creative rather than merely a mechanistic acting out of a socialized norm. The fundamental difference between the kind of *habitus* cultivated by religious methodologies of sanctification and the secularized versions found in the modern world is that the former were grounded in sets of absolute values, whereas for the latter this is not possible. In a 'disenchanted' world of technically efficient means, but no overarching sense of a worthwhile end, reflexivity becomes an act of continual existential renewal of commitment. It is only through an existential 'ethic of responsibility', expressed in a 'calling' or 'vocation', that Weber believed we could avoid the nihilism that follows from Nietzsche's pronouncement of the Death of God. Turner, however, doubts how successfully Weber extracted himself from this problem.

Status groups and social closure

It is important to understand that the formation of *habitus* is not the same thing as socialization into a received body of knowledge, beliefs, values and norms. These might be treated as the *content* of consciousness, as when, in the earlier quote, Durkheim makes a crucial distinction between 'adhering to a particular set of beliefs and specific articles of faith' and 'a profound movement as a result of which the soul in its entirety, by turning in a quite different direction, changes its position, its stance, and as a result modifies its whole outlook on the world' (Durkheim 1977: 29). Bourdieu refers to *habitus* as 'the durably installed *generative principle* of regulated improvisations' (Bourdieu 1977: 78, my emphasis; Nash 1999). In this sense, *habitus* can be understood as the underlying rules, or 'grammar', that structure consciousness (as its 'generative principle') and, as such, regulates the ways in which we categorize, organize, select and configure the material and cultural resources we employ in our social behaviour ('regulated improvisations') – in Durkheim's words, it is 'a more profound condition which determines the others and gives them their unity' (Durkheim 1977: 28). As Bourdieu argues in his major study *Distinction* (1986), the manner in which these generative principles regulate improvisations in everyday social action is revealed through the distinctive *tastes* of different groups: their preferred food and drink, reading matter, approaches to high and popular culture, how they dress, the newspapers they read, and the holiday destinations they prefer. He says: 'Taste classifies, and it classifies the classifier. Social subjects, classified by their classifications, distinguish themselves by the distinctions they make, between the beautiful and the ugly, the distinguished and the vulgar, in which their position in the objective classifications is expressed or betrayed' (Bourdieu 1986: 6).

Taste operates to make (or mark) distinctions between social groups. As the final words indicate, to get it wrong is to be classified as being at varying degrees removed from those whose taste is 'distinguished', and these degrees relate systematically to class structure and its fractions (e.g. between the professional and industrial fractions of the middle class). Bourdieu's concept of 'cultural capital' will be considered in the next section. For Weber, status groups differ from classes in that their members are defined by a shared culture and sense of common identity (to be working-class, in Marx's sense, does not necessarily entail this: class is defined by reference to relationships to the means of production, regardless of how the members of different classes feel about their membership and the life-styles they adopt). Using Weber's concept, Randall Collins defines status groups as follows:

> The basic units of society are associational groups sharing common cultures (or 'subcultures'). The core of such groups is families and friends, but they may be extended to religious, educational, or ethnic communities. In general, they comprise all persons who share a sense of status equality based on participation in a common culture: styles of language, tastes in clothing and decor, manners and other ritual observances, conversational topics and styles, opinions and values, and preferences in sports, arts and media. Participation in such cultural groups gives individuals their fundamental sense of identity, especially in contrast with members of other associational groups in whose everyday culture they cannot participate comfortably. Subjectively, status groups distinguish themselves from others in terms of categories of *moral evaluation* such as 'honour', 'taste', 'breeding', 'respectability', 'propriety', 'cultivation', 'good fellows', 'plain folks', etc. Thus the exclusion of persons who lack the ingroup culture is felt to be morally legitimated. (R. Collins 1977: 125)

Collins's point about the principles of moral evaluation employed by different groups has important educational consequences, in that these principles provide members with a sense of their own value: although the 'cultivated' might consider themselves superior to the rest, for 'plain folk' *plainness* is a virtue that elevates them above cultivation – they have a basic integrity, honesty and authenticity, in contrast to the cultivated, who are seen as effete, over-sophisticated and hypocritical. Each principle tells its own story and provides a particular virtue that places its adherents above others. On this basis, people may aspire to stay as they are, to affirm their membership and its virtues, and to resist the call of education to 'improve' themselves by acquiring the distinctions of cultivation. This recalls the issue raised in chapter 1 concerning judgements about the existential status of pupils' educational decisions and the *apparent* irrationality of those who choose what seem to be less favourable options. This will become especially significant in the next chapter.

On the basis of this Collins produces a Weberian *conflict* theory of education in opposition to technical functionalism (discussed in chapter 2). Like Bowles and Gintis, he rejects the argument that education produces the neutral technical skills demanded in the economy; but, unlike them, he relates education to status rather than class relations. In this respect (as with Ogbu, discussed in chapter 1) his concern is with educational stratification and its inscription within class and ethnic relations in American economy and society. He describes his basic proposition as follows: 'employers use education to select persons who have been socialised into the dominant status culture: for entrants to their own managerial ranks, into elite culture; for lower levels employees, into an attitude of respect for the dominant culture and the elite that carries it' (R. Collins 1977: 127). Collins demonstrates that the products of the elite and non-elite educational institutions are systematically distributed in different ways across the occupational structure in the USA: 'the organisations most clearly dominated by the WASP upper class are large, nationally organised business corporations, and the largest law firms' (ibid. 129). By contrast, members of ethnic minority groups tend to be concentrated in smaller and more local businesses in manufacturing and in solo legal practices. Similar divisions are to be found in local and national government. Hence, it is cultural and social background factors that qualifications index, rather than particular skills. Elite groups can attempt to close access to elite positions by preserving the dominance of their life-style cultures (or at least limit access to those willing to assume those characteristics, as with Ralph Turner's notion of 'sponsored mobility' – in racially stratified societies, of course, access becomes impossible if colour remains a criterion).

Collins identifies a crucial dynamic that emerges from the struggle between status groups: (a) because of the way in which education can provide opportunities for mobility all groups strive for access to better education, and (b) status groups are also in competition to advance their own particular 'virtue' and its associated status culture and the situation of their members. The decentralized character of education in the USA and the separation of church and state has made it relatively easy for different ethnic, racial and religious groups to found their own schools and colleges. As a consequence, the system of positions and relationships in education (as defined by levels and types of education) is being continually revalorized.

> In the process, the status value of American education has become diluted. Standards of respectability are always relative to the existing range of cultural differences. Once higher levels of education become recognised as an objective mark of elite status, and a moderate level of education as a mark of respectable middle-level status, increases in the supply of educated persons at given levels result in yet higher levels becoming recognised as superior, and previously superior levels become only average. (R. Collins 1977: 131)

This process of credential inflation will form the main focus of the next chapter. But first it is necessary to look in more detail at the manner in which status culture, and especially the *habitus* of cultivation, works in and through education in the work of Pierre Bourdieu and his concept of 'cultural capital'.

Pierre Bourdieu and Cultural Capital

So far this chapter has considered ways in which the development of the education system in modern societies can be related to state formation and the distribution of different kinds of education associated with different degrees of 'status'. The issue of the relationship between class and status was raised. It is in the ideas of the influential French sociologist

Pierre Bourdieu that it might be possible to draw these two strands together. As Calhoun et al. say: 'Class and status, emphatically separated by Weber, are interrelated according to Bourdieu' (1993: 5). Bourdieu does this through the manner in which he presents the relationship between 'economic' and 'cultural' capital – that is, in how he sees the relationship between 'disinterestedness' (those qualities associated with status and education for cultivation) and the *obvious* interests vested in economic capital. Cultural capital, he argues, is a 'transformation' of economic capital and cannot be understood, as a social phenomenon, independently from it. Hence, both forms of 'capital' need to be located within a more general theory of exchange.

> So it has to be posited simultaneously that economic capital is at the root of all the other types of capital and that these transformed, disguised forms of economic capital, never entirely reducible to that definition, produce their most specific effects only to the extent that they conceal (not least from their possessors) the fact that economic capital is at their root, in other words – but only in the last analysis – at the root of their effects. (Bourdieu 1997: 54)

Bourdieu's work is complex and extensive. He is concerned with fundamental theoretical issues, such as attempting to resolve the relationship between structure and agency (through the idea of *habitus*) and covers a wide range of issues and areas. He trained originally as an anthropologist, and his earlier work is within the structuralist perspective. He became dissatisfied, however, with the manner in which this approach (in the work of Lévi-Strauss and Althusser, for instance) impoverished the concept of human agency. His change of focus to culture, taste and education in his own society is associated with these theoretical issues. His use of the key concepts are attempts to draw together within a single framework and method (a *relational* model) those dimensions and levels traditionally separated by the dichotomies of objectivism (e.g. structuralism) and subjectivism (e.g. phenomenology), macro/micro, and structure and agency.

> It is in fact impossible to account for the structure and functioning of the social world unless one reintroduces capital in all its forms and not solely in the one form recognised by economic theory. Economic theory has allowed to be foisted upon it a definition of the economy of practices which is the historical invention of capitalism; and by reducing the universe of exchanges to mercantile exchange, which is objectively and subjectively oriented towards the maximisation of profit, i.e. (economically) *self-interested*, it has implicitly defined the other forms of exchange as non-economic, and therefore *disinterested*. In particular, it defines as disinterested those forms of exchange which ensure the *transubstantiation* whereby the most material types of capital – those that are economic in the material sense – can present themselves in the immaterial form of cultural capital or social capital and vice versa. Interest, in the restricted sense it is given in economic theory, cannot be produced without producing its negative counterpart, disinterestedness. The class of practices whose explicit purpose is to maximise monetary profit

cannot be defined as such without producing the purposeless finality of cultural or artistic practices and their products; the world of bourgeois man,
with his double-order accounting, cannot be invented without producing
the pure, perfect universe of the artist and the intellectual and the gratuitous activities of art-for-art's sake and pure theory. In other words, the
constitution of a science of mercantile relationships which, inasmuch as it
takes for granted the very foundations of the order it claims to analyse –
private property, profit, wage labour, etc. – is not even a science of the field
of economic production, has prevented the constitution of a general science
of the economy of practices, which would treat mercantile exchange as a
particular case of exchange in all its forms. (Bourdieu 1997: 46–7)

Bourdieu's starting point is the view that economics, as conventionally
understood, is narrowly confined to the class of 'exchanges' that he terms
'mercantile': that is, monetary exchanges for profit. He argues that this
should, in fact, be seen as only one aspect of a much wider system of
'exchanges' that includes social and symbolic forms as well as monetary
ones. These might include, for instance, a type of exchange associated
with social reciprocities such as everyday courtesies between strangers
or in the exchange of gifts or the obligations of kinship. All exchanges
entail principles of order and relations of hierarchy and power. They are
associated with expectations regarding appropriateness and equivalence –
we can be as much offended or embarrassed by receiving a gift too lavish
as by one too mean. These different kinds of exchange, though operating
in different systems, should be treated as 'transformations' of each other. A
central task for the more extended 'science' of economics that he proposes
would be to investigate the ways in which different types of 'capital'
undergo 'transubstantiation' from one form to another.

   A consequence of restricting economics to mercantile exchange is that it
creates the false impression that the principles that apply in that area are,
in fact, absent from other types of exchange. The most fundamental effect
of this is to create the notion that the worlds of art, culture and learning
are free from the kinds of instrumentalities and self-interestedness that
characterize purely monetary transactions. In this respect they are seen
to serve no other interest than their own – to serve only principles internal to them: 'truth', 'beauty', etc. These other systems appear to be pure,
sacred realms free of the taint of egotistical materialism. Art is 'art for
art's sake'; scholars pursue knowledge for the sake of truth alone, etc.
These other spheres are perceived to be concerned with values and pur-
suits that are *intrinsically* worthwhile, rather than directed towards some
base, profane end – art and knowledge are ends in themselves. Hence,
a division is constructed between what is merely a means to an end and
what is of intrinsic value. In education, this distinction is associated with
that between vocational education and training and 'education for cultivation'. Disinterestedness is the hallmark of this 'sacred' sphere. The
field of cultural production is, Bourdieu says, 'the economic world reversed' (1993: 29). However, we only really understand the operation of

the cultural and educational fields when we reconstitute the relationship between cultural capital and economic capital as internally related rather than radically discontinuous. Crucial to this undertaking is to understand the role played by the accumulation and mobilization of forms of capital of different kinds and the processes of transubstantiation that link them. In addition to economic capital, represented by wealth, Bourdieu defines, also, 'social' capital and 'cultural' capital.

Social capital is essentially to do with social networks and connections (see Bourdieu 1997: 51–3). It requires 'an unceasing effort of sociability, a constant series of exchanges in which recognition is endlessly affirmed and reaffirmed' (ibid. 52). Recognition is central to this form of capital, because it is intrinsically associated with *membership* and, hence, with groups. In this respect, social capital assumes an institutional form. It endures over time and can become extremely extensive in space (as with extended kinship networks). Membership, and the meeting of obligations as far as reciprocal expectations are concerned, is a kind of 'credit' upon which individuals can draw. It is important to note that this form of capital is collective in character: it is the *group* that is the repository of the capital, and members have a common interest in (and duty to) maintaining and accumulating it. It is 'cultural' capital that is particularly significant as far as education is concerned.

Bourdieu divides *cultural capital* into three kinds: 'embodied', 'objectified' and 'institutionalized' (1997: 47). In its objectified form it appears as material objects and media: books, paintings, writing, instruments, etc. But in this purely material form, a crucial ingredient is missing: that which enables the individual to 'see' the paintings or films, or to 'read' the books or 'hear' music in the appropriate manner. Cultural capital has value to the degree that individuals are able to 'decode the code' whereby the objectified forms of cultural capital are classified by the dominant principles of those controlling the cultural field. These class-based dispositions are grounded in the 'embodied' form of cultural capital – essentially, in *habitus*, which crucially begins in the home, but is expressed (and endorsed) also in the major 'institutionalized' form of cultural capital: education.

Bourdieu describes embodied cultural capital as 'external wealth converted into an integral part of the person, into a *habitus*' (ibid.). Crucially, the acquisition of this capital, the formation of *habitus*, takes place over a long period of time. It is a kind of 'work' done on the self – a *transformation* of the self as Weber and Durkheim described it. In this sense, it could be seen as a long-term investment. Primarily, it is measured in terms of length of time in education, though Bourdieu stresses that this must also take account of the primary *habitus* of the family ('early domestic education') and its 'distance from the demands of the scholastic market' (ibid.). Although associated with *formal* instruction through the educational process, it is important to stress that the most significant feature of embodied cultural capital is the *tacit* form of its acquisition and the apparent 'naturalness' of its manifestations. Formal instruction *in itself* is the medium through which acquisition occurs: it is not the content of what is taught that counts, but the underlying tacit principles of classification and selection. For those most distanced from 'the demands of the scholastic market', no amount of formal instruction will compensate for a primary lack of those dispositions necessary to assimilate the tacit codes beneath the surface of the educational process.

Economic capital is transformed into cultural capital essentially because those with more of the former are able to support their children through the lengthy process of education whereby the *habitus* of distinction is acquired. Cultural capital already stored in the primary *habitus* of the home provides the children of the upper classes with a head start. This is because their 'talent' appears entirely natural. Their ability to learn appears as an innate ability rather than as a product of the home and its surrounding culture. The transformation of economic capital into cultural capital *via habitus* disguises both the primacy of the economic field as the basis of cultural capital by 'naturalizing' what is in fact an economic advantage and doing so by asserting a principle that proclaims itself the *opposite* of the vulgar materialism of the economic. In this manner education reproduces the economic relations of society precisely to the degree that in its most cultivated forms it presents itself as most distant from those relations: '*pedagogic conservatism*', according to Bourdieu and Passeron, 'is the best ally of *social and political conservatism*' (1977: 198).

Cultural capital in action

Amy Stuart Wells and Irene Serna (1997) employ Bourdieu's concepts in an examination of resistance to detracking in racially mixed schools in the USA. In particular, they are concerned with the manner in which local elites operate with an 'ideology of entitlement' (p. 718) that in effect disguises their privilege by making their views generally acceptable as simply 'common-sense'. They summarize their approach in this way:

> In order for elites to employ their cultural capital to maintain power, emphasis must be placed on subtleties of taste – for example, form over function, manner over matter. Within the educational system, Bourdieu argues, students are frequently awarded for their taste, and for the cultural knowledge that informs it. For instance, elite students whose status offers them the opportunity to travel to other cities, states and countries on family vacations are often perceived to be more 'intelligent' than other students, simply because the knowledge they have gained from these trips is reflected in what is valued in schools. When high-status elite students' taste is seen as valued knowledge within the educational system, other students' taste and the knowledge that informs it is devalued. In this way, high-status culture is socially constructed as 'intelligence' – a dubious relationship that elites must

strive to conceal in order to legitimise their merit based claim to privileged status. (Wells and Serna 1997: 720)

Detracking is controversial in US schools because of its connection with race. Wells and Serna say that almost invariably it is white and Asian children in the top tracks, and blacks and Latinos in the bottom. Tracking effectively resegregates schooling. Elite parents will seek to preserve the educational advantages of their children because it is in this manner that economic advantage is translated into cultural capital. The relationship between economic and cultural capital within education 'records and conceals privilege' (ibid. 723). The children of the elite have educational advantage by virtue of their cultural capital, but the official ideology of education records that advantage as 'natural', as a return to innate ability, rather than a privilege ultimately grounded in economic capital. Hence, the defence of tracking and the preservation of high-flier tracks for the 'gifted' can appear as a defence of that provision for children of all backgrounds rather than simply the privileged whose tastes are those tacitly acknowledged by the school.

Diane Reay, in a study of two socially contrasting primary schools in Inner London, also focuses upon the ways in which middle-class families are able to employ cultural capital in order to exert pressure upon schools, by 'mobilising a range of resources to ensure their continuing social advantage' (1998: 205). Within this context, tracking (or 'streaming' in the UK) is not the issue, as most primary schools have mixed ability classes: their interest is in ensuring that the school maintains a sufficiently academic effort to provide their children with access to *selective* academic secondary schools rather than local comprehensive (or 'common') schools. She also highlights another important issue: the way in which in an increasingly competitive educational market, 'charismatic' qualities become increasingly important alongside purely academic ones. These are to do with extra-curricular 'refinements' such as music, drama and dance classes that develop children as personalities. This concern relates to an awareness of the ways in which employers are increasingly concerned with 'soft skills', in addition to formal qualifications, and the growing emphasis on CVs and the presentation of self. This, in turn, is a consequence of the tendency mentioned by Collins, above, towards a devaluing of credentials in a situation of educational expansion: as more and more people acquire degrees, additional factors come into play as ways of distinguishing those with the desired social characteristics. In Reay's sample, middle-class families are expending increasing amounts of time and money on extra academic tuition for their children alongside these other activities. Reay's concern is with the *gendered* character of this activity: it is mainly the work of mothers. She found that 'Some of the middle-class families were spending £100 a week [on such activities], more than a number of the working-class lone mothers received in order to support themselves and their child for the same period of time' (1998: 201). She describes this as a form of gendered, collective class action.

> There is an irony when historically collective class action has almost always been associated with the working classes, that effective class action within the educational field has always been the province of the middle classes. I would argue that the individualistic, self-interested activities of the privileged in society add up to a specific form of class action, but one which is powerfully gendered. The activities of a group of highly individualised middle-class women acting in the same way constitutes class action no less than the collective action of working-class men working for better conditions. (Reay 1998: 207)

The strategy that Reay describes can be seen as part of a broader mobilization of economic and cultural resources whereby middle-class families make a judgement in which they allow the local state-maintained primary school to provide a basic academic education which they then supplement with additional tuition and extra-curricular activities underpinned by the primary cultural capital of the home. Significantly, in an educational market system dominated by Scholastic Aptitude Test (SAT) results and school league tables, it is impossible to disentangle from school results the contribution of these extra-school activities. For some people, this makes a mockery of the league tables and the educational regime of which they are a central component – we can never know whether the success of a particular school is its own or that of the extra tutoring that many pupils receive. The crucial question for such families is the point at which it might be both less expensive and time-consuming to simply move their children across to the private sector. Both these studies demonstrate the complex interweaving of forms of capital and class, gender and ethnicity.

Cultural capital, class and status

Bourdieu's theory and its array of concepts allows for the mapping of complex circuits of transubstantiation whereby things are continually translated into modes that systematically conceal their actual origin, purpose and form. In the educational and cultural fields the tastes of the dominant groups are translated into the independent values of 'truth' and 'beauty' and are sanctified as such by apparently neutral and autonomous agents of those fields. What is in fact merely culturally arbitrary is re-presented as universal by virtue of some inner truth or necessity, and that which is socially acquired is treated as an innate capacity of the person. Through the transmission of *habitus* made effective through the employment of cultural capital, the educational ideology of cultivation reproduces the economic relations of class.

In this manner Bourdieu brings class and status back into a direct relationship. However, this relationship is not simply one of reflection, as would be the case in reductionist approaches. Rather, class and status stand to each other in a relationship of reversed institutional, cultural and ideological distanciation. On this basis the educational and cultural fields can achieve relative autonomy based upon principles internal to them ('truth', 'beauty', rather than profit) and evolve in complexity through the realization of possibilities immanent within them. The educational and cultural fields are effective in their role of reproducing class relations precisely to the degree that they appear to have nothing to do with them. The key agents of these fields (whom Bourdieu defines as the subordinated fraction of the dominant group) do not in any manner see themselves as involved in class reproduction; rather, they see themselves as producers of truths quite independent of class relations and interests (as when claiming scholarly objectivity).

In short: the process of the *transubstantiation* of the forms of capital enables the institutional, cultural and ideological *distanciation* of fields of symbolic production (such as education and culture) from that of material economic production, so enabling the *autonomization* of those fields on the basis of their own principles and interests as realized through the evolution of positions *immanent as objective possibilities* in every particular configuration of the field, given its *structure of positions* and the *strategies* and *trajectories* associated with them. Hence, writing of the field of cultural production, Bourdieu says:

> The *space of literary or artistic position-takings*, i.e. the structured set of the manifestations of the social agents involved in the field – literary or artistic works, of course, but also political acts or pronouncements, manifestos or polemics, etc. – is inseparable from the *space of literary or artistic positions* defined by possession of a determinate quantity of specific capital (recognition) and, at the same time, by occupation of a determinate position in the structure of the distribution of this specific capital. The literary or artistic field is a *field of forces*, but it is also a *field of struggles* tending to transform or conserve this field of forces. The network of objective relations between positions subtends and orients the strategies which the occupants of the different positions implement in their struggles to defend or improve their positions (i.e. their position-takings), strategies which depend for their force and form on the position each agent occupies in the power relations. (Bourdieu 1993: 30)

This is not easy! More clarity might be gained by defining what *type* of theory Bourdieu's is in terms of its basic principle – which points to a major problem. The extract above indicates that this is a *relational* model of the field of cultural production (as is his model of the educational field). This means that any position within the field (e.g. a type of novel or painting, a type of school or course, or the choice of cuisine or decor) has meaning *only* by virtue of its relationship to the *other* positions in the field. In the earlier extract, for instance, Bourdieu says that '[t]he class of practices whose explicit purpose is to maximise monetary profit cannot be defined as such without producing the purposeless finality of cultural or artistic practices and their products; the world of bourgeois man, with his double-order accounting, cannot be invented without producing the pure, perfect universe of the artist and the intellectual and the gratuitous activities of art-for-art's sake and pure theory' (1997: 46–7). The one presupposes, and can only be understood in relation to, the other. To put this the other way around, no position has meaning by virtue of some property *intrinsic* to it (e.g. such as its being true or beautiful). What is at issue here is suggested by Randal Johnson in his Editor's Introduction to Bourdieu's *The Field of Cultural Production*:

> At stake in the literary field, and more specifically in the field of criticism is, among other things, the authority to determine the legitimate definition of literary work and, by extension, the authority to define those works which guarantee the configuration of the literary canon. Such a definition is both positive, through selection of certain literary values, and negative through its exclusion of others. The establishment of a canon in the guise of universally valued cultural inheritance or patrimony constitutes an act of 'symbolic violence', as Bourdieu defines the term, in that it gains legitimacy by misrecognising the underlying power relations which serve, in part, to guarantee the continued reproduction of the legitimacy of those who produce or defend the canon. (Johnson in Bourdien 1993: 20)

In this manner we come to see Bourdieu's approach as an instance of a much wider perspective which is concerned with what Karl Mannheim called the 'unmasking' of truth claims (see chapter 6). This is where truth claims of various kinds are 'deconstructed' in such a way as to demonstrate that they are in fact representations of the views of particular groups and that, further, they serve the interests of those groups against the interests of others. In the Marxist variant, such an analysis would reveal school knowledge as 'bourgeois' and serving the interests of capitalism, and in the feminist version, as androcentric and serving the interests of men. Relations within the educational or cultural fields are *officially* presented by reference to ('in the guise of') some higher value such as being true, but this obscures the way in which such claims represent relations of power (misrecognition).

Bourdieu appears to achieve the task of reuniting class and status in such a way that status can retain a degree of autonomy on the basis of its association with the distinction of educational cultivation – it is not simply reduced to class. But it remains the case that the ultimate principle of intelligibility of the relations of symbolic fields remains that of the relations of the economic field. Although at a distance from it, and reversed, the logic of symbolic fields is *homologic* with that of the field of economic production (Alexander 1995). Once we have described the relational position structure of the educational field and the possibilities objectively immanent within it, and once we have grasped that it is no more than the transubstantiation of the economic field and its class relations, then there is nothing more to say about it – nothing in terms of *knowledge* itself. As

Alexander points out, the principle of 'homology' presents each field as 'a microcosm...of the social system' (1995: 160). Knowledge is the translation and scholarly consecration of the tastes of the dominant group. To the degree that symbolic fields are autonomized, they have principles internal to them; but they do not have principles that are *intrinsic* to them in the sense of belonging to them *in themselves* according to their own specificity as sites of symbolic production (e.g. of knowledge or of the aesthetic). We cannot understand knowledge relations in the educational field by reference to knowledge itself, but only in terms of power relations grounded in the economic field. These power relations are realized in the educational field through the differential effects of the class-based distribution of cultural capital and its further refinement in the secondary *habitus* of the school, and it is through *culture* rather than epistemology that we can make those relations and effects intelligible.

It could be argued, however, that the relationship between the cultural field and its distinctive principles and capitalism is *asymmetric*, not homologic. This field (like that of the philosophical canon, for instance) has a history of its own that stretches back over millennia and which contains values, procedures, positions and problems that maintain continuity despite radical changes within the kinds of societies within which it is active. The problem with relational theories is that if the system changes, *everything* changes – all positions and their relationships are revalorized. The new state of the system (and the relative values of positions within it) is radically discontinuous with what went before. But everything does not change. We are able to recognize that the literature produced in the capitalist era is in a fundamental respect continuous with that which went before (in the enduring centrality of Shakespeare to the Western canon, for example, and the influence of the classics). At the same time, fields can transform internally *independently* of any corresponding transformation elsewhere. Fields have logics of their own, whose trajectories are independent of the social probabilities and positionings that Bourdieu describes. Developments in the field of mathematics, for instance, respond to the critical condition of the field itself as a *problem* field, and are not merely strategically mediated transformations of changes in the economic field. Hence, rather than homology, it is the *asymmetry* of relationships between fields that is significant: continuities endure within fields despite changes in systems, and fields change while systems endure.

The fundamental issues at stake here are epistemological in character, and will form the main focus of chapter 6. The production of symbolic goods (including knowledge) is as much based in specific *relations of production* as is the production of material goods. This fact has important implications for considering *reproduction* within education, because (a) it provides an *intrinsic* (rather than simply a distanciated internal) principle of autonomy; and (b) because this, in turn, enables pupils and students (and their teachers) to interact with knowledge *itself* rather than simply with transubstantiated forms of capital. The concept of *habitus* will be revisited in chapter 5 through Durkheim and his *emergent* theory of knowledge, and its implications will be contrasted with both Bourdieu's relational model and varieties of standpoint of reductionism.

Conclusion

This chapter has related the development of mass education systems to state formation. It was stated at the beginning that this should be seen as complementary to, rather than as an alternative to, those approaches that relate it to the economy. Hence, the issue of the relationship between economic development and nation-states is central: essentially, how far are they themselves linked deterministically (e.g. with economic development driving state development), and to what extent is there indeterminacy or asymmetry in the relationship? A key feature of the development of the state was shown to be the manner in which it incorporated and promoted a very distinctive *type* of education: that of 'cultivation', or *Bildung*. This, in turn, was (and still is) associated with a major social division *within* the middle class that is constitutive of an important class fraction that owes its position to the possession of an education of this particular kind. The situation of this group is defined by its particular *status*, associated with a certain 'style of life' expressed primarily through cultural attributes. Bourdieu presents the 'distinction' of this culture as a symbolic transformation of economic relations. In this manner, Bourdieu ultimately links intellectual and cultural fields to the economic field. However, this move fails to account for crucial *asymmetries* in their relationships to the economic field (a problem traced back to the 'relational' character of Bourdieu's model). These asymmetries, in their turn, point to possible sources of autonomy for intellectual fields (but also for social actors) which suggest that it is better to preserve a sense of independence between them and the economic – though one calling for proper theorization.

More substantively, shifting attention from the economy to state formation better accounts for two things: (a) *when* education systems emerge and (b) key *differences* between, e.g., how 'hybrid' they are or how far they form coherent and integrated national systems. Contrary to the 'logics' of industrialism and capitalism, the emergence of modern education systems, when related to state formation, is associated not just with the 'new' problems of economic change, but, as the example of the Chinese literati suggests, some very old (or endemic) ones. When considering the relationship between the development of modern education systems in the West and economic change and state formation, what we see is the manner in which the 'old' problem of regulating the relationship between central and peripheral power is refracted through the 'new' problems of industrialization and modernity. However, states change *over time*. The nineteenth century was pre-eminently the age of the nation-state. That is, nation, economy and state were coterminous within a geographically bounded (and *relatively* culturally homogeneous) territory. There are significant differences between nineteenth- and twentieth-century states and between Western states and those in industrializing and industrialized nations in the global economy of the twenty-first century.

4

Positions, Strategies and Change

Introduction

The previous three chapters have described the major patterns of social differences associated with education in relation to educational processes *internal* to the education system; logics of economic development and *class* structure; state formation, *status* and educational stratification. This chapter is concerned with the *dynamics* of educational change, and the way in which patterns of social difference are structured within an *evolving* system of positions and relationships expressed through differential participation rates and levels of attainment. The approaches to be considered suggest how synthesizing theoretical perspectives and integrated research programmes might be developed – how, for instance, the plethora of small-scale qualitative studies of the classroom and school might be reconstituted as 'segments' within the structure of an evolving system of positions, and how the conditions of that dynamic might provide a general or background principle of intelligibility of the findings of qualitative research. However, as was suggested in chapter 1, there are deeper epistemological issues beneath the surface here and these will be addressed in the final chapter.

There are three broad areas to be explored:

• The first has to do with what can be termed *structural-dynamic models* of educational change. In particular, Raymond Boudon's work will be considered as an exemplar. Part of the interest of Boudon's analysis is that he provides what appears to be a convincing explanation of the key problem highlighted in chapter 1: the long-term stability of class differentials in educational attainment. The obvious next step is to consider whether this type of account might also throw light on the contrary phenomenon of the gender revolution. What are the general implications and possibilities of structural-dynamic models for understanding the relationship between educational and social differentiation and change?

- The second area has to do with pupil *positioning* and *strategies*. It is concerned with approaches and studies that explore not so much the ways in which pupils are positioned *by* education (as in the internalist constructionist theories of educational differentiation reviewed in the first chapter – by 'school masculinities', for instance), but with the ways in which pupils actively position *themselves* in relation to the school. This connects with the previous area in that such positioning occurs within conditions and orientations given by a more general structural dynamic within which education mediates the relationship between pupils' origins and destinations – in other words, that contextualize the questions: What kind of education does someone like me need in order to become the sort of person I want to be? And is it possible? Is it worth it? And what are the alternatives?

- The third area involves the ways in which different groups (children and their families within their particular communities) relate to the school system within their local area. This has become especially significant with the movement in a number of countries towards market-type forms of educational provision. In these circumstances the varying capacities of groups to make more or less effective choices about which schools their children should attend becomes a key concern.

The feature that links these three areas of concern is that of *decision making*: (a) the ways in which the structural-dynamic context both conditions and is driven by the aggregation effects of social aspirations or adjustments to circumstance, (b) the ways in which pupils actively adopt positions in relation to education under those conditions, and (c) the ways in which families and groups orientate themselves towards education given their *local* expectations and resources within the broader dynamic of change. A set of key interrelated processes will be considered: educational expansion, credentialization and credential inflation. This set of concerns includes the problem of how sociological perspectives accommodate individuals *as* active decision-makers – a problem that is, in practical terms, heightened when, under the influence of neo-liberal policy, education has become a market.

Phillip Brown (1987) identified an important omission within internalist differentiation perspectives, one shared by both liberal and Marxist approaches.

> Schooling is understood in terms of the process of educational differentiation that represents little more than the translation of class inequalities into differences in educational attainment and the 'cooling out' of unrealistic expectations. [These perspectives] are also functionalist in that they interpret what happens in schools in terms of the functions the school must perform

for 'society' as they conceive it. Little attention is given to the *conscious-ness and action of the pupils themselves*, and these approaches provide little conceptual space for the study of the groupings, relations, and practices of pupils and educators in contemporary capitalist societies. (P. Brown 1987: 17, my emphasis)

The 'positioning' approach being considered here is distinguished by its concern with 'the consciousness and action of the pupils themselves', and with the relationship between consciousness, action and constraint. Brown's work will be returned to below.

Structural-Dynamic Models

It is interesting that in the 1970s a number of writers on both sides of the Atlantic produced theories that, though located within different paradigms, produced structural-dynamic models of educational change of a broadly similar kind: most notably, R. Collins (1977, 1981) in the USA, Bourdieu and Passeron (1977) and Boudon (1977) in France. The feature of such models is that they attempt to reconstruct educational trend data in term of a complex, interrelated system of positions, rela-tionships, chances and probabilities that evolve over time. It is only in terms of the whole system that any particular element can be properly understood. Consider Bourdieu and Passeron, for example:

> [I]n order to be sociologically rigorous, analysis of the evolution of the structure of chances presupposes that one should also take into account the social significance of the evolution of that structure as a whole. Re-stricting ourselves to the extreme cases, we observe that the chances of access to higher education for workers' sons more than doubled over this period, whereas the chances of senior executives' sons were multiplied by only 1.6; but it is obvious that the doubling of a very low rate of probability does not have the same significance or the same social effects as the dou-bling of a rate thirty times greater. For an accurate assessment of the social consequences of these numerical changes which...amount to an *upward translation* of the structure of the educational chances of the different so-cial classes...one should strictly speaking have to be able to establish the *thresholds* which, in the different regions of the scale of probabilities, are likely to produce significant changes in the agents' systems of aspirations.... Because quantitatively different levels of the rates of collective opportunity express themselves in *qualitatively* different experiences, a social category's collective chances constitute, through the process of internalisation of the category's objective destiny, one of the mechanisms through which that ob-jective destiny is realised. (Bourdieu and Passeron 1977: 224–6)

This features a number of things of different kinds occurring within the 'evolution of the structure as a whole':

- It is observed that the significance of changes in probabilities for different groups relates to the base from which they are starting. The percentage increase might be smaller for a more highly represented group, but that could still result in a *numerical* increase greater than that for a less-well-represented group with a higher percentage increase. Hence, we must look at the population from which students come in order to put into perspective their proportional representation in the university.

- Changes towards greater equality at a lower level of the system can be associated with the preservation of, and even with an *increase* in, inequalities at higher levels through a process of 'upward translation' of differences. This is R. Collins's process of credential deflation referred to in the previous chapter, and is a key factor also in Boudon's analysis. Its implications will be returned to below.

- Quantitative changes in probabilities have different *qualitative* effects for different groups, depending on their historic levels of representation: 'Depending on whether access to higher education is collectively felt, even in a diffuse way, as an impossible, possible, probable, normal or banal future, everything in the conduct of the families and the children (particularly their conduct and performance at school) will vary, because behaviour tends to be governed by what it is 'reasonable' to expect' (ibid. 226). Hence, the way in which different groups *experience* the system of differences reproduces those differences through the manner in which that experience shapes expectations.

Structural-dynamic models put particular positions, relationships and changes into perspective, (a) by locating them within the *system* of positions, relationships and changes, (b) by taking account of the overdetermined character of effects and influences (e.g. as in the way that the whole influences the parts in different ways), and (c) by apprehending the transformations of quantitative and qualitative changes over time.

Boudon's work in this area is of major significance because of the manner in which it systematically pulls together and accounts for an apparently paradoxical set of empirical trends, and does so in a way that radically challenges both liberal and critical sociological assumptions about education's relationship to social differences and inequalities and the possibilities and limitations of educational reform. This is the key issue of the stability in class differentials and the problem it poses for the liberal logic examined in chapter 2. How is it possible to systematically account for counter-intuitive trends in the relationship between educational and social differences and changes?

Boudon develops his analysis through a 'logical simulation model' that employs a set of 'axioms' (rules or assumptions such as 'Assume first that for a population sample, the distribution of individuals according to educational attainment varies as a function of social class background';

Boudon 1977: 188) that constructs a set of conditions defined within specified social and arithmetic parameters.

> I will suggest that once these properties are formalised into a model, one can then reconstitute the distribution of a hypothetical cohort with regard to educational attainment. I will therefore suppose that in our model there exist three social classes (higher, middle and lower), and that in a cohort of 100,000 pupils who finish their elementary education at a given moment,10,000 have a higher, 30,000 a middle, and 60,000 a lower social class background. By correctly formalising the preceding theoretical propositions and by choosing appropriate parameters, it will be possible to show how many pupils from each social background will reach each level of the school system. (Boudon 1977: 188)

By building in further conditions (such as the relative significance of meritocracy and social bias) and a dynamic value for expansion over time, the model can be 'set in motion' in such a way that it is capable of generating virtual educational participation and social mobility tables. Potentially the model could be made increasingly complex by adding further factors, such as changes in the social structure (e.g. in the numbers of places available at different social levels) or class differences in birth rates; but for basic demonstration purposes, Boudon needs to show only that with a simple model constructed around empirically realistic parameters and assumptions, it is possible to demonstrate that an expanding education system reduces social inequalities within education at successively higher levels of the system without reducing inequalities of *social* opportunity as reflected in higher rates of social mobility.

The processes that Boudon's model generates can be explicated in the following way. The fact that the general level of educational attainment improved consistently throughout the twentieth century, while class differentials remained the same, entails that at the lowest and then at successively higher levels of the system, *educational* inequalities between the classes declined. Imagine an examination, similar to the GCSE in England that is normally taken at age 16, at a time when 90 per cent of higher-class, 60 per cent of middle-class and 30 per cent of lower-class pupils pass it. If ten years later, significantly more of *all* pupils have passed the exam, then those extra passes will be drawn disproportionately from the three groups, because whereas the upper-class group had only 10 per cent without a pass, the middle group had 40 per cent, and the lower group 70 per cent. As the pass rate of, first, the upper, then the middle group reaches saturation point, additional passes will come increasingly from the lower group – the only ones left. If a point is reached at which 95 per cent of uppers, 90 per cent of middles and 75 per cent of lowers are all passing the exam, then clearly educational inequality *at that level* has been significantly reduced. At the next educational level above (e.g. in England, 'A' level) the same pattern of change is being repeated, but starting at a *later* point in time. It could be that the differences between the classes at *that* level at the later point in time are like those for the lower examination at the earlier point in time. Within certain time frames inequalities at the higher level could actually be *increasing*, whilst those at the lower level are decreasing!

Over time three things have happened:

1 the mean level of education for each generation has risen;
2 the *relative* differences between the classes (at successively higher levels) have been preserved;
3 this despite an absolute decline in inequalities at the lower levels (see also Halsey et al. 1980: ch. 8, esp. pp. 140–1).

The structure of class differences is *maintained* over time through a continually changing pattern of educational relationships. For instance, at an earlier time the difference between the lower, middle and upper classes might have been registered in the differences between leaving school for work with no qualifications, leaving school for work with qualifications, and leaving school with qualifications for university. At a later point in time, when there is a general expectation of attending university, those same social differences will be registered through differences in the status of the institution attended and the courses studied. At the same time, employers will utilize a more subtle range of indicators in selection, looking for those charismatic qualities of cultural capital referred to in the previous chapter, rather than simply the possession of a degree as such. In short: educational inequalities decrease, but social inequalities remain the same, though mediated through changing educational and social modalities of differentiation. Furthermore, this is not a peculiar anomaly, but a 'normal' feature of the model. The failure of the liberal logic and the expectations of educational reform associated with the advanced industrial society model of chapter 2 were not fulfilled because they *could not be* – the logic was (and in contemporary versions remains) fatally flawed! However, the question remains: What is it that drives the dynamic that Boudon illuminates in his structural model?

Credentialism and the labour market

The reason why there is no necessary gain in social opportunities concerns two related consequences of the dynamic processes that Boudon describes. The first is that of *credentialization* (whereby as more and more people gain qualifications, more and more jobs require qualifications). The second is *credential inflation* (whereby the value of qualifications in the labour market declines over time as more gain them). As more and more people acquire a given level of qualification, the less useful it becomes for employers as a basis for selection. Employers, consequently, demand higher and higher qualifications for the same job. As R. Collins demonstrated (1977, 1981), the steadily increasing demand for higher levels of qualification in the labour market cannot be explained in terms of increasing skill requirements of jobs in themselves (contrary to the logic of human capital theory and technical functionalism). Rather, employers raise credential demands in pace with the increasing qualification level of groups from which they wish to recruit employees. At the same time, successive generations of students have to gain higher levels of qualification to keep pace! The expansionary dynamic creates a vicious upward spiral, within which each generation needs more education than the one before simply in order to maintain the same occupational level. Bourdieu and Passeron describe this dynamic thus:

> [T]he conception of education so long accepted by the upper classes, in which the baccalauréat is simply a ticket to higher education (stated negatively in the formula, 'the *bac* means nothing') is tending to spread to the level of the middle classes: the image which formerly induced many to withdraw from education after the baccalauréat, especially the sons of middle-rank managerial staff and above all the sons of clerical workers, who confined their ambitions to overcoming the barrier that had held back their fathers' careers ('you can't do anything without the *bac*'), is tending to give way to the opposite image ('the *bac* gets you nowhere nowadays'), a conception founded, moreover, on real and realistic experience, given that the baccalauréat ... has become the sine qua non for access to many jobs which the previous generation was able to reach by 'the backdoor' (Bourdieu and Passeron 1977: 227–8)

They are presenting in the French context the situation in America described by R. Collins in the earlier extract (chapter 3). This is also the manner in which quantitative changes *qualitatively* revalorize positions and relationships and the expectations of groups regarding education (see Bourdieu and Passeron 1977 as quoted above). Rather than improving social opportunities, educational expansion imposes greater costs for no net mobility gains, and the basic structure of differentials remains unchanged.

Broadly speaking, as described in chapter 1, 'internalist' approaches attribute *strong* effects to particular sets of educational arrangements and processes of educational differentiation. Such arrangements and processes are seen, in the first instance, as reflecting social inequalities between the classes, the sexes and ethnic communities or racial groups. In the second instance, they are seen as actively reproducing those inequalities through the differentiated outcomes of educational arrangements and processes. This process of reproduction need not be seen as totally mechanistic – within internalist approaches, the education system can be granted a degree of 'relative autonomy' from the state and the economy, and pupils can 'resist' reproductive forces within education. It is these assumptions of *strong* linkages and effects that Boudon's model calls into question in a radical way. Relationships that in reproduction theories are seen to carry a high degree of necessity are revealed by Boudon's analysis to be largely *contingent*.

The contingency lies in the fact that there is no enduring, given relationship between *levels* of educational outcome (and, crucially, the long-term educational career paths leading to them) and prospective *positions* in the system of social stratification (stratification by gender and ethnicity as well as by class and occupation). Consequently, it is difficult to maintain that differentiated educational career paths in some way *prepare* pupils for given positions in the stratification system (whether in its economic or gender relations). What is significant is not so much the *type* of education that different groups receive (whether defined through formal content, the hidden curriculum or the social relations of education), but the relative differences between the *amounts* and *status* of education *regardless* of content or form. Certainly, different groups receive different educations, but successive generations of each group also receive a different education from those before them. In the case of class, where differentials have remained surprisingly constant, it is the *pattern* of differences, the relationship between relative positions, that is reproduced, but those positions (as group averages) correlate with different educational career paths as they move up the system, with typical working-class pupils following at a later time what earlier had been the typical 'middle-class' educational trajectory. In the case of gender, girls began to move progressively into 'male' areas and to out-perform boys there, and changed their relative position in doing so. Rather than the structure of educational differentiation being generated from *within* the system by the kinds of things explored by internalist accounts, it is more that the expansionary dynamic of credentialization and devaluation pulls *all* groups onward and upward through the system, *revalorizing* positions and their relationships as it does so. The evolution of the system of social differences within education is pulled by the inflationary dynamic of expansion and credentialism rather than pushed by changes to and within the education system, whether in its institutional forms or in its processes of differentiation.

The contrast being drawn between Boudon's structural-dynamic model and internalist perspectives is essentially to do with assumptions about *strong and weak links and effects* in education and its societal relations. This is not necessarily to question the accuracy of internalist (e.g. anti-sexist or anti-racist) *descriptions* of education or to deny an *educational* rationale for, say, an anti-sexist and anti-racist curriculum. Rather, from a sociological point of view, the problem is that of moving from homologies to explanations on the basis of unexamined assumptions about social causality and effectivity.

The gendering of school knowledge might be 'like' gender divisions in society, but this does not mean that either is a cause of the other. Gender relations in society, the attainments of girls in education, and gender constructs in the curriculum can each change or fail to change with a high degree of independence one from another and without significant consequences one for the other – as the gender revolution demonstrated. What at any point in time counts as the typical middle-class or female, etc., education is whatever education middle-class or female, etc., pupils typically acquire under prevailing conditions, and has very little to do with any *intrinsic* features of the education itself (e.g. that the curriculum or pedagogy is in some manner 'male' or 'female'). When conditions changed in the appropriate manner, females had little difficulty in moving into 'male' areas and out-performing males in those areas (Hakim 2000). However, it still remains to be seen how a Boudon-type model of *weak* linkages and internal effects defines the locus of the *strong* links and effects in the matrix of relationships between social groups, education and society.

The Educational Decision Field

A second dimension of Boudon's theory has to do with the manner in which he incorporates the individual into his account. It is here that the question can be raised concerning the implications of his model for gender and ethnicity. His starting point is a criticism of the view that differences in attainment levels between classes reflect differences in cultural values relating to aspirations and motivation. Such theories presume that working-class pupils have *lower* aspirations than middle-class ones – they aspire only to lowly working-class jobs, whereas middle-class pupils aspire to higher, middle-class ones. Boudon argues that this approach mistakenly assumes a common baseline against which both groups can be measured. In fact, he contends, we should start where pupils themselves are coming from. The child of a doctor who aspires to become a doctor has no greater 'degree of aspiration' than that of a garbage collector who aspires to become a garbage collector. In any case, it is not differences in aspiration that really count, but differences in the *costs* calculated to be associated with realizing aspirations. Hence, two pupils from different classes could be alike in ability, attainment and potential, and even have common aspirations, but will differ in their capacity to bear the costs of extended education. It is this feature of Boudon's work that is currently capturing most attention, particularly in relation to Rational Action Theory.

The problem with Rational Action (or Choice) Theory (RAT) for many people (e.g. Hatcher 1998) is its narrowly economistic model of rational calculation. However, the virtue of Boudon's approach is that, in contrast to both externalist deficit theories that see working-class (or black) pupils as lacking educability and internalist theories that see them as the largely passive victims of discriminatory processes of educational differentiation and discursive positioning, it acknowledges pupils as *active* subjects, thinking about what they are doing within particular economic and social parameters. These parameters he terms the 'primary and secondary effects of social stratification' (Boudon 1974). The former include many of the material and social differences shaping educability between the classes in externalist approaches. Those of educational significance have, Boudon believes, historically diminished in importance (but see below). It is the *secondary* effects that are most significant, and it is these that contextualize calculations made within the 'educational decision field' of different groups. All actors are doing the same *kind* of thing, but under different conditions within the evolving structural dynamic of educational expansion. Boudon is sceptical about the influence of internal processes of educational differentiation, because the great majority of lower-class pupils who leave education early do so not because they lack the qualifications to go further, but because they *choose* not to continue. Also, the significant minority who remain in the system do just as well as higher-class students. For example, there are no significant class differences in performance at degree level – in England privately educated students do slightly *less* well than undergraduates from state schools: they lose the advantage they enjoyed at secondary school level. Social differences are active at the point of entry into higher education, but *not* at points of exit.

Pupil positioning and the school

Pupil positioning can be understood in terms of how different groups adapt to the circumstances of education, given the relationship between the form of educational provision and the more general circumstances in which they live. Theory of this type has its origins in Durkheim's *Suicide* (1952) and in the way in which he defined different *types* of suicide in terms of differing states of social solidarity. In the 1940s, the American sociologist Robert Merton (1959) further developed these ideas by constructing a 'typology of adaptation' relating to how different groups in American society could relate to the official values of achievement and success and the means whereby those aims could be officially pursued. Some could both support the ideals and have the legitimate means of achieving them. Others might also support them, but not have the approved means, and so turn to deviant or criminal means. Yet others might withdraw from the entire pursuit, because they reject both ends and means, or might seek to change the game completely through radical social change. The approach was applied to subculture formation and to the investigation of pupil subcultures in schools. A classic study by Hargreaves (1967) accounted for the formation of an anti-school subculture amongst lower-stream secondary modern school boys in terms of their adaptation to a system of streaming that branded them as failures. The internal structure of differentiation in the school positioned these pupils in such a way that they were alienated from its official culture and goals and sought alternative sources of identity and achievement. There is a process of differentiation and polarization. As we have seen, the idea of 'school masculinities' is used in the same way today.

Schools, 'Lads' and ordinary kids: orientations

A study by Phillip Brown (1987) provided a significant contribution to this tradition in education because of the way in which it identified a number of problems in earlier approaches and attempted to develop a method that both controlled for those problems and systematically enabled a more complex modelling of positions and processes.

Brown took as his starting point some reservations concerning Paul Willis's classic study *Learning to Labour* (1977). Willis's main concern was with how 'working class kids get working class jobs'. To recall issues raised in chapter 1 concerning the existential status of pupil decision making, the issue here is the *apparent* irrationality of pupils leaving school at the first opportunity to go to work in hard, poorly paid, low-status jobs – in the case of 'the Lads' studied by Willis, in the iron foundries of the English Midlands – when education could offer an escape. The group that Willis focused upon were anti-school, working-class white boys at a single-sex secondary modern school. Unlike Hargreaves in his earlier internalist study of streaming, Willis argued that it was cultural values *outside* the school that were important, not internal structure or processes. In an extremely influential analysis he concluded that the key lay in the boys' values concerning masculinity and class. For them, hard manual labour (or 'graft') was a sign and celebration of manhood. More deeply, they saw manual work as exemplifying a masculine principle of acting upon the world and transforming it. This is in contrast to the female principle that is essentially passive – 'women's work' (in the home) merely puts things back together again in a repetitive manner. They associated intellectual work (including school work) with this feminine principle and, as a result, contemptuously dismissed boys who conformed at school as 'ear'oles'.

Within the broader research context and debate around anti-school subcultures, Willis concluded that it was the relationship between the boys' notions of sexuality and different kinds of work that was significant (Arnot 2003a, b). Given this, there was in fact very little the school could do about such Lads. Indeed, Willis pays tribute to their teachers and the efforts they made to accommodate the Lads, rather than attempt to discover internal alienating features of schooling that if only they were changed would incorporate them. He also argued that there were significant continuities between the Lads' behaviour in school and the subversive culture of the shop floor in the kinds of jobs they aspired to. They heard from their fathers how they 'had a laf' at work, skiving and outwitting their supervisors. (A poignant feature of the book lies in the interviews with the Lads' fathers who had learnt the hard way that such work is in the end physically destroying and unrewarding, but cannot get their sons to see that they should not follow in their footsteps.) In this respect, the Lads' behaviour in school *was* a kind of preparation for work, but in a quite different way from that argued for in Bowles's and Gintis's 'correspondence principle'.

Ogbu (1997) argues that Willis's study was important because of the way in which it directed attention to the 'day-to-day attitudes and behaviours or "lived culture" of students' (p. 770). He argues that 'The Willis study introduced "resistance" as a force of human agency in the process of the reproduction of class inequality through schooling' (ibid.). There is, though, a paradox here. In contrast to other types of theory, such as that of Bowles and Gintis or internalist constructionist approaches, Willis *does* see the Lads as conscious decision-makers who act rather than are simply acted upon. But it is precisely their *choices* that impel them into these jobs and that in effect reproduce their inequality. Although the decisions are *theirs*, they are decisions that can be seen as ultimately acting against their better interests. Ogbu goes on to outline a further complication with respect to black children: a paradox in that 'Black youths accepted academic work and schooling, but behaved in ways that ensured that they would not, and did not, succeed' (ibid.). Ogbu accounts for this paradox as an aspect of *symbolic adaptation* by black Americans to white racial stratification:

> Thus, for some blacks cultural and language differences between blacks and whites are consciously or unconsciously interpreted as symbols of group identity to be maintained, not barriers to be overcome. Moreover, they tend to equate the school culture (e.g., the curriculum and required behaviours) and standard English with white culture and language. They therefore perceive school learning not as an instrumental behaviour to achieve the desired and verbalised goal of getting a good education for future employment, but rather as a kind of linear acculturation or assimilation, detrimental or threatening to collective identity. Some are afraid to behave according to what they see as the white cultural frame of reference for fear it may result in loss of minority cultural identity. (Ogbu 1997: 774)

Willis's Lads had no interest in education from the beginning; so, unlike the black youths in Ogbu's case, were not caught in this more complex ambiguity. Research in the UK indicates that black youths there are in much the same position as those in the USA (Youdell 2003). However, as will be discussed below, black girls are much more able to engage in a strategic instrumental adaptation to the school and gain a good education for future employment.

Brown's observation concerning Willis's Lads is that they are not, in fact, *typical* of working-class pupils. In reality, boys of this type are only ever a minority. What about, the majority of 'ordinary kids', he asks, both boys and girls? It is these who form the focus of his study. His research was set in a large urban centre in South Wales, to which he gave the name 'Middleport', and drew upon pupils in the upper years of three mixed-sex comprehensive schools. Coming ten years after Willis's study, Brown's took account of the significant decline in employment opportunities for young people that had occurred over that period. He adopted a Mertonian-type 'adaptations' model, but one that, he argues, overcomes problems in the original and in later applications to education (see P. Brown 1987: 48–53). He produces a model that distinguishes between different types of attitude towards the formal culture of the school: some pupils might treat school as an end in itself, because they find study intrinsically interesting; for others it is a means to an end that they 'use' instrumentally in order to get a desired job; for yet others it is merely a 'condition' that has to be endured because it is compulsory (ibid. 50). As the extract below illustrates (see Brown 1987: 49, fig. 3.1), Brown defines four 'orientations' towards schooling:

1   *normative*: where the pupil accepts the formal culture as intrinsically worthwhile;
2   *normative instrumental*: where pupils accept the academic demands of the school as a means to an end (especially that of achieving white collar employment);
3   *alienated instrumental*: where pupils accept practical (i.e. vocational) aspects of schooling as occupationally relevant;
4   *alienated*: where pupils reject both intrinsic and instrumental approaches and simply put up with the school as a 'condition' to be endured, because they have to.

Brown's use of the term 'orientation' is significant. The sense in which he uses it derives from an earlier labour market study by Blackburn and Mann (1979), which used the concept of an 'orientation profile', which 'includes a set of expectations and relative priorities which *moves away from the idea of a "cost–benefit analysis"* being conducted by the individual' (Brown 1987: 49, my emphasis). In other words, the idea of an 'orientation' indicates something broader (or 'weaker') than the kind of calculative approach adopted by Rational Action Theory. In this respect, Brown's model of decision making differs from that of Boudon and addresses the reservations of those who wish to treat pupils as decision-makers whose actions and intentions should enter into sociological explanation but who reject an economistic calculation paradigm.

   These 'orientations' towards the formal culture of the school are embedded within broader formations that Brown terms 'frames of reference' (FORs) (see table 4.1). In the case of working-class pupils, he identifies three such FORs: 'getting out', where the pupil aspires to be upwardly mobile *out* of the working class; 'getting on', where the aspiration is to be upwardly mobile *within* the working class; and 'getting in', where the desire is to *remain* within (and *celebrate*) an inherited working-class

Table 4.1

Frame of reference (FOR)	Orientation towards formal culture of the school	Pupils known as
Getting out	Normative	Swots
Getting on	Instrumental (normative or alienated)	Ordinary kids
Getting in	Alienated	Rems, Lads, etc.

position and tradition (e.g. skinheads). Willis's Lads are examples of that minority committed to 'getting in' (a type called Rems, short for 're-medial', among the pupils in Brown's study). The majority of 'ordinary kids' want simply to 'get on', and a third minority group ('swots') to 'get out'.

Brown stresses the centrality of occupational aspirations within the FORs and, consequently, the importance of the structural context given by the local labour market. These concepts and issues are developed by Brown in the passage below:

> It is now possible to specify four orientations to school which apply to all pupils irrespective of gender or social class. Pupils who are orientated to the academic elements of the formal culture of the school, we will describe as having a *normative* orientation. Here schoolwork is seen as an *end* in itself, that is, the intrinsic value of 'education' is accepted for its own sake. There is a propensity for such pupils to accept what the school is seen to stand for . . . a normative orientation to school only applies with respect to the academic curriculum given the bias towards such studies and the high status teachers attach to academic endeavour . . . .
>
> Opposed to a *normative* orientation is that characterized by those pupils who develop an anti-school subculture . . . . [I]t is important to recognise that the development of an *alienated* orientation is a *necessary* but not a *sufficient* condition for the development of an anti-school subculture . . . An alienated orientation is characteristically held by non-examination pupils who are neither orientated to the school as an intrinsically valuable learning experience nor as a means to his or her individual ends, for what he or she can get out of it. A normative or alienated orientation to the formal culture of the school can be understood in terms of pupil acceptance or rejection, but where an orientation is adopted to the school as a *means* (i.e. as an instrumental orientation), it cannot easily be located along the same con-tinuum. *Instrumental* responses to school represent an analytically distinct dimension. These pupils' primary orientation to the school is explicable in terms of their perceptions of its ability to facilitate desired individual ends, most notably by qualifying them for entry into certain types of employment. (P. Brown 1987: 51–3)

The distinction between 'normative', 'instrumental' and 'alienated' ori-entations to the school has significant implications for these internalist approaches, which stress the ways in which pupil identities are constructed by educational discursive processes. Brown's study underlines the fact that the great majority of pupils treat school *instrumentally* – they simply don't care much about it or the views of their teachers. Indeed, we should note that this could be as true for the academically able as for any other group (Power et al. 2003). The relatively few studies of such cases show that some pupils can be *intrinsically* committed to learning for its own sake, but still adopt a 'rebel' position in relation to the school's normative culture. In the humanities, of course, the role of the artist and intellectual as subversive and rebel is a dominant modern *motif* and identity. In the sciences, also, 'boffins' are not simply conformist, but are often eccentric 'outsiders' (the stereotypical mark of the 'genius'). It is not only the alienation of Rems and Lads that creates an oppositional position for pupils – the academically able and committed (as the student revolution of the Sixties vividly demonstrated) can also adopt a counter-cultural posture. Thoroughly normative conformists are as much a minority as Willis's Lads, and are often condemned by teachers themselves as lacking that difficult spark of creativity and originality that presents the real professional challenge and ultimate satisfaction – pupils can be too *good* as well as too bad!

Brown locates FORs in 'the conceptual space between pupil orientations and strategies in school and class location' (ibid. 32) – the concept, in this respect, lies within the theoretical plane of *habitus*. Like Boudon, Brown brings together, on one side, the circumstances of the pupil's family and, on the other, the pupil's understandings of what it is to become and be an adult through the crucial transition into work. Unlike Boudon, he steps back from the informed calculative (cost–benefit) model of RAT to the more provisional and speculative position of an orientation shaped within a 'frame of reference'. He also emphasizes that there is never just *one* way of being working-class or a working-class pupil.

> Therefore, working-class culture needs to be understood as a stock of commonly available cultural *resources* which people in the same class location use in different ways to order their social conduct and make sense of their changing life histories and social situations. It follows that the range of working-class responses to the school cannot be explained simply as the expression of working-class culture because pupil responses to the school will, at least in part, reflect a *selection* from that culture, unless we regress to a form of explanation relying on differences in working-class family 'types' or condemn the majority of Middleport children to the lowly status of ideological dupes as the price for celebrating Willis' lads as cultural heroes. (P. Brown 1987: 34)

As with Stone's earlier (1981) critique of identity theory in relation to black pupils, Brown's approach to 'ordinary kids' recognizes their (and their families') capacities to mobilize cultural resources in their own right according to circumstance and aspiration. It renders more problematic the relationship between agency and constraint and the notion of 'choice'. The flexibility of this contrast between 'resources' and 'selection' also opens the space within which individuals can 'change their minds' – something very difficult to accommodate within identity theories of educational differentiation. Interestingly, Willis's Lads give accounts of when and why they *decided* to become Lads, and in some cases why later they decided to stop and to rejoin the mainstream – becoming, in effect, 'ear'oles'!

A subtle but significant point underpins Brown's approach. The issue is: Does such complexity require a multiplicity of explanatory approaches (class analysis for males, feminism for females, etc.), or is there something in *common* that can be accommodated within a broadly unifying perspective? The point of an approach such as Brown's is that pupils are not doing different *kinds* of things because they differ in class, sex or ethnicity: they are all doing the *same* kind of thing, but under different conditions and in different ways because of their class, sex or ethnic membership. These things make a *difference* to what they do, but *what* they are doing is not fundamentally *different*. To further develop this point, I will now consider a study of black schoolgirls by Heidi Safia Mirza (1992).

Young, alienated, female and black: strategic careers

Mirza's (1992) study focused on black female pupils in secondary schools in south London. However, her investigation also included black and white boys and white indigenous and Irish girls as points of comparison. She begins with a detailed review of the manner in which research in the race area has systematically ignored the achievements of black girls. The 'myth of black underachievement' (Reeves and Chevannes 1988) was in reality about black *boys*. She notes a number of distinctive features about black girls:

• They tend to have high occupational aspirations relative to the other groups (in her study, working-class white boys had the lowest). But, most significantly, they also had high *expectations* of realizing those aspirations. The relationship between aspiration and expectation is an important feature of Mirza's analysis. Even when members of the other groups also had high aspirations, they differed from the black girls in *not* expecting them to be realized. What differed most significantly between the groups were their views of what could *realistically* be accomplished.
• They were also very conscious of the ways in which *discrimination* in the labour market could operate against them. Consequently, they tended to select initial career paths with great care, concentrating upon those areas (e.g. certain caring professions) where black women were

already well established. They tended to see this as a first step in a longer process of social career development where by they would obtain further qualifications enabling them to be mobile and also step sideways into new (and more desired) areas of work.

- Crucially, although their occupational choices could be seen as tending towards traditional female types of employment, this was not because of their having a traditionally gendered subjectivity. Their decisions were self-consciously *strategic*. In fact, in terms of cultural values, they did not recognize a strong division between 'male' and 'female' work and they accepted unproblematically the right of women to be fully economically independent in work of their choosing.

- In relation to the school, these girls adopted what in Brown's terms is a position of 'normative instrumentalism' – that is, they accept for their own purposes the formal goals of academic learning but distance themselves from the school's normative culture in other respects. Like Brown's 'ordinary kids', they conform sufficiently to get by, given what they want to get out of the situation, but with the aim of long-term mobility.

The orientations that the girls brought with them into the school enabled them to position themselves (however precariously) on a trajectory between the occupational and educational systems: 'Clearly what these girls were doing was attempting to achieve upward mobility through a strategy that rationalised the various constraints that they encountered' (Mirza 1992: 14). Mirza summarizes the situation as follows:

> One major constraint was the existence of a racially and sexually segregated labour market which ensured limited occupational opportunities to young black women. The black girls chose careers that were 'gendered', not so much because of the nature of the job but because that was the only type of work in their experience and knowledge that was available to them. However, in choosing these jobs they used the stated educational requirements as a vehicle for obtaining more or better qualifications, in order to enhance their career prospects and satisfy their desire for credentials. Their willingness to move into 'non-gendered' careers can be largely explained by the combination of the notion of relative equality between the sexes, which meant that there were no cultural limits on attempting to do non-traditional female work, and the motivation to succeed, which encouraged the search for opportunities wherever they were or however they might be defined by others. (Mirza 1992: 145)

Mirza's analysis weaves together a complex set of factors, but at the same time presents the black girls in her study as *consciously* positioning themselves in relation to the school as part of a longer-term personal strategy of social career development. She stresses the importance of being sensitive to the specificities of context and tradition and the problems of generalizing from spuriously universalistic categories such as 'the culture of femininity' (see ibid. ch. 7). However, she also stresses that despite significant differences in the orientations and expectations of different categories of female pupils, it still remains the case that the labour market is racially and sexually segmented. It is not schooling that reproduces those divisions; they persist even when certain girls depart from the position supposedly constructed for them in the system of educational differentiation and aspire to 'inappropriate' positions in the world of work. The primary forces generating and reproducing such social differences and inequalities are structural, rather than cultural. In addition to the earlier argument concerning the weak effects of processes of educational differentiation and discursive positioning, it can be suggested that the major dimensions of social inequality do not to any significant degree depend upon education for their reproduction as structures – they persist because their sources are elsewhere.

Studies of pupil positioning and strategic adaptations can be located within the space defined by Boudon's 'educational decision field'. They are positioned within the structural dynamic of the systemic relations between family structures, education and the occupational system, and are magnified by class and ethnic cultural traditions which provide the frames of reference within which pupils envision their futures and strategically adapt to the circumstances of their schooling.

Choice and the Primary Effects of Social Stratification

Boudon gave principal attention in his model to the 'secondary effects' of social stratification affecting class survival rates *inside* the education system. He tended to see primary effects as material inequalities declining over time. Halsey et al. (1980), however, argued that primary effects were influential at significant *entry* points into the school system. In their study this related to the kinds of schools that children from different classes tended to enter in the old tripartite system in England and Wales (established by the 1944 Education Act). Studies of the market impact of the 1988 Education Reform Act suggest that this is as true today, and that market forces in an increasingly differentiated school system could be *increasing* the significance of primary effects in this respect through cultural capital. Whether the concern is to select, simplistically, the 'best' school in terms of league tables or more 'effective' schools, clearly 'locals', as Ball et al. (1977) call them will have less scope than active 'cosmopolitans' (below). Similarly the kind of collective action explored by Reay (1998) could have a differential effect in orientating schools towards the particular agendas of particular groups. The logic of marketization is that schools could become more socially segregated as the primary effects of social stratification become more significant in determining *which* schools pupils attend and how schools respond to pupils of different types (Gillborn and Youdell 2000).

The earlier discussion of pupil positioning strategies concentrated on the situation of pupils *within* the school. However, it is also important to take account of the position of different groups of pupils relative to *schools*, especially in view of the fact, as discussed earlier, that some schools are more effective than others (chapter 1). The reason why this question is important relates to the impact of New Right education policies in the UK (and elsewhere) in the 1980s that introduced market forces into education and increased the capacity of parents to *choose* the schools their children attend. How pupils position themselves in relation to the system of educational differentiation relates to the schools they find themselves in, and this, in turn, relates to the differential capacities of families to optimize choice in an educational market-place. If it is indeed the case that school does make a difference, then the differential capacities of families to select or access the better schools may be a significant feature of social *stratification* in education.

The logic of the marketization of schooling is to empower parents as *consumers*. However, parents inevitably differ in their *powers* as consumers. As Stewart Ranson put it:

> The market is formally neutral but substantively interested. Individuals come together in competitive exchange to acquire possession of scarce goods and services. Within the market place all are free and equal, differentiated only by their capacity to calculate their self-interest. Yet, of course, the market masks its social bias. It elides, but reproduces, the inequalities which consumers bring to the market place. Under the guise of neutrality, the institution of the market actively confirms and reinforces the pre-existing social order of wealth and privilege. The market is a crude mechanism of social selection. (Ranson 1990: 219–20)

In what ways might families differ in terms of their capacities to compete in the educational market?

- First, they will be unequally equipped in their capacity to gain information and make judgements about the relative merits of different schools.
- Secondly, they will vary significantly in their material capacity to exercise choice in terms of things such as simply having the time, money or means to transport their child to their preferred school. Families in rural areas will be especially disadvantaged in this respect.
- Thirdly, they will differ in their capacity to individually and collectively influence school policies and practices and to put resources into their children's schools through fund-raising activities.

It must be stressed that all of these things were true to a degree in the social-democratic comprehensive system of provision that preceded the New Right reforms. The difference lies in the fact that the universalistic principle of social-democratic provision *aspired* to provide all children with the best possible education in whatever school they attended (as a citizenship right), whereas a market approach is content to abandon this egalitarian principle in favour of individual consumer self-interest. Education is redefined as a private rather than a public good, with the individual acting on the basis of self-interest rather than as a citizen with a sense of the common good and of social responsibilities to others. The logical expectation of the introduction of market principles to schooling is that schooling will become more socially (and racially) segregated and polarized than it was previously. Consequently, educational researchers in the 1990s turned attention to monitoring these divisive possibilities of marketization.

Choice and the education market

In a major study from the early 1990s, Ball, Bowe and Gerwirtz (1997) attempted to move beyond simple empirical descriptions towards providing a theory of class-related parental choice in the educational market. Drawing upon Bourdieu and Boltanski, they wish to 'place the education market' sociologically in terms of strategies of reproduction (p. 419).

> [T]hree factors 'trigger' or provide for the increased emphasis on strategic choice within the middle class families reported here. First, there is the steady inflation of academic credentials and their correlative devaluation. Second, and related, is the increased democratisation of schooling, by comprehensivisation. Both of these pose threats to the maintenance of class advantage by reducing educational differentiation and by changing patterns of access to higher education and the labour market. Third, is the new possibilities offered in and by the policies of school specialisation and increasing selection and choice within a market framework, being pursued by the Conservative government. That is to say, the middle classes here are making the most of the new opportunities which these policies offer to re-establish their historic economic advantages or newly achieved status position. (Ball et al. 1997: 419)

A significant aspect of the complexity that they uncovered in their investigation has to do with the importance of locality. This is not simply about the need to be sensitive to the local context of the education market: space needs to be built into any theory as part of the broader conceptualization. Education markets have a *spatial-temporal* form that varies between groups. At one level this is reflected in the practical constraints of time budgeting for different groups – how much time they can give to travel, for instance. But at another it relates to how groups envisage their children's social careers as developing within a familiar locality and in familiar ways, or whether they have a 'cosmopolitan' orientation which adopts a longer-term perspective in which the children move beyond the local into unfamiliar spheres and possibilities.

The study, which focuses on secondary schools, was undertaken in 1991–2 in three adjacent LEAs in London. In order to achieve their goal, Ball et al. needed to be able to classify both schools and parents. They decided that there were 'three clear circuits of schooling which relate differently to choice, class and space' (ibid. 410). Different groups of parents 'plug into' these circuits in different ways, and each circuit has a different power in the provision of life chances to pupils. The first circuit is that of 'local' schools, which tend to recruit from a particular area and have 'highly localised reputations' (ibid.). These local schools tend to be LEA mixed comprehensives, favoured by working-class parents, but less so by middle-class ones. The second circuit is that of 'cosmopolitan, high-profile, élite, maintained schools' that have reputations beyond their immediate localities and recruit from much further afield. The third circuit is that of local 'day' (i.e. non-boarding) independent schools that to some degree compete with the elite maintained schools. These different circuits reflect, in part, the increased diversity of school types that emerged from the Conservative reforms of the 1980s when schools were given the opportunity to 'opt out' of the LEA service (while still maintained by public funding), and the area included a new City Technology College. The second two circuits practice more or less formal processes of academic selection.

As far as parents are concerned, Ball et al. distinguish between 'cosmopolitans' (mainly middle-class) and 'locals' (mainly working-class). The first major difference between the two groups is that the 'locals' do not '*see*' the cosmopolitan circuit (ibid. 411). The 'cosmopolitans' have a broader conception of the scale of their education market and are more active as 'choosers' within it. For 'locals', being local is valued in its own right. As indicated above, this has both a practical aspect reflecting time–budget constraints, but also a cultural dimension to do with relating to the familiar and its attachments. For both types of reasons, working-class families need schooling to be adjusted to the needs of the family, whereas middle-class parents are more willing and able to adjust the family to the school. Ball et al. stress that this is not a cultural deficit model of the working-class family, but recognition of the way in which 'Choice of school [is] "embedded" in a complex pattern of family demands and structural limitations' (ibid.).

The authors emphasize 'time horizons and the imagination of time' (ibid. 413). By the latter they mean that 'The middle-class "cosmopolitan" families are more likely to "imagine" their children as dentists or accountants or artists, at university, in the sixth form; whereas the working class "locals" will "wait and see" and they are less likely to speculate about the future of their offspring' (ibid. 413). Ball et al. identify different *discourses* of educational choice: 'A working class discourse dominated by the practical and the immediate and a middle class discourse dominated by the ideal and advantageous' (ibid. 419). The class distribution of cultural capital constructs a system of educational stratification based upon socially differentiated and largely discontinuous circuits within the educational market-place. Class differences in choice are not, then, just to do with differing capacities; they are associated with different types of discourse significantly structured by spatial-temporal orientations – different types of *habitus* – and their imaginative potentials for envisaging possible futures.

Segregation and the index wars

Although increased segregation would appear to be the obvious logic of marketization (see Noden 2000: 372–4), the issue has to be settled empirically by asking the question: Has education *in fact* become more socially segregated? The answer is not as straightforward as it might seem. There are two (possibly interrelated) problems. The first is that empirical studies in different localities seem to give different pictures: some do show evidence of increased segregation, but others don't. The second problem is a technical one, to do with how social segregation between schools (or social differentiation in education more generally) is measured. In a discussion of these issues, Gorard (2000) says that there are two commonly used but 'substantially different methods' for measuring these things: 'The interesting thing about these two common methods is that they give totally different results from the same raw data' (p. 392)! Hence, one reason why the empirical studies may give contrary findings is that they use different methods.

Gorard summarizes the situation as follows:

> [U]sing the most popular method of comparing groups over time, there appears to be a crisis in British education. Differences between social groups, in terms of examination results expressed in percentage terms, are increasing over time, and so education is becoming increasingly polarised by gender, class, ethnicity, and income. Using the second method, when these differences are considered in proportion to the figures on which they are based, the opposite trend emerges. Achievement gaps between groups of students defined by gender, ethnicity, class and income actually appear to be declining. Education is becoming less polarised over time. This is the 'paradox of achievement gaps'. (Gorard 2000: 393)

The intention here is not to engage in any way with the mathematical technicalities of these debates, but to make some more general observations.

The first is that, as Noden (2000) points out, notions of attainment or segregation are not simple: they do not have single meanings. They might be defined in different but equally valid ways in different cases for different purposes. Secondly, different measures might be better suited to different cases and purposes. Consequently, it is a mistake to expect any simple, single measure of differences. Thirdly, given the importance that

Ball et al. (1997) and others are giving to the significance of *local* factors, it is highly possible that different things *are* happening in different places for locally contingent reasons (regardless of measures employed). Fourthly, it would be wrong to assume that such factors remain unchanged over time. Although, initially, middle-class families might be advantaged by market reforms, working-class families might begin to catch up through experience, and become more skilled and resourceful 'choosers': in the first instance segregation might increase, but subsequently it might narrow as the market and its modes of behaviour become established and more familiar (Gorard and Fitz discussed in Noden 2000: 383).

Throughout this chapter, the approaches and research discussed have moved in the direction of increasing complexity in the relationship of pupils to their schools and of families towards the schools their children might attend. Ball et al. illustrate this in the conclusion to their paper. As they say, 'the keynote is complexity'.

> What we are describing here was an already highly complex and differentiated system of schools – with hierarchy, specialisms, selection, and oversubscription all present. Within this system space, distance and transport all play a part in making some schools more 'get-at-able' than others. History and reputation make some schools more desirable to some choosers. Schools are more or less well placed in spatial terms and so are some families. Patterns of choice are generated both by choice preferences and opportunities and capacities. Thus in making choices, reputation and desirability are played off against other factors, like distance, and like matching. For some parents it is not the general characteristics of a school that are important but the specific match or fit between the school and their child. For working-class parents the child's wishes are often more decisive but family organisation is a constraint. For middle-class parents family organisation seems to be less a constraint but the child's input into the choice process is more limited. The individualisation of choice is different in each case. In all the ways noted above the market is strongly related to social class differences. (Ball et al. 1997: 419)

The relationships between families' 'position to' the school, the manner in which pupils might be 'positioned by' the school, and how they strategically 'position themselves' *within* the school form a complex matrix that is itself positioned between two structural dynamics: the first that of the education system itself and the processes of expansion, credentialization, inflation and the 'upward translation' of differentials, and the second that of exogenous changes in the world of work and in family organization. Although these things affect different groups in different ways at different times, there are nevertheless shared conditions: for all education is located between an origin and a destination, between some place and somewhere; but the education system itself is also on a journey. Its own dynamic of change is not simply reducible to the deliberated effects of educational policy and reform. As Boudon indicates, it is within the structural dynamic of the system itself that the key to the sociological understanding of how education works lies.

Conclusion

This chapter has reviewed the problems of social differences in education in terms of perspectives that are concerned with (a) the dynamic of the system of positions in education and (b) the ways in which pupils position themselves in relation to education. Following Phillip Brown, the concern has been with pupils as active subjects operating strategically within an evolving educational context, the position system of which is continually being revalorized by the combined processes of credentialization in the labour market and credential inflation. If the kind of 'strategic positioning' approach of investigators such as Willis, Brown and Mirza is related to Boudon's idea of the 'educational decision field' and his simulation model of educational expansion, then it appears possible, with some degree of satisfaction, to account for dominant empirical trends in education and provide a plausible account of how those trends are generated through the combination of changes in the system of positions and the explication of the strategies of particular groups.

More specifically, Boudon's model systematically accounts for the way in which (a) educational inequalities at lower levels of the system can decline, while (b) overall differentials remain the same, and (c) the average level of attainment rises. Most significantly, it demonstrates that there is no necessary logic whereby reductions in *educational inequalities* generate greater equality of *social opportunity*. The spread of qualifications in the population does not increase opportunity; it devalues the qualifications (the GCSE examination in the UK is currently reaching this point, with elite schools dropping it for their pupils). The link between educational opportunities, social opportunities and social mobility is inherently *weak*; hence there is a limit to how far education can operate as a more general instrument of social policy. This means that policy should not overburden education with social objectives that are beyond its capacity, and that other kinds of mechanisms for promoting opportunity and social equity should be addressed (Brown and Lauder 1997).

As far as pupils and schools are concerned, the focus upon strategic positioning suggests that the types of factors considered in the externalist and internalist accounts have weak effects relative to those associated with the ways in which pupils themselves act in relation to the school. As the examples of the gender revolution and the more specific case of black girls indicate, pupil positionings and strategies, under circumstances shaped by family structures and labour market conditions, are the more powerful factors in shaping the system of social differences in education. This is not to say that schools have no effect; but as school effectiveness research illustrates, it is restricted and, in any case need not affect educational and social inequalities (chapter 1). As the work of Ball et al. shows, how families are positioned in relation to schools is probably of more significance than the ways in which pupils are discursively positioned by schools (though school selection procedures might be influential here). In relation to equal opportunities concerns, exploration of frames of reference and their relationships to education markets and labour markets is likely to be of more value than the deconstruction of educational discursive processes, whether at policy or curriculum level.

An implication of these arguments is that if the *instrumental* capacity of the education system to realize certain kinds of economic and social policy objectives is weaker than has often been thought, then there is less justification for restricting the flexibility of schools in realizing intrinsically *educational* objectives. Initiatives such as anti-sexist and multicultural education have educational justifications that are intrinsic, regardless of how far they contribute to ends beyond themselves (however desirable those ends are thought to be). The gender revolution in education owes far more to changing family structures, labour markets and the feminist revolution in society than to anti-sexist education in the schools; but that is not a reason to stop promoting anti-sexist education on *educational* grounds. The final implication of these sociological accounts might well be that the best reasons for doing things in education are *educational* reasons, and that educators are best employed pursuing these intrinsic aims rather than being harnessed to external objectives.

5

The Structure of Pedagogic Discourse

Introduction

This chapter returns to issues raised in the third chapter in the discussion of Weber, Durkheim and *habitus*. Attention was drawn there to the distinction that Durkheim makes when he writes: 'underlying the particular condition of our intelligence and sensibility there is in each one of us a more profound condition which determines the others and gives them their unity; and it is this more profound condition which we must get at if we are truly to do our job as educators and have an effect which will be durable' (Durkheim 1977: 28). It is this 'more profound condition' that is now the central concern, as it was for Durkheim himself (for reasons to be given below). In order to provide a sense of what is at issue here, another distinction drawn by Basil Bernstein can be considered:

> It is a matter of some interest that the sociology of education has rarely turned its attention to the analysis of the intrinsic features constituting and distinguishing the specialised form of communication realised by the pedagogic discourse of education. Many of the analyses of the sociology of education, especially those carried out by the diverse group of theories of reproduction, assume, take for granted, the very discourse which is subject to their analysis. These theories, in particular, see pedagogic discourse as a medium for other voices: class, gender, and race. The discourses of education are analysed for their power to reproduce dominant/dominated relations external to the discourse but which penetrate the social relations, media of transmission, and evaluation of pedagogic discourse. It is often considered that the voice of the working class is the absent voice of pedagogic discourse, but we shall argue here that what is absent from pedagogic discourse is its own voice. (Bernstein 1990: 165)

'It is as if', Bernstein says, 'pedagogic discourse is itself no more than a relay for power relations external to itself; a relay whose form has no consequences for what is relayed' (ibid. 166). He asks the question: 'How is it possible to make a distinction between a relay and what is relayed?' This distinction is not identical to Durkheim's, but both are of the same form and have to do with the same thing.

Basil Bernstein, until his death in 2000, was the pre-eminent British social theorist working in the sociology of education, and his work is likely to remain for many years its most substantial intellectual achievement. It is not possible here to adequately summarize the complexity of Bernstein's system and its development from his first published paper in 1958. Rather, the focus will be upon two issues: (a) what is distinctive about Bernstein's theory and (b) what that can tell us about the production of knowledge and the structuring of intellectual fields (Moore and Muller 2002). The first question will be pursued by considering two seminal papers from the 1970s, respectively on 'classification and framing' and 'visible and invisible pedagogies' (Bernstein 1977: chs 5 and 6), and the second question will be examined through his later writings concerning 'languages of description' and 'vertical and horizontal knowledge structures' (Bernstein 2000). Bernstein stands out amongst social theorists in that his theory has generated an impressively wide range of *empirical* work amongst researchers across the world (e.g. Morais et al. 2001; Power et al. 2001; Arnot 2002: ch. 11; *British Journal of Sociology of Education* 2002). This was made possible because his theory sought to generate concepts that enable a close engagement with data (Bernstein 2000: ch. 6), and the particular character of that theory is what requires examination. This points forward to the deeper epistemological and theoretical issues of the next chapter.

The implication of Bernstein's statement above is that the sociology of education has been in a significant manner one-sided. It has paid considerable attention to the ways in which forces such as class and gender differences are present within or relayed through education, but has neglected something that is intrinsic to education itself: the *voice* of pedagogic discourse. The 'voice of pedagogic discourse' and the 'more profound condition' are aspects of the same thing, but, unfortunately, it is not possible to give a simple and immediate illustration of what this is. However, an everyday observation might provide an initial sense of what is involved. As I am writing, my television set is showing the play between the English and South African cricket teams. I can see the pictures and hear the commentary – they are *what* is being relayed by the broadcast. But there is also something else, a *relay* (a signal), that makes this possible, and this I cannot see or hear, but without it I would see or hear nothing at all! It is this invisible condition for that which *is* visible that Durkheim and Bernstein are concerned with.

The problems here are compounded, alas, by others to do with the 'visibility' of Durkheim and Bernstein themselves! Bernstein throughout his work emphasizes his debt to Durkheim:

Durkheim's work is a truly magnificent insight into the relationship between symbolic orders, social relationships and the structuring of experience. In a sense, if Marx turned Hegel on his head, then Durkheim attempted to turn Kant on his head. For in *Primitive Classification* and in *The Elementary Forms of the Religious Life*, Durkheim attempted to derive the basic categories of thought from the structuring of the social relation. It is beside the point as to his success. He raised the whole question of the relation between the classification and frames of the symbolic order and the structuring of experience. (Bernstein 1973: 194)

Bernstein speaks of Durkheim's 'truly magnificent insight', but he was also very much aware of the way in which Durkheim's thought had been successively recontextualized through a series of reinterpretations that fundamentally misrepresented his concerns and his theory – he was (and is) commonly presented as a conservative and a positivist, whereas he was actually a socialist and a rationalist. Bernstein's former tutor at the London School of Economics, Donald MacRae, in his Foreword to the 1973 edition of the first volume of *Class, Codes and Control*, says of Bernstein's work:

Its concerns, but not its procedures, are Durkheimian and the relation of Bernstein to Durkheim – and not the Durkheim of the textbooks – would be worth serious exploration. For Durkheim raises questions that the other great sociological theorists from Ferguson to the present have either not seen or have avoided. In a way what Bernstein does is to attack the questions of *The Elementary Form of the Religious Life* but in terms of categories forged not out of Kantian categories but out of categories derived from the half-century of sociology since Durkheim's death, from the author's own thought and feeling, from his researches, and, by a circuitous route, from the neo-Kantianism of Ernest Cassirer. (Bernstein 1973: p. xiv)

Bernstein also had a 'truly magnificent insight' – an insight into Durkheim and his project that is very far removed from the 'Durkheim of the textbooks', and in order to properly understand Bernstein, it is necessary to recover Durkheim in something like the sense that Bernstein had of him, which involves reversing the movement that in the early 1970s positioned Durkheim at the conservative, positivist pole of the intellectual field.

Durkheim and the Science of Education

Of the founding thinkers of sociology, it was Emile Durkheim (1858–1917) who devoted most attention to education. Furthermore, education was at the core of his theory. Karabel and Halsey, in their authoritative 1977 review of the sociology of education, say of *The Evolution of Educational Thought* (Durkheim 1977) that 'No sociologist of education has yet surpassed – in depth or in breadth – this investigation of the relation-ship between social structure and the process of educational transmission' (Karabel and Halsey 1977: 74; also 87–8). This verdict remains valid to-day. Durkheim's theory does not have just historical priority; it maintains a powerful intellectual claim on the centre of the sociology of education. But there are considerable difficulties in pressing this claim on his behalf, given the various ways in which his thought was refracted and recontex-tualized in the major sociological debates in the post-war period.

Durkheim's influence on the sociology of education has been extensive, and has sometimes assumed contradictory forms. He provided a major source for the American normative functionalism that was the dominant sociological paradigm of the 1950s – the time when sociology was strug-gling to become institutionalized in British universities. Associated with this was a particular model of 'advanced industrial society' (see chapter 2), related to his ideas on 'organic solidarity', which powerfully influ-enced thinking about education in sociology. This functionalist model became the object of intense criticism in the late 1960s and early 1970s with the rise of subjectivist, humanist sociologies such as phenomenology and ethnomethodology (associated with the New Sociology of Educa-tion). These approaches portrayed Durkheim as a conservative positivist, and formulated their own positions in *opposition* to his. In this sense, Durkheim's influence was negative, in that this school constructed their approaches on the grounds that they were *not* Durkheimian, as they un-derstood and represented him. In a more specialized way, his classic work *Suicide* (1952) provided, via the work of Robert Merton, the basis for a set of classic studies of pupil subcultures in English secondary schools (through 'typologies of adaptation', discussed in chapter 4). These studies played a pivotal role in shifting attention from the macro-level concerns of structural theories to the micro-processes of schooling. However, this set of influences only partially represent Durkheim – filtered as they are through secondary, Anglophone, reinterpretations.

There is a more authentic, though less frequently acknowledged, in-fluence reflecting Durkheim's seminal position in the development of French social science. Despite recent enthusiasm for structuralist and post-structuralist thinkers, it is rarely recognized that, through what Bourdieu called 'a strange ruse of intellectual reason', these ideas (e.g. of Claude Lévi-Strauss, Louis Althusser, Michel Foucault) have their roots in 'the Durkheimian philosophy of man' (Bourdieu 1988: p. xxiii). This alterna-tive, but more 'subterranean' influence (Alexander 1990: 4–6), surfaces in crucial ways throughout the sociology of education. Understanding Durkheim in this way enables us to see, for instance, the manner in which Foucault's concerns range across the terrain mapped by Durkheim in *The Division of Labour in Society* (1933) and what his thinking owes to Durkheim's critique of humanism (Cladis 1999). From this perspec-tive, Durkheim can be presented in a way very different from the received conventions of 'the textbooks'.

Context and background

In locating Durkheim, it is important to have a sense of his time and the circumstances of the French Third Republic. They bear directly upon the particular ideas that he chose to develop and the manner in which he did so. Durkheim's writing is deeply polemical (though this is not necessarily obvious to us as contemporary readers; Lukes 1973). He took as his major task that of establishing sociology as a *science*. The particular model of science that he supported (an 'emergent' model – see chapter 6) was one which enabled him to advance the claim that 'the social' exists as a distinct domain of the real requiring its own distinctive discipline: sociology. His attacks upon empiricism and utilitarianism are made on behalf of sociology as an aspiring science. These arguments are also *political*, in that he saw a direct link between 'the science of society' and the anti-clerical, secular morality that he supported within the Third Republic and promoted through his thinking on education (Durkheim 1973)

Durkheim was a deeply committed and passionate defender of individual liberty and dignity: he possessed a strong sense of social justice, was an egalitarian republican, militant anti-clerical rationalist, and an internationalist. These attitudes were channelled into his academic work and informed both his own teaching and his approach to education and its role in society. He was, by all accounts, a dedicated and inspired teacher, who placed his immense intellectual powers at the service of educational reform in France, for the purpose of improving the general social condition.

> Let us therefore make use of our liberties to seek out what we must do and to do it, to smooth the functioning of the social machine, still so harsh on individuals, to place within their reach all possible means of developing their abilities without hindrance, to work finally to make a reality of the famous precept: to each according to his labour! Let us even recognise that in a general way liberty is a delicate instrument which one must learn to handle; and let us train our children accordingly. All moral education should be oriented to this end. (Durkheim 1973: 55–6)

It is no accident that the great theorist of *la république des professeurs* should put education at the centre of his thinking and activity. Durkheim's theory of knowledge underpinned the secular rationalism that Clark (1973) describes as the 'predominant cultural pattern' of the militant supporters of the Third Republic.

Education, Society and the Problem of Knowledge

Durkheim was in the first place a *rationalist*. His rationalism has its origins in the ideas of the great German Enlightenment philosopher Immanuel

Kant (1724–1804; see Scruton 1997). This must be the starting point for understanding the centrality of education to his theory and the character of that 'profound condition which determines the others and gives them their unity'. Kant attempted to reconcile the ancient conflict in Western philosophy between *empiricists* and *rationalists* (or 'apriorists'; Durkheim 1995: Introduction). The basis of this distinction can be summarized as follows. Empiricists are those who believe that *experience* is prior to knowledge, and that knowledge is ultimately based upon sensory experience. In many cases (especially for the 'logical positivists' of the early twentieth century; chapter 6), such sensory phenomena (or sense data) are seen as the objective basis of scientific knowledge. One important consequence of this belief is that it disallows any knowledge claims that cannot ultimately be grounded in sensory experience.

The problem with empiricism is in accounting for the remarkably orderly and structured nature of thought in the light of the disorderly and potentially random character of empirical (or experiential, subjective) association. Following Kant, Durkheim was concerned with the 'compulsive' way in which human beings invariably experience reality in terms of basic *categories* (concepts and intuitions) such as space, time, causality and extension. As Ernest Gellner says, 'The empiricists could not account for this compulsion. They have great trouble with *any* compulsion: their world is, so to speak, floppy and *loose*. It coagulates by accident, like a snowball' (Gellner 1992: 31–2). In essence, the logic (or rather, illogic) of associationism is simply not sufficient to account for the enduring structured regularities of human thought. 'Association is law-less, it can establish links *anywhere*. Our concepts, by contrast, are astonishingly well disciplined. How on earth could anarchic association engender such well-drilled concepts and produce such an orderly and stable world?' (ibid. 34).

Whereas empiricists see knowledge as *a posteriori*, as coming *after* experience, rationalists see its crucial dimensions as *a priori*, as *preceding* experience (Scruton 1997: 32–3). That is, the fundamental categories of experience such as time and space that *structure* our experiences exist prior to experience, and provide experiences with their basic organizing principles. Kant referred to these basic, *a priori* categories as 'transcendental', meaning that they are the universal and necessary pre-conditions for any experience and for knowledge, and are revealed by means of *deduction* rather than being empirically established (see chapter 6 on 'transcendental arguments' and Scruton 1997: 39–42). Although both culturally and individually *time* can be known and subjectively experienced in many ways, we cannot but experience reality in terms of time in some form or other. The *category* is fundamental and necessary, though its form is open to variation. Kant views these categories as a universal property of the human mind (a 'transcendental ego'), and they are the condition for our individual experiences.

Durkheim shared this basic Kantian *a priorism*. However, he also saw a fundamental problem in Kant. The 'apriorists' are genuine rationalists;

however, 'they have to ascribe to the intellect a certain power to transcend experience. But for this singular power, they offer neither explanation nor warrant. Merely to say that it is inherent in the nature of human intellect is not to explain that power' (Durkheim 1995: 14). In the final analysis, the transcendental ego explains nothing, because how can we explain the transcendental ego itself? The solution offered by Kant is simply that (as Gellner puts it; 1992: 36) 'the mind did it'. Durkheim addresses this problem through the radical suggestion that the basic categories of thought are *social* in origin: essentially, the transcendental categories of Kantian epistemology are derived from the principles of social order. In these terms, the 'social self' (see below) in Durkheim stands in place of Kant's 'transcendental ego'. As he says: 'Philosophers have often speculated that, beyond the bounds of human understanding, there is a kind of universal and impersonal understanding in which individual minds seek to participate by mystical means; well, this kind of understanding exists, and it exists not in any transcendent world but in this world itself' (1977: 340).

Durkheim's definition of education

Durkheim's definition of and approach to education have, in the first instance, to be understood in these Kantian terms. Education is defined as the 'methodical socialisation of the young generation'.

> *Education is the influence exercised by adult generations on those that are not yet ready for social life. Its object is to arouse and to develop in the child a certain number of physical, intellectual and moral states which are demanded of him by both the political society as a whole and the special milieu for which he is specifically destined.*
>
> ... It follows from the definition that precedes, that education consists of a methodical socialisation of the young generation. In each of us, it may be said, there exist two beings which, while inseparable except by abstraction, remain distinct. One is made up of all the mental states that apply only to ourselves and to the events of our personal lives: this is what might be called the individual being. The other is a system of ideas, sentiments and practices which express in us, not our personality, but the group or different groups of which we are a part; these are religious beliefs, moral beliefs and practices, national or professional traditions, collective opinions of every kind. Their totality forms the social being. To constitute this being in each of us is the end of education. (Durkheim 1956: 71–2)

We must note here that this is a broad definition of 'education', and is not restricted to what happens within modern education systems or schools. Durkheim associates this process with the formation of a 'social self' that owes its origins entirely to society: socialization 'creates in man a new being'. Education, in this broad sense, mediates between society and the self, and is the process whereby the 'outer' (social) becomes the 'inner' (self). Education is the process (the formation of *habitus*) whereby the social comes to be inscribed within the individual as the structuring principles of consciousness that provide the framework and conditions for the individual, 'personal' self. Durkheim (or at least his English translators) uses the term *habitus* relatively rarely, but once the character of his project is properly understood as the sociologizing of Kant in the manner described, the *concept* is seen to be fundamental to his theory and ubiquitous in his writing.

Understood with reference to Durkheim's Kantianism, we can see that his central concern is not so much with the *content* of knowledge and beliefs, as with the fundamental *generative* categories of thought (as noted in chapter 3). It is by virtue of being generative that these categories carry the possibilities of creativity, reflexivity and innovation. These possibilities find their fullest expression in what Durkheim called 'reflection', and are most highly refined within the sciences. By seeing these principles as social in origin, Durkheim also sees them as socially and historically variable, rather than universal. He expresses this view in the following, where he also makes a fundamental distinction (echoing that considered earlier) between societies' 'external forms of life' and 'the fundamental substance of their way of conceiving the world'.

> Far from being immutable, humanity is in fact involved in an interminable process of evolution, disintegration and reconstruction; far from being a unity, it is in fact infinite in its variety, with regard to both time and place. Nor do I mean simply that external forms of life vary, that men do not everywhere speak the same language, wear the same clothes, or observe the same rituals. Rather I mean that *the fundamental substance of their way of conceiving the world* and conducting themselves in it is in a constant state of flux, which itself varies from place to place. The view that there is one single moral system valid for all men at all times is no longer tenable. (Durkheim 1977: 324, my emphasis)

The main features of Durkheim's approach to sociology of education, and his historical materialism, can be summarized as follows:

- humanity is socially and historically developed;
- education is the process whereby the young are made into social beings under particular historical circumstances;
- central to that process is the inscription of the basic generative categories of thought;
- these categories are principles of social order translated, through education, into the structuring principles of consciousness;
- because these principles vary as societies vary, and because there is no universal human nature, there can be no universal pedagogy;
- the purpose of the science of education is to explicate the links between particular forms of social order, forms of education and forms of consciousness.

The sociologizing of the Kantian categories brings into play the concept of *habitus* – 'the fundamental substance of their way of conceiving the world' – as that which mediates between the inner and the outer and that transcribes the principles of social order as the generative principles that structure consciousness through the medium of pedagogy.

The duplex Self

The formation of *habitus* through pedagogy must be seen in terms of Durkheim's distinctive model of the self (a 'duplex' Self) and of the relationship between the self and the social. Durkheim's definition of education (above) includes the following:

> In each of us, it may be said, there exist two beings which, while inseparable except by abstraction, remain distinct. One is made up of all the mental states that apply only to ourselves and to the events of our personal lives: this is what might be called the individual being. The other is a system of ideas, sentiments and practices which express in us, not our personality, but the group or different groups of which we are a part. (Durkheim 1956: 71–2)

The distinction being made here between the social and the personal self constitutes the 'duplex' model of Self (e.g. Durkheim 1974: 325–40). He relates his model to the traditional division between the body and the soul that he sees as an intuitive awareness of this state ('The old formula *homo duplex*'). 'Far from being simple, our inner life has something that is like a double centre of gravity. On the one hand is our individuality – and, more particularly, our body in which it is based; on the other is everything in us that expresses something other than ourselves' (Durkheim 1973: 154–5). Durkheim's preoccupation with the *social* side of the equation is probably the cause of the main criticisms of his work: that he reifies society and produces an objectified, deterministic model of the person. If it is society that constitutes the self, is there any space left for individual freedom and voluntaristic social action? It is important, especially in relation to education, to understand properly Durkheim's view of the relationship between individuality and the social.

Paradoxically, it is precisely because Durkheim *does* define the social as a reality in its own right that his theory opens up an effective space for both individual freedom and collective human influence over society and history. The starting point is the fact that 'the social' is both external to us and also 'within' us. The social 'within', however, is not identical with our subjective experiences or the *content* of our values and beliefs (it is, as it were, 'tangential' or 'refracted' in the way that speech and language are not identical). The generative structure of *habitus* should not be confused with the *output* of *habitus* any more than language should

be confused with speech. This 'gap' between experience (personal subjectivity) and generative principle opens the space for what Durkheim calls
'spontaneity', and enables a voluntaristic view of the individual. The point
has been well made by Poggi (1972: 223–4), who differentiates between
'norms' and 'instincts' by saying that the latter are both 'within', and
from within', whereas norms are 'within' but do not *come* from within
– their source is external. However:

> The externality of norms is the externality of mental things and they can only
> affect action by being continually transformed into 'internalities' through
> the *mediation of the individual's active subjectivity*. This mediation involves
> an irreducible element of freedom in the relationship between the norm and
> the behaviour that the norm evokes. It cannot be said, in a strict sense, that
> the norm *determines* the behaviour, although Durkheim's treatment of this
> point sometimes seems to suggest that it does. To this extent, some degree
> of 'spontaneity' is a necessary element of compliant behaviour, but one that
> Durkheim construes in a rather austere manner. (Poggi 1972: 225–6, my
> emphasis)

What Poggi refers to as the continual transformation of the external into
the internal through the mediation of the individual's active subjectivity
is fundamental to Durkheim's view of education. In a sense, education
is the socially legitimated and regulated form of this process. Experience
and subjectivity are *structured* by the social (the social self), but not determined by it. Precisely because the 'personal self' (the self of individual
subjective experience) is not identical with the 'social self', there is an
irreducible space within the Self that is the space of individuality, spontaneity and creativity. The tangential relationship between consciousness
and experience (between the social and the personal self) constructs an
arc that is continually mediated by active subjectivity. Durkheim's view,
Poggi says, is that 'society is at bottom a "conditional" reality, inescapably
dependent on norms that in principle can only be observed freely, and by
the same token need not be observed at all' (ibid. 228). Durkheim's 'so-
ciologism' leads not to a determined but to a 'conditional reality'. From
this point of view, the 'problem of order' is endemic to society, because
its roots are intrinsic to the ontology of the duplex Self. The individual is
both socially constituted but also continually at a distance from and with
inclinations often in deep conflict with the social. Social order is never
given, but always needs to be worked at to be sustained because of this
'inner contradiction' in our nature.

Human beings, for Durkheim, are socially *contained* rather than determined, and this condition becomes an increasingly urgent issue in modern
societies in which social change actively requires innovative 'spontaneity' and the space of individuality is continually enlarged. Because of
the way in which 'spontaneity' figures in the relationship between norm
and behaviour, 'in a sense all societies are suspended over the abyss of
chaos; they possess a purely conditional existence' (Poggi 1972: 266).

Durkheim's personal experiences and his perceptions of his own time (the political instability of the previous decades in France and the cataclysm of the First World War) led him (not unreasonably) to fear that the 'abyss of chaos' loomed all too near. When his son André was reported missing in action, he wrote of 'the image of this exhausted child, alone at the side of a road in the midst of night and fog... that seizes me by the throat' (Lukes 1973: 555). This poignant image condenses Durkheim's fears of the consequences of the breakdown of social order. Historical circumstances, both general and deeply personal, do much to explain what Poggi aptly describes as Durkheim's 'austere' approach, but can also, unfortunately, make his style and priorities initially less than convivial to modern readers.

Durkheim's sociological translation of Kant locates his categories within social order. But they reappear in the social self as the constitutive principles of consciousness and experience. This continual translation between the outer and the inner is the work of *habitus*: the pedagogic formation and regulation of the self in the mediation of the individual and society. In the context of Durkheim's project for sociology and the science of society, it should also be noted that the duplex model and the idea of a *social* self resists the possibility of psychological reduction – crucially, the self, in this respect, is as much an object for sociology as for psychology, and in the distinctive way appropriate to it as an autonomous science of society.

The Structuring of Order

Following on from the sociologizing of the transcendental categories of Kant's philosophy and the observation that rather than being universal, they will differ as societies differ in terms of social order, it then becomes necessary to theorize and model the transformations of social order. Durkheim attempts this task through the concepts of 'mechanical' and 'organic' solidarity. However, the terms appear only in his first major work, *The Division of Labour in Society* (1933), where he associates these two forms of solidarity with simple and complex societies at the opposed points of an immense arc of human social evolution. It only takes a moment's reflection to see that neither mechanical nor organic solidarity could ever exist in an exclusively pure form. Durkheim is describing two contrasting *principles* of social integration that must always be present to varying degrees and always together. Schmaus argues that the *concepts* denoted by 'mechanical' and 'organic' reappear in his next work, *Suicide*, as 'social integration' and 'regulation', and, similarly, the term 'social representations' replaces 'collective consciousness' in the later book. Schmaus sees these changes as 'terminological' (1994: 174), in order to avoid certain confusions that arose concerning the argument in *Division of Labour*.

Consider how Durkheim describes the different situations of primary and secondary school teachers:

> In the first place, secondary education is a more complex organism than primary education. Now, the more complex an organism is, the more it needs reflection in order to adapt itself to its environment. In the elementary school, at least in theory, every class is in the hands of one and only one teacher; consequently his teaching tends to have a quite natural unity which is very straightforward and therefore does not need to be intellectually planned: it is indeed the unity of the person teaching. The same is not true of secondary schools, where the same pupil is generally taught by a variety of teachers. Here there is a genuine division of pedagogic labour.... How, short of a miracle, can unity emerge from this diversity, unless it is contrived? How can all these different teachers adapt to one another and complement each other so that they create a unified whole if the teachers themselves have no notion of what the whole is? It is not a question, especially in secondary schools, of producing mathematicians and men of letters, physicists and naturalists, but of developing the mind through the medium of literature, history, mathematics and the natural sciences. But how can each teacher fulfil his function, as he regards his own specialised part in the total enterprise, if he does not know what this enterprise is and how his various colleagues are supposed to collaborate with him in it, in such a way that all his teaching is related to it? People often argue as if all this went without saying, as if everybody knew instinctively what is involved in developing a mind. (Durkheim 1977: 6)

In the first place, the basic distinction that Durkheim is making between the elementary school and the secondary school is a form of the distinction between those principles initially termed 'mechanical' and 'organic' solidarity. But here they are co-present at different levels within the same institution in the same society at the same time in history. The point at issue has been well made by Randall Collins:

> To grasp this, it is necessary to treat Durkheim's theoretical statements analytically rather than concretely. That is to say, when he speaks of the principles of a 'society' and its integration, we should not take this to mean that *empirically* this necessarily refers to a 'whole society' as conventionally defined (which in practice usually means a political unit, especially a nation state). Instead, we should take 'society' in its generic sense, as any instance of prolonged sociation, whatever its boundaries in space or time. In this sense, a social class may well be a 'society', though it need not always be; in fact, the Durkheimian theory shows us the variable conditions under which its integration and moral solidarity is greatest or weakest. (R. Collins 1990: 109)

So, Collins suggests, 'society' should be understood in the 'generic sense' as 'any instance of prolonged sociation' (society in the sense given by 'I belong to the College Debating Society' or, more loosely, in the phrase 'high society' or the statement 'He craved the society of others'). Durkheim uses the term 'society' in this way, for instance, in *Moral Education* (1961: 79) in relation to the family and the manner in which the school provides the link between the family and the nation. Collins concludes that 'we arrive at a conception of modern stratification, in which the entire stratification order is a line-up of different types of 'societies' (1990: 110).

Secondly, having identified the complex division of labour in the secondary school, Durkheim raises the key issue of how to *theorize* it. What kind of 'unity' should emerge from the diversity of the teachers' specialized pedagogic roles? What should be the social form of their complementary activities? Durkheim argues that this issue is central to educational theory, and that the need to answer it in a 'methodical' and scientific manner justifies 'educational theory' and its teaching to student teachers.

Thirdly, he makes a distinction between teaching subjects in order to produce 'mathematicians and men of letters, physicists and naturalists' and 'developing the mind through the *medium* of literature, history, mathematics and the natural sciences' (my emphasis). Remembering that the crucial issue here is how to form the complementary relationships between the specialized subjects and that each teacher, through his or her specialism contributes to 'the total enterprise', it is the *structuring* of this enterprise that 'develops the mind' through the 'medium' of the disciplines – the formation of *habitus*, 'a more profound condition which determines the others and gives them their unity'.

Social order and individuality

The general historical movement in social evolution is towards greater complexity in the social division of labour. The key point is where the balance between the 'shared' and the 'idiosyncratic' element of consciousness shifts from the former to the latter, tipping the principle of solidarity towards the organic pole. The development of complexity within the social division of labour is realized through:

1   *differentiation* of institutions,
2   *specialization* of their activities,
3   *autonomization* of their fields,
4   *interdependence* of their relationships.

A consequence of this is that the principle of the self is increasingly detached from any particular, localized social base, and becomes concomitantly more abstract and 'universal' (see Lukes 1973: 155–7; Poggi 1972: 185–9). This is associated with the rise of what Durkheim refers to as a 'cult of personal dignity' (Lukes 1973: 156) that transcends the crude individualistic egotism of utilitarianism, empiricism and those he refers to as 'the economists'. This higher form of individualism has three main features.

- First, it is *abstract*: it elevates humanity in general, as a principle, rather than identifying any *particular* category of person. It is universal and egalitarian.
- Secondly, despite its individualism, it maintains a strong sense of the *collective*. It is not an egoistic individualism of the utilitarian type. All its great thinkers (Kant and Rousseau, Fichte, Hegel, Marx) asserted both the individual and the collective, and Durkheim associates this with an inherent socialism.
- Thirdly, it has the aura of the *sacred*. It not only proclaims the rights of the individual but inspires the individual with a sense of higher purpose and a source of moral value and worth extended to all human kind. '[I]ndividualism thus extended is the glorification not of the self but of the individual in general. It springs not from egoism but from sympathy for all that is human, a broader pity for all sufferings, for all human miseries, a more ardent need to combat them and mitigate them, a greater thirst for justice' (Durkheim 1973: 48–9).

However, these great prophets of the higher form of individualism, each in his own way, fail to properly reconcile or integrate the *individualist* and *collectivist* dimensions of their systems. It is at this point that the argument takes a distinctively original, but typically Durkheimian, twist. That these two things so frequently occur together within the same philosophy suggests that they 'must depend on a single social state of which they are probably only different aspects' (ibid. 48). The reconciliation occurs when it is recognized that individualism itself is social in origins and character. Individuation comes about as 'societies become more voluminous and expand over vaster territories' (ibid. 51), and is the culmination of the evolution of social complexity.

Hence, in just the way that Durkheim sees his theory as providing a solution to the problem of Kantian epistemology, so he sees it as reconciling the tension between the individual and the social in the theorists of the higher form of individualism. A particular historical development of the social is the *condition* for the emergence of the individual, and this is crucial for modern education.

[I]ndeed, once the individual personality has become an essential element of the intellectual and moral culture of humanity, the educator should take into account the germ of individuality that is in each child. He should seek to foster its development by all possible means. Instead of applying to all, in an invariable manner, the same impersonal and universal set of rules, he should, on the contrary, vary and diversify his methods according to the temperaments and the configuration of each intelligence. But to be able properly to adapt educational practices to the variety of individual cases, it is necessary to know what they are, what are the reasons for the different processes that constitute them, the effects which they produce in different

circumstances; in a word, it is necessary to have them submitted to pedagogic reflection. An empirical, mechanical education cannot be other than
repressive and levelling.... Now, the only way to prevent education from
falling under the yoke of habit and from degenerating into mechanical and
immutable automatism is to keep it constantly adaptable by reflection....
Reflection is the force *par excellence* antagonistic to routine, and routine is
the obstacle to necessary progress. (Durkheim 1956: 105–6)

For Durkheim, there is no inherent conflict between the collective and
the individual. A particular historical development of the collective is the
condition for the emergence of the individual self in its modern form.
The individual and individualism are the quintessential expressions of the
complexity of modern society. The manner in which the modern education system solves the problem of configuring the relationship between
specialization and totality is crucial, because, as the paradigm of the more
general social order, the structuring and processes of its *habitus* ('of developing the mind through the medium of literature, history, mathematics
and the natural sciences') constitute the principle whereby the individual
manages in practice the complexity of modernity. And for educators to
properly meet this end, sociology must deliver a 'science of education'.

Returning to Bernstein's comments on Durkheim's 'magnificent insight'
quoted above, he says that 'Durkheim attempted to derive the basic
categories of thought from the structuring of the social relation', and adds
that 'He raised the whole question of the relation between the classification and frames of the symbolic order and the structuring of experience'
(Bernstein 1973: 194). In the first instance he acknowledges the Kantian
character of Durkheim's sociological project in the manner described
above, but in the second he embeds terms of his own – 'the classification
and frames of the symbolic order' – within the account as if they are
quite naturally at one with Durkheim's own thinking, as if he has simply
given those names to concepts at work in Durkheim's thinking, rather in
the way that the concept of *habitus* is a recurring motif even when not
named in that manner. Bernstein's own magnificent insight was to read
Durkheim, apparently at the very beginning of his own intellectual career,
in a manner quite at odds with 'the textbooks' of his time and for long
after, to highlight and conceptualize principles at work in Durkheim's
system and continue with his own distinctive and original elaboration of
that project. The above reading of Durkheim is through a Bernsteinian
lens and attempts to recover Durkheim in a manner that makes sense of
Bernstein's own Durkheimianism, in order to read on now into Bernstein
himself.

Bernstein: Class, Codes and Control

There is a crucial difference between the concerns of Durkheim and those
of Bernstein. As an educationalist, Durkheim was seeking to define the

type of educational system appropriate to French society in his day – a task he believed to be of some urgency – whereas Bernstein's major focus has been the ways in which symbolic resources are differentially distributed amongst groups and within and through education. In this respect *power* is a central concern in his work in a way that it is not in Durkheim's. Del Hymes, has observed that 'Bernstein, a sociologist working in a complex society, recognised both linguistic form and social relations, but necessarily in terms of a plurality of styles and social positions. Styles and social positions are only sometimes side by side. More often, they are superimposed, stratified. Some control others' (Hymes 1995: 3–4). Hymes's essential point is that Bernstein is looking at the ways in which different modes of 'solidarity' (principles of order) interact and are *differentially* distributed in complex, modern societies. This comment by Hymes resonates with the way in which R. Collins (above) defines Durkheim's 'generic' use of the term 'society'. In this respect, Bernstein's interest was in the distribution of modes of sociality and their regulative principles and relationships.

It is not easy to classify Bernstein's theory, and he was dismissive of what he called 'epistemological botany' that attempts to pigeon-hole theories (2000). Commentators who know his work well stress how it weaves together threads from various disciplines and approaches. Hasan suggests that his is 'a type of theory whose primary allegiance is not to the mores of some recognised discipline: rather it is committed first and foremost to the investigation and explication of its central problematic' (2001: 128; Bernstein 2000: 125). Similarly, Diaz says that 'Bernstein cuts across paradigmatic positions in his concern with how society is inscribed within the individual and how what is written becomes a grammar for society' (Diaz 2001: 84). The question of the inscription of the social within the individual is at the centre of the problematic. In this respect, as Bernstein continually stressed, the starting point is in Durkheim. Bernstein summarizes his problematic as follows:

> Basically the theory addresses forms of symbolic control as regulators of cultural reproduction and of its change. In particular it addresses those forms of symbolic control institutionalised formally or informally as pedagogic practices. It seeks to understand how such practices, directly or indirectly, relay power and control and, more specifically, relay the distribution of power and principles of control which are a function of class relations. Thus there are two elements: one modelling agencies, agents, practices and specialised forms of communication, so as to reveal varieties or modalities of regulation and their organising principles as cultural relays; the second showing how such principles are themselves, directly or indirectly, media for the reproduction of class relations. (Bernstein 1996: 126)

Diaz argues that Bernstein 'provided a model for the understanding of how social class and power distribution become internally shaped means of recognition and cognition', and that 'mediating these relations was a *semiotic device* that implies a socially produced potential of meanings, contexts of internalisation, and unequally distributed realisations' (Diaz 2001: 84, my emphasis). This 'semiotic device' mediates between the inner and the outer in the process of inscription/realization, and its principles and forms are what Bernstein sought to describe and model. It constitutes the central focus of his analysis, and the concepts he develops are designed to delineate its variations and modalities: 'Irrespective of the question of the intrinsic logic of the various forms of public thought, the *forms* of their transmission, that is their classification and framing, are social facts' (Bernstein 1977: 87). Hence, Bernstein's theory has a distinctive *object* ('forms of transmission'), and the purpose of his theory is to make this object visible.

Bernstein created a radically new language for talking about the curriculum and pedagogic processes: a theoretically grounded, conceptual language the terms of which would engage with both underlying principles and the ways in which those principles manifest themselves in systematically varying, but conceptually specifiable, forms of social practice. At one level, *particular* concepts must be able to describe empirical instances as examples of their type (in order that we may know that type when we see it, or recognize its absence), and at another, principles must be described theoretically such that they can be modelled as the *generative* principles of those types actualized in particular instances. These aspects of the theory were explored by Joseph Solomon in an interview with Bernstein (Bernstein 2000: Postscript).

Solomon suggests that the 'position of interpretation' in Bernstein's theory is 'rather weak'. 'Instead, the need to produce accurate "descriptions" of practices of educational and cultural production and reproduction, and especially of educational practices, is permanently stressed' (ibid. 274). He goes on to say that 'you work very much by creating models of relations, mechanisms and transformations. In your texts, very often, concepts and their meanings are condensed, expressed in the form of an actual diagram. What is the function of these models? How do they link with the empirical research that is supported by the theory?' Solomon posed here a crucial set of questions, and elicited from Bernstein one of the most explicit statements of this fundamental dimension of his approach (2000: 209; see also 114–15).

In an earlier paper Bernstein described his type of 'model' when discussing certain interpretations of his theory:

> It is often said that the theory works by producing opposing dichotomies in which each side functions as an ideal type: elaborated/restricted, positional/personal, stratified/differentiated, open/closed, visible/invisible, collection or serial/integrated. That these are opposing forms (models) I certainly agree. That they are ideal types I certainly disagree. Classically the ideal type is constructed by assembling in a model *a number of features* abstracted from a phenomenon in such a way as to provide a means of analysing the presence or absence of the phenomenon, and a means of

analysing the 'workings' of the phenomenon from an analysis of the assembly of its features. Ideal types constructed in this way cannot *generate* other than themselves. They are not constructed by a principle that generates sets of relations of which any one form may be only *one of the forms* the principle may regulate. (Bernstein 1996: 126)

Bernstein's theoretical language is always attempting to move in two directions at the same time: crossways, as it were, between concept and description, and also vertically between levels.

Classification and framing, visible and invisible pedagogies

In volume 4 of *Class, Codes and Control* (1990), Bernstein developed a distinction between approaches that treat education as a 'relay' for power relations external to education (mainly reproduction theories – standpoint, interest, voice theories, etc.) and an approach that focuses upon the *intrinsic features of pedagogic discourse*. The difference is between perspectives that are concerned with *relations to* and those concerned with *relations within* pedagogic discourse. This is not simply to do with differences in interests or foci of concern (Moore and Maton 2001). It is to do with perspectives operating in distinctive theoretical modes and using different 'languages of description' (Bernstein 1977: ch. 7; 2000: chs 7 and 9). The distinction is between what is relayed and an underlying 'pedagogic device' (Bernstein 2000: 114) that structures and organizes the content and distribution of what is relayed. The key process is recontextualization, whereby knowledge produced at one site, that of knowledge *production* (mainly, but not exclusively, the university), is selectively transferred to sites of *reproduction* (mainly, but not exclusively, the school). This process is not straightforward and cannot be taken for granted. Bernstein's distinction is between the message (that relayed) and the 'grammar' of the pedagogic device (the relay) that makes the message possible by drawing into a specialized relationship knowledge and people, time and space, context and performance according to rules of distribution, recontextualization and evaluation (ibid.).

Bernstein describes the 'pedagogic device' as a 'symbolic ruler, ruling consciousness, in the sense of having power over it, and ruling in the sense of measuring the legitimacy of the realisations of consciousness' (ibid.). It is through its realizations that the pedagogic device reveals itself, and the theorization of its form and principles entails the production of concepts that can describe realizations as phenomena of its generative possibilities. Diaz indicates how:

> In essence, boundaries are the critical point for definitions of knowledge and practice, as well as for the subject. The more the boundaries, the more the distribution of unequal spaces and the more the distribution of inequalities

between positions, discourses, and practices. Thus, there is a close relation in Bernstein between boundaries, power, social groups, and forms of identity. Bernstein's analysis of power and boundaries provokes questions about their force, duration of spacing, ordering of internal forms and sites for knowledge, flows of identity, and relations with changes in the collective basis of society. (Diaz 2001: 84–5)

The concepts of classification and framing are crucial. The device is approached through categories and boundaries, the explicit and the implicit. It is not the *content* of pedagogic discourse that concerns Bernstein, but the structuring of relations *within* the field of discourse and the manner in which it associated with the contextual regulation of practice and consciousness for groups differentially positioned in terms of family, work and state. From this point of view, the content of a progressive and a traditional curriculum may be similar, but the structuring of their *forms* is radically different. These differences are expressed in relations between *context*, *meaning* and *practice*, and Bernstein defines *code* as 'a regulative principle, tacitly acquired which selects and integrates' these three features.

> From this general definition it is possible to conceptualise specific code modalities by a process of translation of the above three elements.
>
> - *context* translates as interactional practices
> - *meanings* translate as orientation to meanings
> - *realisation* translates as textual productions.
>
> Different distributions of power and principles of control differentially shape interactional practices according to different classification and framing values and thus give rise to different orientations to meaning, forms of realisations and so 'texts'. The formulation, above, shows visually the possibility of the produced text having consequences for expected meanings and their generating interactional practices. (Bernstein 1996: 194)

The differential regulation of context, meaning and realization through tacitly acquired codes active within an educational transmission process regulated by the principles of a particular pedagogic device generates a complex position system and its relations of power and control. The issue of 'translation' will be returned to below.

The possibilities or forms of regulation are given by the relationships of classification and framing. 'Classification' refers to the *relationship* between contents or contexts and the degree of boundary maintenance or insulation between them. 'Framing' is to do with the pedagogical relationship between the teacher and the taught, and the amount of control and the range of options each possesses over the '*selection, organisation, pacing and timing of the knowledge transmitted and received*' (Bernstein 1977: 88–9). Classification and framing can vary independently ($+C/+F$, $+C/-F$, $-C/+F$, $-C/-F$) and are *relative* in terms of strength or weakness (hence, this does not mean that there are only four given types of pedagogy). Strong classification and framing can be represented by a 'traditional' curriculum and pedagogy, with well-defined subjects and the pupil having little control over selection, organization, pacing and timing of the knowledge. Where both principles are weak, there is low insulation between subject categories, and pupils have a higher degree of control over the pacing of acquisition.

The key difference between 'strong' and 'weak' classification and framing is *not* to do with the presence or absence, or number or flexibility, of rules regulating a teaching situation. It has to do with the degree to which the rules are *explicit* or *implicit* from the point of view of the *pupil or student*. On this basis, Bernstein also distinguishes between 'traditional' and 'progressive' in terms of 'visible' and 'invisible' pedagogies (Bernstein 1977: ch. 6). The difference between the two is that the rules governing the hierarchical relationships between teacher and taught, control of sequencing of transmission, and the criteria used to evaluate the success of acquisition are *more or less* visible (or explicit). Bernstein's theory and its concepts aim to model (and reveal the principles giving rise to) systematic variations in the configuration and appearances of a complex set of relational properties structuring pedagogic discourses and codes.

> I started with classification because classification, strong or weak, marks the distinguishing features of a context. For example, some children when they first go to school are unaware or unsure of what is expected of them. They fail to recognise the distinguishing features which provide the school/classroom with its unique features and so particular identity. Such a failure in recognition will necessarily lead to inappropriate behaviour. On the other hand, some children are extensively prepared and are aware of the difference between the family context and the school context. In this case they are able to recognise the distinguishing features of the school, or class, even if they are not always able to produce the range of behaviour the school expects. Inasmuch as some children recognise the distinguishing features of the school, relative to the children who do not, those that do are in a more powerful position with respect to the school. It is likely that those who do recognise the distinguishing features of the school are more likely to be middle-class children than lower working-class children. The basis of such recognition is a strong classification between the context of the family and the context of the school. In our example the strong classification between the family and the school is a product of the symbolic power of the middle-class family. This power is translated into the child's power of recognition with its advantageous outcomes.... We can therefore set up a relationship between the principle of the classification and the *recognition rules* for identifying the specificity *or* the similarity of contexts. As the classification principle is established by power relations and relays of power relations, then recognition rules confer power relative to those who lack them. (Bernstein 2000: 104–5)

This illustrates how Bernstein typically attempts to refine his concepts by a process of 'translation' that drives concepts from initially abstract to increasingly more substantive forms such that they can be recognized and recovered in the world (effectively displayed at the beginning of the paper on visible and invisible pedagogies (Bernstein 1977: 116–20)). Hence, in the first instance, classification has to do with the degree of insulation between family and school (strong classification); but in order for this to be a differentially effective property of context, pupils must possess 'recognition rules' which identify the *specialized* character of the educational situation and its demand for an appropriate response (appropriate, that is, to the evaluation criteria operating in the school). Further, pupils must be equipped with the 'realization rules' that enable them to perform in the appropriate manner. Bernstein (2000: 106–8) describes work by Harry Daniels and others in which the concepts of recognition/realization rules are translated into research devices enabling their substantive investigation in the classroom – where these ideas can be recovered in terms of what teachers and pupils actually *do*. It is this feature of Bernstein's work that, in contrast to that of many other high theorists, enables it to ground such an impressive array of independent empirical research.

Bernstein (see above) describes *two* ways in which groups of pupils might be positively oriented towards the school context in the case of invisible pedagogies. The school might be recognized as either *similar* to the context of the home (weak classification between them) or in terms of its *specialized* character *vis-à-vis* the home (strong classification). It is the *recognition rule* that is important. Certain groups, at certain points in time, are *doubly* advantaged in that their children are symbolically equipped to operate effectively in both the progressive primary school (similar context, $-C/-F$) and the selective, academic secondary school (specialized context, $+C/+F$). These children are primarily those of the 'new' middle class, the 'agents of symbolic control'. Such children are able to recognize differences *between* contexts of different types and also to realize performances appropriate to criteria *within* contexts of different types (Power et al. 2003).

The subtlety of Bernstein's approach relates not so much to differences *between* classes, but to variations *within* classes and the ways in which those variations are contextually regulated. At no point, for instance (contrary to some interpretations), did he argue that working-class people speak only in a 'restricted' code, and middle-class people only in an 'elaborated' code favoured by the school. Rather, his concern was to identify the conditions under which members of different groups (class *fractions*) tend to realize restricting or elaborating variants and potentials – what are the orienting conditions whereby particular groups come to recognize the specialized features of *contexts* that call for elaborating discourses and how effectively can they meet the criteria (Bernstein 1973: chs 8 and 9).

The distinction between elaboration and restriction relates to that between the explicit and the implicit, and to (Durkheimian) modes of sociality grounded in principles of difference and similarity. The 'restriction' upon restricted codes is not cognitive, but cultural and contextual: meaning is restricted to those 'in the know', who share basic cultural values, assumptions and understandings. Meanings can be conveyed in ways that are highly condensed symbolically, in few words or in gestures that 'speak volumes'. Formal religious ritual, for example, is an intensely condensed code through which complex layers of profound meaning can be conveyed through stylized gesture or display to those who *know* the rules. A lecture, by contrast, works by unpacking or expanding meaning, by making explicit (elaborating) what is unclear (from the point of view of the listeners): 'Today I am going to talk about Bernstein's concept of elaborated code. What he means by this is . . . .' Ideally, the exposition progresses through moves that successively break down broad abstract concepts into constituent elements that enable the listeners to configure what they do know with what they formerly did not. What are differentially distributed between groups are the recognition and realization rules and orientations to meaning whereby they can successfully distinguish between that which can be assumed and taken for granted and that which is calling for a *demonstration* of understanding within a specialized context such as a classroom, tutorial or examination. These issues of recognition and realization become problematic for many children when the *ideology* of the pedagogy (as with progressivism) denies that such demands are being made, as if the child itself is free to be the 'author' of the text (Bernstein 2000: 110). In this respect, pedagogic processes regulate 'normativity' (Cladis 1999). The pedagogic regime requires continual display – display that is always measured against the calibration of the 'symbolic ruler'. But not all know that they are, in fact, on display!

Against the conventional view that aligns 'traditional' education (strong classification and framing) with the dominant classes and presents it as inherently conservative, and 'progressive' education (weak classification and framing) with the subordinated classes and presents it as inherently emancipatory, Bernstein's model produces a more nuanced perspective.

> I argued that the conflict between visible and invisible forms was an ideological conflict between different fractions of the middle class about the forms of control. One fraction, located in the field of production, carried out functions directly related *to the economic base* of production, circulation and exchange. The other fraction was located in what I called the field of symbolic control. Members of this fraction related directly to *specialized forms of communication* . . . . Agents of symbolic control could be said to control discursive codes, whereas agents of production (circulation and exchange) dominate production codes. It also follows that agents of symbolic control could function in specialised agencies of symbolic control or in the economic field. Similarly agents of production could function in the economy or in specialised agencies of symbolic control (e.g. accountants, managers). I propose that location, hierarchical position in the field of symbolic control or in the economic field would regulate distinct forms of consciousness and ideology *within* the middle class. In essence I was distinguishing between a complex division of labour of symbolic control and a complex division of labour in the economic field. (Bernstein 1996: 112–13)

Bernstein's focus has mainly been on mapping intra-class variations and contradictory positionings (see also Bernstein 1977: ch. 8, and Bernstein 2001) of groups and families between the private and public sectors and between material and symbolic production and control. Progressivism (at least in the form it took in Britain in the 1960s and 1970s) comes to be seen as a pedagogy promoting the interests of new middle-class and *liberal* professional groups against those of both working-class and *managerial*-based middle-class fractions (Power et al. 2003). This is linked to the culturally conferred capacity of the children of these 'agents of symbolic control', with their expertise in 'specialized forms of communication', to successfully read (decode) the often contradictory and implicit messages of progressive pedagogy. That is, what these pupils possess is a capacity to see through appearances to that which is rendered ideologically or rhetorically *implicit* in invisible pedagogy – the demand for highly specialized performances by pupils requiring equally specialized recognition and re-alization rules, as expressed in *appropriate* forms of play, for example. They can 'see' the rules that *implicitly* regulate the pedagogy by virtue of principles tacitly acquired in the family, but which remain invisible to other children who lack such tacit cultural resources. By focusing upon (modelling) the *structure* of pedagogic discourse rather than *interpreting* its content (as in constructionist approaches), Bernstein reveals invisible pedagogy, in this particular form, to be a highly specialized code favouring and sponsored by the new middle class, rather than the universalistic, emancipatory project that it claims itself to be.

By contrast, visible pedagogies, precisely by making their rules explicit (even if the rules themselves are arbitrary), are *more* open and available to children from a variety of social backgrounds. The explicit character of the rules also clearly delineates the 'space' of consciousness that is the concern of the school. For example, in a 'traditional' pedagogy, there is strong classification and insulation between work and play, whereas in 'progressive' pedagogy – especially for young children – play (or, rather, a specialized construct of 'play') is a central category of the theory of learning and is incorporated into the field of the teacher's surveillance and evaluation of the child. In this respect, progressivism both extends the scope of education's regulation of the subject (its symbolic ruler) and intensifies its normative demands (Hargreaves 1989; Walkerdine 1984). Because the rules and criteria are *implicit* ('invisible'), they are not available to *all* pupils and their families in the same way. This concern with normativity in Bernstein's work parallels that in Foucault and, for both, that in Durkheim (Gephart 1999).

Bernstein's distinction between the relay and that which is relayed, and his theorization of the relations *within* pedagogic discourse, provide a critical model of relations *to* pedagogy that radically revalorizes the conventional ideological default settings of the curriculum debate. It calls into question received views of the relationships between particular pedagogies and social groups and the potentials of different pedagogies for emancipation or control. He rejects simple dichotomizing, essentialist models of curriculum and pedagogy, such as middle-class/working-class, male/female, black/white, etc., and the view that any given curriculum form has automatic effects by virtue of its *intrinsic* character. There is a *complex* interplay between pedagogic discourse and positioning.

Languages of Description and Knowledge Structures

Bernstein's method distinguishes between two qualitatively different (though not *radically* discontinuous) languages in theory and research (2000: ch. 7). On the one hand, there is the language of a theory itself – a language *internal* to it – and, on the other, the language that describes those things outside the theory within the field it investigates, an external language of description. Crucially, it must be possible to read one language in terms of the other – to specify what it is in the world that corresponds to terms and operations in the theory. It is within this space that Bernstein's theory is most methodologically demanding.

There must be a 'discursive gap' (Bernstein 2000: 125–6, 209) between the internal language of the theory and the language that describes things outside it (otherwise, as with constructionism or discourse theory, descriptions are merely circular, and theory simply constructs its own objects). This second language must not only be able to describe what is outside the theory in terms relevant *to* the theory, but also be capable of recognizing what is *beyond* the theory. It must submit to an external *ontological* imperative (the principle of ontological realism, see chapter 6) that allows that which is outside to 'announce itself' (ibid. 316) in such a way that the theory is independently tested against reality and open to systematic modification in the light of that testing – a principle of falsification. As Bernstein says in the interview with Solomon:

> When the model is referred to something other than itself, then it should be able to provide the principles which will identify that something as falling within the specification of the model and identify explicitly what does not so fall. Such principles we can call the *recognition rules* for identifying an external relevant something. However, this something will always generate, or have the capacity to generate, greater ranges of information than the model calls for. The *realisation rules* of the model regulate the descriptions of the something. They transform the information the something does, or can put out, the language of enactment, into data *relevant* to the model. However, if the realisation rules produce descriptions which are limited to transforming only that information into data *which at that time* appear consonant with the model, then the model can never change and the whole process is circular. Nothing exists outside the model. (Bernstein 2000: 209)

The discipline that Bernstein imposed upon his theory was exceptionally rigorous. Within the research context, this means designing research instruments that are sufficiently precise and robust that they can engage with data in such a way that (a) the theory can 'recognize' its concepts in the world, and (b) the world can 'announce' itself to the theory in such a way that the theory can be modified in the light of experience. Bernstein (2000: chs 6 and 7) provides detailed examples of this method in practice from his own research and that of collaborators (see also Morais et al. 2001, especially the papers by Hasan (ch. 2), Daniels (ch. 4), Morais and Neves (ch. 8) and Singh (ch. 10)). Understanding the discipline imposed by the requirement of a 'discursive gap' between the internal and external 'languages of description' (of describing what is *outside* the theory in terms that can acknowledge what is *beyond* the theory) is central to understanding Bernstein's method, and also to locating his system within the broader context of current debates in social theory. It is precisely the discipline of the 'discursive gap' that is denied by constructionism and abandoned across a wide range of post-modern, feminist, multicultural-ist and post-colonialist standpoint approaches. As the anti-realists say, 'there is nothing but the text'. For Bernstein, however, the quest for va-lidity must extend, as Habermas puts it in a strikingly similar analysis in critique of Foucault, 'beyond the boundaries of the text' (Habermas 1995: 223; Moore and Muller 1999, 2002).

The distinction that Bernstein makes between those sociologies that treat education simply as a relay for forces outside it and that which is concerned to theorize the internal forms and principles of pedagogic dis-course operate in different theoretical *modes* (Moore and Maton 2001). Essentially, 'relay' approaches, through reduction, redescribe education *empirically*: Bowles's and Gintis's correspondence principle is a device that takes the liberal account of education (as meritocratic, open, universalis-tic, etc.) and translates its language into an alternative set of terms (as anti-egalitarian, closed, particularistic). In a similar fashion, feminist accounts redescribe it as patriarchal, androcentric, sexist, etc. But these transla-tions are at the *same* level – one empirical description replaces another. They operate through processes of alternative *interpretation*, rather than through modelling in the sense described above. Educational processes are not translated into a *theoretical* language the terms of which are internal to the theory itself. Liberal becomes 'bourgeois' or 'male', but not $+C/+F$ or $-C/-F$. In reductionism, the mind, in Durkheim's terms, does not go 'outside itself' through theory, but takes a step to the side, as it were, and sees a familiar object from a less familiar angle – it claims that we have simply misrecognized the object; we thought it was one thing (a duck), in fact it is another (a rabbit). The *principles* of pedagogic discourse cannot be translated in this manner. They can *only* be expressed conceptually in terms that are discontinuous with empirical descriptors: e.g. the way that Bernstein produces the concept of 'invisible pedagogy' as $-C/-F$ through a set of transformations that *begin* with an empirical description that is then theoretically translated into a term wholly conceptual in character, a term within an *internal* language of description.

Through the concepts of 'vertical' and 'horizontal knowledge structures' Bernstein (2000: ch. 9) provides a means of understanding these differences of modality in terms of the structuring (and possibilities) of intellectual fields. Initially, there are two observations to be made regarding these concepts. First, although they appear formally in his final volume, these ideas clearly have their descriptive origin in a paper from the early 1970s ('The sociology of education: a brief account'; Bernstein 1977: ch. 7). Secondly, it is interesting that Bernstein's fellow Durkheimian Randall Collins employs much the same language in *The Sociology of Philosophies* (2000). To begin with Collins:

> At times the density of debating factions floods the attention space with contending positions; this excess of horizontal density is fateful for the abstraction-reflexivity sequence too, because it generates epistemological scepticism. This faction takes the meta-stance of 'a plague on all houses', denying on reflexive grounds the very possibility of knowledge. This in turn provides a foil for a cognitive move, providing new transcendental grounding for epistemological-metaphysical systems. This 'horizontal' crowding of the network's collective conscience has a counterpart in the 'vertical' crowding which takes place if continuing factional wars are kept up across the generations. Such long-term debates drive up the abstraction-reflexivity sequence by raising the level of reflexivity concerning the categories of argument: names, universals, particulars, radical contingency. (Collins 2000: 845)

The condition of 'horizontal crowding' and 'epistemological scepticism' that Collins describes corresponds to the field of post-modernism and to post-structuralism's proliferation of hyphenated identities. In Bernstein's terminology, this is a 'horizontal knowledge structure with a weak grammar'. Bernstein (2000: ch. 9) makes two distinctions: (a) between vertical and horizontal *discourses*, and (b) between vertical and horizontal *knowledge structures*. The distinction between discourses has to do with that between 'common-sense' knowledge that is local, context-dependent, specific and tacit (essentially, that which operates with a *restricted* code) and vertical discourse that 'takes the form of a coherent, explicit and systematically principled structure, hierarchically organised as in the sciences, or it takes the form of a series of specialised languages with specialised modes of interrogation and specialised criteria for the production and circulation of texts as in the social sciences and humanities' (ibid. 157). Vertical discourse, consequently, entails the distinction between vertical and horizontal knowledge structures, and this difference, in turn, is expressed in terms of *strong* and *weak* grammar (Moore and Muller 2002).

The crucial difference between vertical and horizontal knowledge structures has to do with their relative capacities for *integration* and *abstraction* (the strengths of their 'grammar') – in Collins's terms, to generate 'abstraction-reflexivity sequences' in which knowledge is systematically integrated at successively higher levels of abstraction and generality. The exemplar of a vertical knowledge structure with a strong grammar is physics, and of a horizontal knowledge structure with a weak grammar, the sociology of education (Moore and Maton 2001). How is this so?

Bernstein illustrates the difference between the two structures visually (ibid. 161). The strong grammar form is represented by a triangle the apex of which signifies abstraction/integration. The weak form has a *segmented* structure – it is a series of cells, and in this respect reproduces the form of a horizontal *discourse* (where L = 'language'):

$$L^1 L^2 L^3 L^4 L^5 L^6 L^7 \dots L^n$$

> Thus in the case of English Literature, the language would be the specialised languages of criticism, in Philosophy the various languages of this mode of inquiry, and in Sociology ... the languages that refer for example to functionalism, post-structuralism, post-modernism, Marxism, etc. The latter are the broad linguistic categories and within them are the ideolects (theories) of particular favoured or originating speakers. *Horizontal Knowledge Structures*, unlike *Hierarchical Knowledge Structures* which are based on integrating codes, are based upon collection or serial codes; integration *of* language in one case and accumulation of *languages* in the other. (Bernstein 2000: 161–2)

In the earlier paper (1977) Bernstein refers to these 'broad linguistic categories' as 'approach paradigms' (p. 158). In this language and in the above, approaches are identified as theoretical perspectives. Today, they could be personified as the 'particular favoured or originating speakers' of post-modern discourse theory – in terms of the hyphenated identities of post-structuralism. These segmented knowledge forms with their specialized, and exclusive grammars are congenitally restricted in their capacities to generate cumulative, progressive knowledge integrated at successively higher levels of abstraction – in their post-modern version this possibility is systematically denied. Post-modern voice discourses can *proclaim* a position, but they create little 'news' (Bernstein 1977: 157). Under such conditions of 'horizontal crowding', it is not that more gets said, but that more come to say the same thing ('integration *of* language in one case and accumulation of *languages* in the other').

The manner in which Bernstein's theory *works* is represented in research by others across a range of areas. People *other* than Bernstein can take it, or aspects of it, and apply and develop it in their own ways for their own purposes. This capacity for the theory to detach itself from its originator has to do with the process of 'translation' whereby concepts at the most general theoretical level come to be systematically redefined as terms which engage with the world and which initiate a research process in which the world can 'announce' itself to theory. It is in this respect that Bernstein's thought stands out from that of so many other theoreticians.

Conclusion

This chapter has attempted a number of things: first, to examine the manner in which education is *central* to Durkheim's theoretical system and his project. This follows from the manner in which that project was concerned with sociologizing Kant. In order for the outer (principles of social order) to become inner (as the generative principles of consciousness), there must be a 'device' that achieves that transformation and structures the process whereby it is achieved and sustained over time – a *habitus*. Durkheim repeatedly points to this through distinctions concerning that 'more profound condition which determines the other [aspects of consciousness] and gives them their unity'. Within the complexity of his thinking, this condition is associated, on the one hand, with his 'duplex' model of the self and, on the other, with his determination to establish sociology as an autonomous science, and the social as a distinctive domain of the real. The way in which Durkheim places education at the centre of his system could, at the same time, be seen as placing Durkheim at the centre of the sociology of education through the sheer scale, ambition and originality of his thought. But, as Karabel and Halsey (1977) indicated, and as Bernstein was very much aware, this requires a major programme of recovery.

A second objective was to understand Durkheim in a manner that informs the sense in which Bernstein declared himself to be a Durkheimian, so as to better understand Bernstein himself. Bernstein's own project systematically conceptualized principles that are, as it were, at work below the surface of Durkheim's writing (in the way that *habitus* is), and to do so in such a way that those concepts could be refined into research devices that can engage with the world. His success in this respect, as measured by the quality and extent of the research inspired by his ideas, is remarkable.

Thirdly, in his concern with the 'voice' of pedagogy, he was not simply exploring a particular area of sociology of education, he was exploring it in a distinctive theoretical mode. In his last papers he began to construct a new theoretical language for analysing intellectual fields – fields of knowledge *production*. In doing so (in the distinctions between vertical and horizontal knowledge structures and strong and weak grammars), he was also producing a description of his own mode of theorizing (Moore and Muller 1999, 2002). This can be explicated through his accounts of the 'languages of description'. The sociology of education conducted in this Durkheimian/Bernsteinian manner indicates differences in the ways in which fields of knowledge production can be organized and *be* productive (Moore and Maton 2001). The broader context for these considerations is to be found in the underlying epistemological concerns to be explored in the next chapter.

6

The Problems of Knowledge

From the fact that it isn't possible to make science perfect, it doesn't follow that we shouldn't try to make it better.

Susan Haack

Introduction

At the heart of the educational process lies the curriculum and the crucial question, 'What should we teach?' Whatever we intend to do with education, or believe is happening because of it, occurs by virtue of the transmission of knowledge intended to transform the learner. This points to something broader than teaching method: a curriculum is an organization of knowledge involving the selection of content and *also* the structuring of the relationships within the content. The distinction between 'traditional' and 'progressive' forms of education, for instance, depends not just upon what is taught, but upon how the different elements are interrelated. Typically, a traditional curriculum is organized by well-defined subject categories with strong boundaries, whereas a progressive curriculum promotes integration and has weak boundaries. The content could be much the same, but the organization very different. Pupils may come to have similar bodies of knowledge, but to acquire quite different principles regulating knowledge relationships, and these principles could have broader social and personal connotations. The traditional form could be seen as instilling respect for the purity of categories and hierarchy, keeping things apart and in their proper place, and the progressive form as celebrating the mixing of categories and seeking innovative reconfigurations. In this way different forms of curriculum might be seen as representing different principles of social order. The traditional versus progressive debate has been conducted as a conflict about society itself, as reflecting a tension between social order and change, respect for tradition versus 'permissiveness'.

Sociological approaches to the curriculum start from the recognition that it is socially produced and historically located. These facts bear upon the key questions: What is in the curriculum? How is it organized and transmitted? To whom and by whom? How is success evaluated? And how and by whom are these issues settled? The last of these questions is treated by some as the most fundamental, because, it is argued, the 'who' issue effectively settles the rest. However, the sociology of education must be concerned with the *production* of knowledge as well as with its repro-duction. In key respects these two things raise very different issues, but one particular approach to how knowledge is produced, or 'constructed', has had a major influence upon sociology of education in terms of un-derstanding reproduction. In that sociology is itself a form of knowledge, the sociology of knowledge entails (or at least implies) a view as to how sociology forms itself – how it makes sociology. This in turn, is associated with how the social is understood, within different sociological perspec-tives. If knowledge is held to be socially produced, then what this means will be influenced by how 'the social' is understood, and this will depend upon the perspective adopted and how it defines sociology itself. The in-terlocking sets of concerns covered in this chapter can be seen in terms of the following areas and issues.

What is entailed by the recognition that knowledge is socially produced? This can be understood in different ways that carry different implications. One that has been especially influential is the perspective known as 'con-structionism'. This view treats knowledge in a *reductionist* manner by tracing it back to its point of origin within relationships between groups – relationships of *power* in particular. On this basis, knowledge relations are rewritten as power relations, and knowledge is understood in terms of the *interests* of those who produce it. Hence, knowledge is 'named' with reference to those it is seen to serve: e.g. 'bourgeois' or 'male' or 'white', etc. This perspective is often referred to as 'standpoint theory', and is associated in part with Marxism and, today, especially with feminism.

The constructionist approach provides a major challenge, in that it calls into question the truth status of knowledge as normally understood (it adopts a *sceptical* position). It denies that the concept of truth has any real objectivity. The idea of truth is treated as a 'mask' disguising the interests that lie behind it. Hence, this approach is to be contrasted with other views that do not see knowledge as compromised in this way, and that retain concepts of truth, objectivity, rationality, etc. It is generally the case that this latter position is referred to as 'positivism' in the constructionist lit-erature and this view (exemplified by science) is seen as placing knowledge *outside* history and society in a way that makes its claims absolute and cer-tain. Knowledge is presented as objective to the degree that it is *not* social.

This contrast between constructionist relativism and positivist abso-lutism reflects a more general tension between the sociology of knowledge and *epistemology* (the branch of philosophy that deals with knowledge). The latter declares that objective knowledge depends upon its *not* being social, whereas the former says that this condition is impossible, hence there is no knowledge (in the absolutist, positivist sense). The tension lies in the fact that, traditionally, epistemology has approached these issues in a formal way through defining the *logical* conditions for justified true belief (knowledge is those beliefs we are justified in holding because they can be demonstrated to be true). Knowledge is treated abstractly, independent of the social conditions under which it is produced and held.

The situation described above constitutes what has been termed 'the epistemological dilemma' (see below) whereby we seem to have only a stark choice between the two extremes of relativism and absolutism. In order to put this situation into perspective, it is necessary to review a range of developments within the philosophy of science and epistemology over the past thirty years or so. These developments are associated with what is known as 'naturalized epistemology': that is, epistemology that recognizes that knowledge is social but does not take this as meaning that it cannot also be true in an objective manner. How this is so is illustrated by a third position, known as 'critical realism'. Critical realism treats knowledge as social and seeks the conditions for truth not in abstract forms of logic (as with logical positivism), but in the material conditions (the collective social relations) under which it is produced. Against relativism and absolutism, realism adopts a 'reliablist' position, which says that of all the different ways in which we (i.e. humanity) go about producing knowledge, some have been proved more reliable than others, and that it is to these that we should look for truths that are *not* certain beyond question but *less fallible* than others produced in less reliable ways.

The debate about knowledge has been structured by the opposition between constructionism and positivism, and these two perspectives are treated as mutually exclusive. Indeed, constructionism presents itself as the radical critique of positivism (which is generally held to be conservative and, today, to be white, male and Western). How does the introduction of critical realism change things? First, by its focus upon the *social relations* of the production of knowledge, it throws into relief fundamental things that constructionism and positivism share: both reduce knowledge to *knowing* and subjective *experience*, and both employ *linguistic* models of knowledge. The introduction of the realist perspective both presents alternatives to the problems presented by positivist absolutism and constructionist relativism and reveals both to be, in fact, two sides of the same coin, rather than the opposites they are taken to be. Realism is more thoroughly sociological than constructionism, in that its concern is with enduring collective *relations of knowledge production* rather than with subjectivity. In this respect, the realist solution to the epistemological dilemma reconfigures the field of debate about knowledge in the sociology of education and provides new ways of thinking about the curriculum and about sociology of education.

The major purpose of this chapter is to review the principles and positions underlying debates about knowledge in the sociology of education by examining different approaches to the relationship between knowledge and the social. It poses questions about the implications of how knowledge is produced for how we can approach the *reproduction* of knowledge and the curriculum, and the key issue: what to teach. By focusing upon the production of knowledge from a critical realist point of view, new questions can be raised about the relationship between the sociology of knowledge and epistemology and the implications of naturalized epistemology for the investigation of knowledge production by the sociology of education. Although most of the material considered here is relatively recent and reflects responses in philosophy of science to Kuhn's seminal work *The Structure of Scientific Revolutions* (1970), the basic position represented by contemporary critical realism has a longer history. It can be related both to Marx (on certain representations) and to Durkheim. Durkheim's theory of science and the 'emergent' model that he adopted will be considered in detail later (see Schmaus 1994).

Constructionism

Constructionism became particularly influential in the sociology of education in the early 1970s, through the influence of the New Sociology of Education (often called the 'sociology of knowledge' approach at the time and criticized for its relativism). Constructionism had its roots in qualitative approaches such as phenomenology, symbolic-interactionism and ethnomethodology. Today it is found under the general headings of post-modernism and post-structuralism. In between, it adopted (and still holds) a range of feminist, multicultural and post-colonial forms. Its basic principle of *anti-realism* has been described by Muller as 'the claim that there is no reality beyond constructive description, that there is nothing "outside the text" (nothing that is not a product of representation) and therefore science takes its place as a human activity next to all other activities' (Muller 2000: 151). Reality is not 'out there' waiting to be described; it is the descriptions themselves that construct the 'real' of which we claim to have knowledge. Truth is created, not discovered, and is essentially circular. On this basis, those forms of knowledge (sciences) that claim to provide accounts of an independently existing reality (forms of realism) are fundamentally misguided. Their claims to cognitive privilege disguise the interests of those whose standpoints they represent. In constructing a basic distinction between forms of knowledge that are rational and objective and other forms that are not, it is in fact elevating one *group* above the rest (men above women, white men above black people, etc.).

Constructionist perspectives define themselves in *opposition* to forms of epistemological realism exemplified by the sciences. It is on the basis of this opposition that they not only build their distinctive methodology but also claim their special virtue – their capacity to deconstruct dominant, hegemonic knowledge claims and to give 'voice' to those oppressed and silenced by them. How do constructionists construct this 'positivist' Other of which they are the opposite? A representative post-modern version does so in this way:

> The ascendancy of scientific method as the means of establishing knowledge has resulted in a consistent failure to examine science as a social practice and as a historical and cultural product. Science has instead been seen as transcendent and decontextualised. Knowledge, as well as the knowing subject, therefore becomes context free. Rationality is cast as universal and transcendental, operating across all historical and social contexts and practices but independent of all of them. The result is an individualistic epistemology where the solitary individual confronts an independent reality of objects. (Usher and Edwards 1994: 36)

It is in this manner that constructionist approaches define science as being outside history and disembedded from any social context. As the final sentence of the quote demonstrates, this view of the ahistorical character of science is linked with an atomistic model of the individual and the objects of his detached, rational gaze. According to these writers, science is concerned with '"perfect knowledge" which grasps the truth of its object' (ibid.), and its quest is for 'mastery'. It is probably fair to say that virtually *all* scientists, many philosophers and certain sociologists of science would treat descriptions such as this with surprise. J. R. Brown, for instance, writes:

> [F]or the most part, working scientists find sociological analyses of scientific knowledge far removed from anything like their normal experience. In the face of sociological analysis, working scientists are simply incredulous. So even if they don't know where to begin in offering effective criticisms, they feel so alienated from typical constructivist work that they are likely to dismiss it completely. (J. R. Brown 2001: 31)

The more general point is, from *where* do the constructionists get their view of science? Who, other than constructionists, says that science is like this or makes such extreme claims on its behalf? Other ways of talking about science that *are* generally available will be encountered later – this question will be answered in due course. For the moment, the question is: what are held to be the consequences of this hegemonic model of knowledge and what is its alternative?

> To transcend history and culture is to transcend relativistic limitations. To know the world independently of history and culture is to have common measure or standard whereby difference and heterogeneity become sameness and homogeneity. Knowledge therefore becomes a mastery, the elimination of difference. Relativism is feared precisely because in claiming that there is no uniquely privileged position from which to know but a number of different positions each with their own standards, the very possibility

of an authorising centre is apparently destroyed. It implies that difference and heterogeneity cannot be eliminated and knowledge and truth cannot be mastered. (Usher and Edwards 1994: 37)

This passage displays the kind of language outlined earlier: (a) knowledge is presented in absolutist terms as involving certainty and a uniquely privileged position; (b) relativism alone is presented as the alternative to absolutism; (c) knowledge relations are represented as power relationships in terms of the conflict between homogeneity and heterogeneity expressed in the gender-loaded term 'mastery'. This polarization of approaches constitutes what J. C. Alexander calls the 'epistemological dilemma':

> I will call the presentation of these alternatives the 'epistemological dilemma', for it presents the fate of general theory as dependent upon an epistemological choice alone. Either knowledge of the world is unrelated to the social position and intellectual interests of the knower, in which case general theory and universal knowledge are viable, or knowledge is affected by its relation to the knower, in which case relativistic and particularistic knowledge can be the only result. This is a true dilemma because it presents a choice between two equally unpalatable alternatives. I argue that neither pole of this dilemma should be accepted. The alternative to positivist theory is not resigned relativism; the alternative to relativism is not positivist theory. Theoretical knowledge can never be anything other than the socially rooted efforts of historical agents. But this social character does not negate the possibility for developing either generalised categories or increasingly disciplined, impersonal, and critical modes of evaluation. (Alexander 1995: 91)

Viewing the relationship between epistemology and the sociology of knowledge as antithetical has had profound implications for the sociology of education, and is reproduced in the traditional versus progressive debate (Moore 2000; Moore and Young 2001). The purpose of introducing the critical realist approach is to find a way out of these dilemmas.

Post-Modernism and 'Unmasking'

There is no simple definition of 'post-modernism'. It is best seen as a constellation of ideas across a range of fields related by an apocalyptic sense of the character and depth of changes that have occurred in advanced societies in the final quarter of the twentieth century. Post-modernism describes a new order of consciousness which recognizes that the foundational principles and aspirations of the modernist (or Enlightenment) project were not only impossible, but based on illusion in the first place. This radical change in consciousness is associated with profound changes in society at large: economic and political, as well as cultural (Harvey 1990). Here, however, the concern is with 'philosophical' post-modernism and its sceptical critique of knowledge (Lopez and Potter 2001).

The sociologist of science Steven Ward provides a review of the issues raised by post-modern relativism.

> Postmodernism and its conceptual corollaries – deconstruction, intertextuality, discourse, rhetoric and hyperreality – have become the intellectual and cultural buzzwords of the 1980s and 1990s. Such popularisation and proliferation, however, have not resulted in an improved understanding of what postmodernism is about. For instance, in the last fifteen years the term has been used to describe television commercials, urban skyscrapers, feminist theory, poststructuralism, and the gay and lesbian rights movement. Once we clear away the variety of uses, however, it appears that at the centre of the debates surrounding postmodernism, at least many of those occurring in the humanities and the social sciences, lie important and long-standing questions concerning the possibility of obtaining objective, context-independent truth. All varieties of postmodernism are firmly antiepistemological. Postmodernists distrust all modern attempts to ground representation and knowledge in some philosophical or theoretical project, such as the Kantian subject, the perfection of language, or the empirical methods of science. Within the last ten years the antiepistemological stance of postmodernism has created a sea of controversy, debate and confrontation. Critics see it as giving rise to a contemporary crisis of representation – of announcing the end of all fixed meaning and of collapsing the epistemological distinctions between belief and knowledge, science and literature, authenticity and simulacrum, and, ultimately, truth and falsehood. For these critics, postmodernism's levelling of all epistemic distinctions prohibits knowledge practitioners from providing any accurate representations of the real and, as a consequence, any type of definitive truth claim. Politically it also inhibits theorists from offering any guide for the emancipation of oppressed groups. As such, postmodernism's antiepistemological stance leads contemporary thought into a nihilistic, antifoundationalist hermeneutics where perspectivism runs rampant, interpretation piles on top of interpretation, 'anything goes', and progressive political action is impossible. (Ward 1996: pp. xxiii–xxiv)

The implications of the post-modern account affect education most significantly in its historic role as a transformative agent. The purpose of education in 'advanced industrial society' was to facilitate progressive social change by educating citizens for productive and fulfilling lives in affluent, meritocratic, 'open' societies based upon the rational application of science and technology to economic and social life (see chapter 2). The post-modern account rejects the three basic principles of this model:

1 belief in social progress (countered by the rejection of 'grand narratives'),
2 the commitment to reason and science (countered by the critique of 'foundationalism'),
3 the model of the rationally self-determining individual (countered by the claimed 'decentring' and fragmentation of the subject).

Standpoint theory

An important aspect of the constructionist approach can be associated with the analysis of ideology through Karl Mannheim back to Marx. Mannheim referred to this as the 'unmasking' approach that arises when 'I do not even raise the question (or at least when I do not make this question the burden of my argument) whether what the idea asserts is true, but consider it merely in terms of the extra-theoretical function it serves' (Mannheim 1952: 140). This applies to 'whole systems of ideas, to an underlying social reality' (ibid. 144). To treat ideas in this way is, Mannheim says, to 'disintegrate' them. As Ward indicates, similar approaches today are influenced by 'deconstructionism', associated with Jacques Derrida, and post-structuralist forms of discourse theory derived from Michel Foucault (e.g. Weiner 1994: ch. 6; Ball 1992). This position follows from the constructionist principle that, because knowledge is socially constructed, truth is *necessarily* relative to the context within which it is constructed (relative to a culture, a language, a form of life, a paradigm, a discourse, a standpoint, etc.).

For post-modernists, relativism is seen not as a problem – indeed, it can be a cause for celebration! For them, knowledge is always partial, in the double sense of being both limited and biased, and exposing this, it is argued, empowers those groups (women, ethnic and sexual minorities, colonial and indigenous people) oppressed by its false (white male) claim to universalism. In the words of the influential feminist standpoint theorist Sandra Harding:

> An *epistemology* is a theory of knowledge. It answers questions about who can be a 'knower' (can women?); what tests beliefs must pass in order to be legitimated as knowledge (only tests against men's experiences and observations); what kinds of things can be known (can 'subjective truths' count as knowledge?), and so forth. Sociologists of knowledge characterize epistemologies as strategies for justifying beliefs: appeals to the authority of God, of customs and traditions, of 'common sense', of observations, of reason, and of masculine authority are examples of familiar justificatory strategies. Feminists have argued that traditional epistemologies, whether intentionally or unintentionally, systematically exclude the possibility that women could be 'knowers' or *agents of knowledge*; they claim that the voice of science is a masculine one; that history is written from only the point of view of men (of the dominant class and race); that the subject of a traditional sociological sentence is always assumed to be a man. (Harding 1987: 3)

Knowledge, here, is unequivocally identified with *knowing* as given within the subjective experience of different social categories of knowers. Standpoint theories not only attempt to reveal the limitations of dominant knowledge, but also argue that the socially disadvantaged can have 'epistemic advantage' (ibid.) in that their experiences and position in society provide insights unavailable to those in power. There are 'alternative epis-temologies' (C. Mills 1998) that not only provide new knowledge, but do so in new *ways*, as claimed by some forms of 'feminist epistemology' that contrast female and 'androcentric' knowledge (Holmwood 1995). It should be noted that the term 'feminist epistemology' has come to be asso-ciated with a rather narrowly defined group of standpoint theorists. There is nothing intrinsic to feminism that requires this to be the case. A notable example of a feminist, female epistemologist who does not adopt this posi-tion is the philosopher Susan Haack (see Haack 1998: chs 6 and 7, esp. pp. 124 and 132–3 n. 2). The concern *here* is with standpoint theory, *not* fem-inism. The 'social' is attached to knowledge through analyses that 'name' those whose experience and interests it is held to express (Moore 2000). Alternative forms of curriculum and 'critical' pedagogies are sought, based on the experiences and standpoints of 'subjugated' groups. In this reduc-tive fashion, knowledge tends to be conflated with *knowing*.

Constructionism is appealing because it apparently 'unmasks' false claims to universalism and disinterestedness on the part of the knowledge of dominant groups – it reveals how knowledge is always constructed within the power relations of class, gender and race. This conflation of knowledge with knowing is associated with standpoint and post-structuralist preoccupations with identity and experience. It knowledge is based in experience, then it is incomplete if certain categories of 'knowers' are excluded. From this point of view, what is important is not *what* is said, but *who* says it, because the former is only intelligible when located within the standpoint of the latter (Maton 2000).

The issues raised by the 'unmasking' approach to knowledge are partic-ularly serious as far as education is concerned. A common-sense intuition about the curriculum is that curriculum knowledge has not been selected because of its 'extra-theoretical function' but because of some property that sets it apart from other knowledge current in society that could be included, but is not. There are valid (if contentious) demarcation criteria that distinguish knowledge that should be taught from that which is false, pernicious, trivial or in some other way inappropriate. Post-modern rel-ativism denies the possibility of demarcation criteria. Indeed, relativism calls into question the very intelligibility of the idea of education, because any curriculum becomes in the last analysis a purely arbitrary product of power.

It is the debunking of reason and of a reasoning self that drives post-modernism into relativism. In their critical review of 'the varieties of rel-ativism' (see also Haack 1998: ch. 9), Harré and Krausz (1996) say:

> All arguments for relativisms of whatever strength or variety depend on the observation that there are, as a matter of fact, many languages, many theories for every phenomenon, many descriptions of what can be felt, seen, touched and so on, and many differing assessments of moral and aesthetic

values. From this observation it is concluded that phenomena are relative to which description is chosen, explanations are relative to which theory is favoured and both are relative to which language is used. By a parallel line of argument it is supposed that moral and aesthetic assessments are relative to whatever criteria are current. (Harré and Krausz 1996: 7–8)

But does relativism necessarily follow from the fact that there are 'many languages', etc.? These issues are especially acute for education, because they relate to its most fundamental concern: *What* should we teach?

Knowledge and Society: What Should We Teach?

In order to move beyond the default settings of the curriculum debate, it is necessary to return to the basic issues in epistemology. The current official rhetoric of educational reform draws heavily upon the idea of a 'knowledge society' – that we are moving (yet again) into a higher-order industrial society to which knowledge workers are the key. Education must keep pace with these changes by adapting to produce a new kind of flexible, multi-skilled worker, and that worker in turn must be ready to become a 'life-long learner'. The issues raised by these ideas are profound (e.g. Beck 1999), but as Michael Young (1998) has pointed out, the sociology of education is strangely ill-equipped to contribute to debates about the 'curriculum of the future', because what it crucially lacks is a robust theory of knowledge (Moore and Young 2001). It is for these reasons that this chapter examines the ways in which knowledge is held to be social, by reviewing debates in epistemology and the philosophy of science.

Young has distinguished between the process whereby the growth of knowledge has involved increasing specialization and differentiation and that whereby it has been associated with 'differential *social* evaluation' and 'stratification' (1998: 15–16, my emphasis). Reductionism conflates the two by reducing the former to the latter – the organization of knowledge (its specialization and differentiation) is *no more* than a reflection of social differentiation and stratification. The realist argument is that the growth of knowledge has a logic of its own – though one that is also *social* in character. Young believes that there is no 'necessary relationship between the two processes and that greater differentiation could be associated with reduced stratification in a society where the fragmenting tendencies of differentiation are balanced by the integrative trend of less stratification' (ibid.). In order for this aim to be realized, it is as important that we develop non-reductive understandings of the social logic of knowledge as that we explore the logic of social stratification.

The question 'What should we teach?' can be treated as a form of the question 'What should we believe?', in that it would be inconsistent with any defensible definition of education that we should teach things that we (collectively – and whoever 'we' might be) do not believe to be in some sense true or worthwhile. How can this be determined?

Epistemology is concerned to establish how we can come to hold beliefs that (a) are believed to be true, (b) are in fact true, and (c) can be demonstrated to be true. A basic distinction can be made between 'normative' and 'naturalized' epistemologies. The first is concerned with the *formal conditions* for holding certain beliefs as true (with the *a priori* form of logical justification), and the second with the *social conditions* under which true beliefs come to be produced and accepted as such. As Ilkka Niiniluoto says:

> Logical empiricism is often portrayed as an attempt to establish by logical analysis and rational reconstruction general prescriptions for sound science, or ideal models and norms expressing what science ought to be. Thus, philosophy of science is an *a priori* account of scientific rationality. On the other hand ... 'naturalised epistemology' and the historical/sociological approach to the philosophy of science ... holds that scientific rationality has to be grounded in the actual practice of scientific research. (Niiniluoto 2002: 15)

Normative epistemology attempts to logically reconstruct the *a priori* principles of knowledge, whereas naturalized epistemology seeks the sociological conditions of its production and acceptance – we are justified in holding those beliefs that have been produced in some *reliable* way. According to David Papineau, those operating with a naturalized approach to science do not seek to 'identify principles of scientific rationality on some *a priori* basis ... [but] look to empirical information about the effectiveness of different scientific practices to decide the right methodology of science' (Papineau 1996: 16).

Normative epistemology is 'normative' in the sense that it seeks to establish how knowledge should be produced in order that we might produce better knowledge. It is important to appreciate that naturalized epistemology *shares* this normative aspiration. It is in relation to the *a priori* that the two approaches differ, rather than in relation to the normative (Kitcher 2001). Relativists, of course, reject the very idea of normative criteria – for them, all knowledge is equal.

Normative epistemology can be further divided between 'coherentism', which concerns the ways in which beliefs reinforce or support each other to produce justification, and 'foundationalism', which holds that true beliefs are built upon certain foundational terms or propositions that do not in turn derive their own justification from any other terms or propositions. These might be rational intuitions or, within the empiricist tradition, primary sensory experience or 'sense data'. It is the *empiricist* form of foundationalism, and the school known as 'positivism', that is especially significant here. Positivism was influential as a model of scientific method in the first half of the twentieth century, when the social sciences were establishing, and seeking to legitimize, themselves in the universities (in the

USA in particular, where a number of major European logical positivists fled from the Nazis).

Within this perspective, the meaning of a term is that to which the term refers (usually held to be a 'sensation' rather than a 'thing'). In the first part of the twentieth century, this position was represented in the 'logical atomism' of philosophers such as Russell, Whitehead and Wittgenstein in Cambridge and by the logical positivists in Austria known as the Vienna Circle – the 'logical' part refers to powerful systems of symbolic logic and notation developed by Frege in Germany and Russell in England (Dummett 1993; Klee 1997; Edmonds and Eidinow 2001). However, a foundationalist thread of this type can be traced back through the Western philosophical canon and was important in the development of experimental method in early modern science (Luntley 1995: ch. 1). Foundationalism is significant here because, upon inspection, it becomes clear that the post-modern arguments about knowledge that have been so influential in recent times are almost invariably concerned *only* with foundationalism or, even more narrowly, with positivism (the conflation of science with positivism was also a pronounced feature of similar debates in the 1960s and 1970s). Typically, the post-modern argument inflates foundationalism into the 'Enlightenment project' as a whole, or even the entire Western philosophical tradition!

Foundationalism and positivism

Foundationalism provides an important example of one of three ways in which knowledge can be seen as non-social: where it is held to be received through divine revelation, when it is taken to be intuitively self-evident, and when it is grounded in direct sensory experience. In this last (empiricist) case, the social would be seen as a filtering or mediation of direct experience by received or preconceived prejudices and presuppositions (Klee 1997: 172, fig. 8.1). From Bacon and Descartes in the sixteenth century through to the logical positivists of the twentieth, the social and cultural were seen as what distorts knowledge and truth. The chief source of distortion was the imposition and uncritical acceptance of received authority in a variety of forms: religion, metaphysics, superstition, common sense, etc. Rather than promoting a conservative doctrine, positivists saw themselves as challenging received authority.

Positivism sought the perfection of language through non-mediated meanings founded in one-to-one and transparent relationships between words and sensations – the word means what it names or 'pictures' – and distinguished between knowledge and belief in terms of meanings that are or are not mediated (distorted) by the social. Knowledge is that which can be justified through a pure observation language methodologically realized through the operationalization of concepts and the empirical verification of propositions. The form of this language is propositional logic. The critique of positivism centres on the possibility of such a non-mediated, presuppositionless language of perception and its associated methodology. Positivism foundered in the mid-twentieth century because arguments from a number of different sources (some internal to positivism itself; R. Collins 2000: 717–30) demonstrated that such a language was not possible.

Dogmatic scepticism and the 'all-or-nothing' fallacy

There are two basic responses to recognition of the social locatedness of knowledge. One is to say that positivism is simply wrong as a theory of knowledge: we know we do have knowledge and that it is social. The task is to produce non-positivistic theories of knowledge – all knowledge is socially produced, but there are fundamental differences in how, and *this* is the key issue. This is the path followed by 'naturalized' epistemology and is, in a number of forms, the mainstream position today (Muller 2000: ch. 9).

The other response is to say that positivism is right, but that because its conditions can never be met, we cannot have knowledge. This is the position adopted by post-modernism. Essentially, post-modernism claims that, because all knowledge is socially mediated and contextualized, all truth claims can only ever be relative to the context of their construction – hence there can be no knowledge. All beliefs are cognitively equal, because none can claim the *necessary* epistemological privilege of *not* being socially constructed. However, this follows only if there is an implicit acceptance of positivism's principle that knowledge is only knowledge when *not* socially constructed. Niiniluoto (2002) has referred to this position as 'dogmatic scepticism':

> Thus, a typical 'dogmatic' sceptic is not a philosopher who denies the absolutist conception of knowledge. Instead, he assumes this strong conception, and then proceeds to argue that knowledge (in this sense) is impossible.
> This mode of thinking could be called the *All-or-Nothing Fallacy*. Its different forms propose a strong or absolute standard for some category (e.g. truth, knowledge, conceptual distinction), and interpret the failure or impossibility of satisfying this standard as a proof that the category is empty and should be rejected. (Niiniluoto 2002: 81)

It is important is to understand how constructionism shares (dogmatically) foundationalism's demand for the conditions for knowledge, but then draws the (sceptical) conclusion that, because such conditions cannot be met, there is no knowledge. This link between the two perspectives has been noted by Ian Hacking: 'The roots of social constructionism are in the very logical positivism that so many present day constructionists profess to detest' (Hacking 2000: 42–3). The disagreement between post-modern constructionists and positivist foundationalists is not the truly radical difference that post-modernists proclaim it to be, and it is necessary to be clear about what they *share* as well as how they differ.

A good sense of what is involved here is provided by A. C. Grayling (2001) when discussing the problems with the positivist model developed in Wittgenstein's *Tractatus*:

> But the most important point is the one selected by Wittgenstein himself for particular attack when he came to work out his later philosophy, namely the fact that the *Tractatus* oversimplifies and distorts language. And it does this by claiming that language is the sum of propositions, that it has a single essence, that this essence is describable in terms of predicate logic, that language and world have parallel structures which connect by means of the picturing relationship, and that sense attaches to what we say (and therefore think) only if what we say is a picture of a fact. Wittgenstein came to reject all of this. (Grayling 2001: 61)

This summarizes the basic features of positivist foundationalism. It contains within it those things rejected by post-modernists, suggests the grounds for that rejection, and indicates that the crucial debate is around the possibilities of *language*. Grayling poses the problem of why it was that Russell, Wittgenstein and others were so 'beguiled into thinking about language and the world in terms of a particular model' (ibid. 60) – the atomistic one summarized above. Robert Klee (1997) suggests why when discussing the Vienna Circle. He begins with an observation especially relevant to the present concern: 'The positivists held that a scientific theory is a *linguistic* representation, not of external reality (which they were not sure was a notion that even made sense) but of actual and possible human *experiences* (p. 28, my emphases). The terms 'linguistic' and 'experience' begin to suggest the underlying points of contact between positivism and constructionism. In a similar way to Grayling, Klee also wonders why the positivists were 'so smitten with mathematical logic?':

> The answer is, because they understood mathematical logic to be a universally applicable, maximally precise cognitive tool, a tool that could be used to analyse successfully a host of abstract, difficult-to-understand concepts, problems and issues. And a successful analysis ends our mystification about whatever it was that puzzled us by showing us how to understand it in terms of other things that we already understood previously.
>
> The universal applicability of mathematical logic is due to the fact that it is a *subject-neutral language* that can be used to capture and express the claims of any special subject matter. And the precision of mathematical knowledge is due to the fact that the main symbols of this subject-neutral language can be provided with *mathematically precise and unambiguous meanings*. In short, you can use mathematical logic to talk about anything under the sun, and the claims you produce with it each have a unique and computable meaning. This is a splendid outcome because, as generality

and precision increase, confusion and ambiguity decrease. It is no surprise then that this relatively new 'toy' of mathematical logic was taken by the positivists to be a kind of philosophical wonder drug with almost Herculean powers. (Klee 1997: 30)

It becomes clearer what it is that the post-modernists are getting at in their accounts of a supposed dominant, hegemonic form of knowledge that is outside history, etc. It is the normative *a priori* of foundationalist epistemology: the formally constructed subject-neutral language of mathematically precise and unambiguous meanings. But this was never more than the elusive ideal of a particular (albeit for a time an important and influential) project in *philosophy*. In reality, positivism never achieved even a stable form, let alone hegemonic dominance. Post-modernism rhetorically inflates the scope and significance of this project (the 'Enlightenment project', etc.), and in standpoint theory it is personified as hegemonically Western, white and male. Yet these approaches remain unaware of how their radical scepticism entails the dogmatic acceptance of positivism's own normative *a priori* as the only acceptable condition for knowledge. As Boham points out:

> The standard list of contrasts between the natural and human sciences had all derived from a positivist and empiricist view of scientific knowledge: the neutrality of observation and the givenness of experience; the ideal of a univocal language and the independence of data from theoretical interpretation; the belief in the universality of conditions of knowledge and criteria for theory choice. (Bohman 1991: 2)

By insisting that positivism *alone* provides the model for science, post-modernism treats its demise as that of science itself, and fails to appreciate the way in which post-empiricist naturalized epistemology provides the basis for alternative understandings of science and knowledge in general. As Luntley observes: 'In a peculiar way such postmodernists are not really postmodernist enough, for they still hanker after the idea that unless knowledge can be founded upon certain foundations it cannot exist at all' (1995: 140). One of the most decisive blows against positivism was Popper's demonstration (1994) that it does not reconstruct the logic of scientific discovery. The post-modern critique of the 'dominant view of science' is in this major respect fundamentally misguided: it is a critique of *positivism*, but positivism is *not* science, and in any case has long been superseded. Bohman says that 'With the rejection of positivism and its thesis of the "unity of method", many of the historic reasons for defending the sharp distinction between the sciences have simply disappeared' (1991: 2). The task for social theory, then, is to reconsider the possibilities of social *science* under the conditions of post-empiricism, rather than to lapse into the relativism of post-modern dogmatic scepticism (Lopez and Potter 2001).

Positivism and constructionism are located in the same theoretical plane, but at opposite ends. Both reduce knowledge to knowing by identifying it with the manner in which language constructs meaning within the consciousness of a knowing subject (for positivism, one language and a unitary subject; for constructionists, many languages and a decentred, fragmented self). Dummett (1996: 5) identifies the 'first clear example' of the 'linguist turn' as Frege's *The Foundations of Arithmetic*, published in 1884 (see also R. Collins 2000: ch. 13). Semiotics, now associated with discourse-theoretic models based in cultural studies, has its origins in mathematical logic ('the very logical positivism that so many present day constructionists profess to detest'; Hacking 2000: 42–3) (R. Collins 2000: 675–9). The 'linguistic turn' frequently identified with post-modernism is not a turn to language for the first time, but a series of shifts in which the semiotic exemplar migrates across disciplinary boundaries, from (positivist) mathematical logic and scientific method, to (structuralist) linguistics and cultural anthropology, to (post-structuralist) discourse theory in the humanities and literary criticism. As Collins says, 'the postmodernism of the late 1900s loudly echoes the themes of the mathematical foundations crisis, for those who have ears to hear' (2000: 855; see also pp. 10–15). Contemporary post-modern forms of constructionist relativism are the transformation of positivism, rather than the radical alternative implied by the rhetorical 'post' prefix.

Recovering Knowledge and the Incoherence of Relativism

The epistemological dilemma can now be seen as reflecting two sides of the *same* coin. The way out is to identify an alternative to the things that positivism and post-modernism *share*: the centrality of language to the problems of knowledge (the 'linguistic turn') and the reduction of knowledge to knowing. They also share the foundationalist principle that knowledge, in order to count as knowledge, must be *certain*: both assume an *infallibilist* position. They differ over whether such certain knowledge is possible. It is in this respect that Luntley (above) says that post-modernists are not post-modern enough: they remain within the positivist doxa as a sceptical heterodoxy to its orthodoxy. In a similar fashion, Niiniluoto describes them as 'disappointed absolutists': 'A dogmatic epistemological realist claims that we may gain absolutely certain knowledge about reality. A *critical* realist admits that both truth and certainty are matters of degree. Thereby a critical realist avoids the All-or-Nothing Fallacy typical of the sceptical doctrines favoured by disappointed absolutists' (Niiniluoto 2002: 95).

What this involves can be indicated by contrasting infallibilism with the *fallibilist* interpretation of the classical definition of knowledge. Niiniluoto does this in the following way ('iff' means 'if and only if'):

According to the *classical definition* of propositional knowledge,

(a) X believes that h iff   (1)
(b) h is true
(c) X has justification for h.

An infallibilist interprets condition (c) in the strong sense where justification implies certainty:

(c_1) X is certain that h.
        (Niiniluoto 2002: 80)

Fallibilism, within limits, weakens (c). Niiniluoto (ibid. 83) gives the following examples of 'weak' fallibilism: 'h is more probable or more acceptable than its rivals on the available evidence'; 'h is obtained by a reliable process'; 'X has the right to be sure that h'. In the last case he says that an example would be knowledge obtained from a teacher, because a teacher is someone who 'has the *duty* to tell the truth about h . . . . Lay knowledge about scientific matters is normally based upon such information from scientific "authorities" or experts' (ibid.).

Niiniluoto says: 'realism in epistemology should employ the fallibilist conceptions of probable, conjectural and truthlike knowledge – and thereby avoid the Scylla of infallibilism and the Charybdis of scepticism' (ibid. 85). The way out of the epistemological dilemma is to recast the absolutist formula for knowledge in a 'strong' fallibilist form:

X knows that h iff   (2)

(a') X believes that h is truthlike
(b') h is truthlike
(c') X has reason to claim that h is more truthlike than its rivals on available evidence.

(Ibid. 84)

What is being demanded by both positivism and post-modernism is a strong definition of knowledge that insists that it is certain beyond doubt – a 'grand' truth. But, as Luntley asks, 'How worrying is it that knowledge lacks foundations in this sense? The answer we give to this question depends, in part, on how high we set the standards of knowledge' (1995: 90).

> If the lack of foundations for knowledge amounts to the thesis that there is no mechanical recipe for knowledge, does this really amount to any more than the observation that all our knowledge is fallible? If so, surely this is correct? Our knowledge is fallible. Recognising our fallibility, the fact that for any claim we make it is possible that we could be shown to be wrong, is surely not a problem but a recognition of our humility? Indeed, if we think about it further it would seem odd, if not presumptuous, to think that we could be infallible in our knowledge claims. We are not that good. So, if the loss of foundations amounts to no more than a recognition of our fallibility, what's the problem? It is possible that Copernicus got it all wrong, but I bet he did not! (Luntley 1995: 90)

This is the same point as raised by the all-or-nothing fallacy. Fallibilism sits between absolutism and relativism by rejecting the all-or-nothing view. It recognizes that there is no way in which we can produce knowledge that is certain *beyond doubt*. This fact about the condition of knowledge (the human condition!) does not show that knowledge is impossible, but that it is *difficult*. 'That is to say, the lack of foundations does not show it is impossible to have standards of belief, but it does suggest that the enterprise of trying to gain something usefully called "knowledge" is fragile' (ibid. 87–8). It is fallibilism that puts the 'critical' into 'critical realism'.

The fallibilist approach is not concerned with measuring the truth of statements against the *world* and claiming that some provide a certain picture of how it actually is. Rather, it is concerned with the relative reliability of the *different* ways in which we produce knowledge. Relativism denies that it is possible to make such an assessment, because it holds that all judgements are framework- or standpoint-relative and, furthermore, *incommensurable* (i.e. because all meanings are discourse-relative, the terms of one discourse cannot be translated into those of another). Fallibilism is associated with a second principle: *reliabilism*: the recognition that although there are many ways in which we construct our beliefs, we can still have *standards* of belief by evaluating the reliability of our knowledge-producing procedures. As Muller says with reference to educational research:

> Inferences may be formally the same, but, especially insofar as they are intended as guides to action, as research for policy surely is, they are not all equally commendable. They differ in terms of their 'superempirical virtues' – consistency, explanatory power, fecundity, comprehensiveness and simplicity. They differ, in other words, in terms of *coherence* or 'epistemic gain'...
>
> 'Epistemic gain' is just what the constructivists don't want to concede….The critique of positivism may have displaced views of absolute truth and thereby of absolute epistemic privilege (views which had, after all, more to do with scientific self-image than anything else), but it does not displace the notion that we can discern epistemic gain. (Muller 2000: 152)

We can distinguish between knowledge-producing practices in terms of 'epistemic gain' and qualities such as 'consistency, explanatory power, fecundity, comprehensiveness and simplicity'. But what is it that makes the discernment of epistemic gain possible?

As Muller and others (e.g. Luntley 1995; Collier 1994: 1) point out, posing this issue at all can meet with incredulity – especially from scientists, but also from 'ordinary' people with their the common-sense realism. The reason for this is that what is being questioned is the idea of an independently existing reality, or what is known more formally as the principle of *ontological realism* (Niiniluoto 2002: ch. 2). It is the denial of this principle that is promoted by post-modernism and other varieties of relativism. We can advance on the issues involved here by reconfiguring the frame of reference. Within the circumference of the positivist/post-modern debate the question is: Do we have *certain* knowledge, yes or no? But if we step outside this framework of shared infallibilist presuppositions, that we have knowledge is not in serious doubt – We know we have it. The issues are: *What* is it? *How* do we make it? And how do we *recognize* it when we see it?

There are two kinds of ways in which we *know* we have knowledge. The first relate to the *incoherence* of attempting to deny that we do – the incoherence of relativism. The second concern *why* that denial is incoherent: with conditions that are consistent with both the common-sense and the critical realist conviction that there is, indeed, a mind-independent reality of which we can have knowledge (and which puts the 'realism' into 'critical realism').

The incoherence of relativism

There is a well-known logical objection to relativism: relativists claim that *all* truth is relative, but for this to be the case, there must be one truth that is *not* relative: namely, the truth that all truth is relative. Hence, it is *not* true that *all* truth is relative. To put this another way, in order to proclaim its truth, relativism must covertly exempt itself from its own principle that there is no truth. This covert exemption reappears again and again beneath the surface of relativist-type arguments. For instance, to argue that knowledge represents a male standpoint implicitly assumes (even when explicitly denying) an *independent* standpoint that is not gendered; for to argue that knowledge is male from a feminist standpoint would mean that it is so *only* from that standpoint (if all knowledge is standpoint-specific). Similarly, interest-theoretic approaches are vulnerable to their own principle: they must have an interest of their own (see also J. R. Brown 2001: 162–6 on 'underdetermination'). Arguments of this type are ensnared within an infinite regress in which one standpoint/perspective/interest is unmasked by another standpoint/perspective/interest that is unmasked by yet another standpoint/perspective/interest, *ad infinitum*.

A similar kind of problem arises with the principle of incommensurability: the relativist argument that all knowledge is relative to a framework or standpoint, and that we cannot judge one paradigm against another because the terms of each are non-translatable – in effect, those within different paradigms dwell in different worlds. The problem here is that if this were in fact so, we could never know, because the one thing we would never be able to see would be *difference* (Grayling 2001: 118–22; Fay 1996; Popper 1994). If we can only see other forms of life in terms of the meanings of our own, then we would not be able to see them as *different* – we could only see their meanings in terms of our meanings. Clearly, all cultures (and groups *within* cultures such as the sexes and classes and ethnic groups) are able to recognize difference. We know difference when we see it, are puzzled by it, and can ask the question 'What does this mean?' Rather than being trapped within exclusive, incommensurable standpoints, we can come to see things from the other's point of view – the Other is never quite so 'other' as post-modernists seem to think. It is a peculiarity of post-modernism that politically it makes much of identity, difference and recognition, while proposing an (anti-)epistemological position that renders such things invisible and impossible! The fact that we can be aware of difference shows that meanings are not simply framework-relative, and that frameworks are not incommensurable – meanings can be *meaningfully* transcribed from one framework to another; we can learn from others and 'change our minds' by empathizing with them. We can be persuaded by reason to change our view of the world however we conceive our 'interests'. How is this so?

Ontological realism and the simple truth

The incoherence of relativism points towards a defence of the possibility of knowledge by way of a 'transcendental' argument. This is how Luntley demonstrates the 'simple truth' of a mind-independent reality (the principle of ontological realism) (Luntley 1995: 110–14; Collier 1994: ch. 1; Bhaskar 1975). A transcendental argument has the form: 'Given that X pertains, certain other things, Y, must also be accepted, for these are commitments that cannot be denied, given X.' I will not follow Luntley's argument in detail here. Suffice to say that he legitimates the simple truth of ontological realism by demonstrating that 'the metaphysical model of objects as persisting in time and space is necessary in order that we are able to have thoughts about material objects' (1995: 113).

> The model of the world continuing independently of experience is something we are committed to on acceptance of our ability to have thoughts about material objects. Everyone accepts we have thoughts about material objects; that is not in question. Therefore, the idea of simple truth as outlined is legitimate. It cannot be questioned without denying that we can have thoughts about material objects. (Luntley 1995: 113)

In order to be able to *think* about material objects in the way we do, there must be material objects *existing* independently of our *experience* of them, such that we can make the distinction between a *judgement* and a *truth* (ibid. 28–32): 'The concept of judgement, the idea of saying something or thinking something, commits us to a concept of truth that is independent of us' (ibid. 28). When we make a judgement, we 'lay ourselves hostage to a notion of that which would show us wrong in our judgement'. Whenever we judge something to be the case, there is a state of affairs that could prove us wrong – the way the world actually is, is independent of how we judge it to be. Luntley calls this 'the basic constraint':

Basic constraint: Truth is independent of judgement, for it is a precondition of our making judgements that we acknowledge some notion of independent truth. (Ibid. 29)

It is precisely the possibility of a distinction between a judgement and a truth that relativism denies (truths are simply judgements masked in the service of power). This distinction constitutes the 'discursive gap' between Bernstein's two languages of description discussed in the previous chapter. If the constructionist view were right, then we could never be wrong – the world would be just how we think it to be. It could never, as Bernstein says, 'announce itself' to us. All of the people would be right all of the time, even though asserting contradictory truths.

Luntley argues that 'the scientific world-view' is continuous with our common-sense view: 'that the physical world continues in motion in ways independent of our observations of it . . . is the core common-sense belief that all cultures share, and that first reveals our acceptance of simple truth' (ibid. 129). This 'core common-sense belief' is the open door between cultures through which cross-cultural or cross standpoint communication is made possible. We *can* come to see the Other's point of view. For educators in the liberal-humanist tradition, this is the most fundamental principle for the moral intelligibility of our vocation.

The movement from positivism to post-modernism is one such that commitment to an infallibilist foundational model of truth shifts from optimism to pessimism. Positivists were hopeful absolutists; post-modernists are disappointed ones. Both assume the 'grand truth' of certainty. Against both, realism moves in a different direction: from the grand to the simple truth, from infallibilism to fallibilism, from absolutism or relativism to reliabilism, and on this basis we can carry on talking to each other, come to see things from the other's point of view, and be persuaded to change our minds. We can reject post-modernism's 'anarchic chaos of a plurality of chattering' (Luntley 1995: 124).

Intellectual Fields and the Social Production of Knowledge

The question 'What does it mean to see knowledge as social?' can now be posed again on the basis of the *simple* rather than the grand truth. Philosophically, the framework is established by the principles of ontological realism, fallibilism and reliabilism. Sociologically, the question has to do with how naturalized epistemology can be made substantive through sociological understandings of the forms and practices within and through which knowledge is produced. Avoiding the epistemological dilemma entails the complementarity of (naturalized) epistemology and the sociology of knowledge. The sociality of knowledge is approached through an *emergent* model. The key contrast is between the *reductionism* of constructionist approaches to knowledge and critical forms of sociological realism that define knowledge in terms of the *emergent* properties of knowledge production. Niiniluoto (2002: ch. 2) refers to this perspective as 'emergent materialism'.

An emergent model of the sociology of knowledge recognizes that (a) knowledge is an emergent product of the *systematic* qualities of knowledge-producing practices; (b) the latter are understood as distinct *modes of symbolic production*; and (c) these qualities, in their distinctive and *enduring* collective forms, constitute the *objects* of a critical realist sociology of knowledge. Emergence is crucial, because it grounds the principle of an *irreducible* autonomy to knowledge that is denied by reductionism and is also lacking in Bourdieu's relational model (chapter 3), where autonomy is, in the end, an 'illusion'. Emergence can be taken as bridging the philosophical and the sociological. This position does not deny the significance of external factors working within and upon knowledge, but it does insist that they are working upon something that is *real*: knowledge in its own right. At the same time, *contra* foundationalism, it also insists that knowledge is intrinsically social and historically located: this 'double determination' of knowledge is thoroughly historicized internally as well as externally. There are two issues to be addressed: (a) how to distinguish between knowledge and knowing, and (b) how to understand knowledge as a structured, emergent field of human practice.

Epistemology without a knowing subject

What is the difference between 'knowledge' and 'knowing'? Karl Popper argues:

> Traditional epistemology has studied knowledge or thought in a subjective sense – in the sense of the ordinary usage of the words 'I know' or 'I am thinking'. This, I assert, has led students of epistemology into irrelevancies: while intending to study scientific knowledge, they studied in fact something which is of no relevance to scientific knowledge. For *scientific knowledge* simply is not knowledge in the sense of the ordinary usage of the words 'I know'. (Popper 1972: 108).

Popper illustrates the distinction he is making with a number of examples, including: 'I *know* that Fermat's last theorem has not been proved, but I believe it will be proved one day.' And, 'Taking account of the present state of *metamathematical knowledge*, it seems possible that Fermat's last theorem may be undecidable' (ibid. 110).

Popper is distinguishing between a state of individual consciousness and the state of an intellectual field. The point of his argument is that the latter is not simply reducible to the former. The field of mathematical knowledge is not simply the aggregate of what people who know about mathematics *know*. In any particular state, an intellectual field might (and almost inevitably must) contain problems that no one has noticed or is interested in (Hacking 2000). This might well reflect contingencies such as state and commercially influenced research funding policies, intellectual fashion or, indeed, the class, ethnic and gendered composition of practitioners; but this does not mean that they are not *there* as immanent possibilities of the field. To give another illustration: the *rules* of chess make possible a large but calculable number of chess games. Historically it is contingent which particular ones are actually played and how often (and hence are *instantiated* in the experience of chess-players as knowing subjects). Hence we can distinguish between chess as a *field* of possibilities given by its rules and chess as an *experience* of chess-players, and the former can be described independently of the latter. Chess is not the experiences of people playing chess; it is what makes those experiences possible. In the same way, science is not what people doing science are doing when they do it; it is the condition for their being able to do it in the first instance.

The emergent model of science involves the idea that the 'domains of the real' that constitute the fields of the sciences are discontinuous in the sense here described by Niiniluoto:

> *Emergent* materialists accept the existence of some mental phenomena which are 'emergent', causally efficient properties of sufficiently complex material wholes or systems.... Such emergent properties of a system S cannot be derived by any true physical theory from information concerning the elements of S and their interrelations – in this sense, a whole may be 'non-additive', more than the sum of its parts. This view does not assume any substance outside matter, but acknowledges the existence of non-physical properties – therefore, it is also called *property dualism*. (Niiniluoto 2002: 22)

Particular sciences are specialized by the distinctive ontological properties of the domains to which they refer. It was because of this that Durkheim was so concerned to establish the autonomy of sociology as a science in its own right on the basis of a non-reductive understanding of the social. Hence, rather than a (positivistic) unitary model of science, we have a set of *sciences* that are methodologically specialized to their distinctive domains, but, nevertheless, sharing certain procedural protocols (the demand for logical rigour and consistency, respect for evidence, falsifiability, etc.) in virtue of which each can be seen as a 'science'.

Niiniluoto's reference to 'property dualism' and 'non-physical properties' concerns the fact, previously alluded to in relation to the rules of chess, that 'Cultural entities...are not "things" in an ordinary sense: they have a beginning in time, and perhaps sooner or later they will be destroyed, but they are not located in space. The "Eroica" Symphony does not exist in space, even though its various kinds of physical and mental instances are so located' (ibid. 24; see also Schmaus 1994: 50–1 on Durkheim). In the main, the social sciences are concerned with the description of the generative *principles* of social practice rather than with the generative powers of material *objects*. But such principles are no less *real* in their regulative power and material effects.

Science, Knowledge and Society

Durkheim wanted to be able to define science in such a way that it (a) allows for sociology to exist as a distinctive science in its own right, and (b) in doing so, provides the basis of legitimacy for a social class based in education in this new 'scientific' form. Durkheim originally encountered this 'emergent' model of science in the ideas of his teacher at the École Normale Supérieure, Emile Boutroux (Lukes 1973: 57–8). Durkheim's starting point was the view that 'A discipline may be called a "science" only if it has a definite field to explore. Science is concerned with things, realities. If it does not have a datum to describe and interpret, it exists in a vacuum.... Before social science could begin to exist, it had first of all to be assigned a definite subject matter' (Durkheim 1972: 57).

This argument about science is based upon the view that the universe of natural and social phenomena is made of classes (or domains) of 'things' of different types (what philosophers call 'natural kinds'), and that at least some of these things are open to systematic examination by human beings (Collier 1994). The different sciences are defined by the nature of their 'objects' and the forms of knowledge that we may have of them. Scientific forms of understanding become institutionally autonomized when the pursuit of knowledge becomes an end in itself, organized around the culture and practice of critical rational inquiry. Crucially, science is a historically evolved *collective* practice of systematic reflection, including, with the advent of sociology, reflection upon society itself (Durkheim 1956: 92–3; 1977: 340).

If sociology is to be a science in this sense, then two conditions have to be met. The first is that 'the social' does in fact constitute a distinctive domain of the real. Society is, as much as anything else, a part of nature, but a distinctive part with its own properties and principles and requiring its own science. The second condition is that for sociology to be an *autonomous* science, social phenomena must also be *irreducible* to lower-level phenomena such as those studied by psychology or biology. However adequate those disciplines may be for *their own level* of reality, they always leave a significant type of social phenomenon unexplained. This 'residual' (or 'emergent' level) constitutes the domain of sociology and its basis as an autonomous discipline. Sociology, and only sociology, can explain 'the social' (see the previous chapter and the 'duplex Self'). If the basis of a science is that it has a distinctive 'object' or field of phenomena, then for sociology to be 'the science of society', the social must exist as an independent domain that is in some crucial respect *external* to the individual – is 'thing like'. This idea of the social as 'external', as a *sui generis* reality, has provided one of the most intractable problems in the interpretation of Durkheim's theory, and it is especially important to see that Durkheim did not mean these things in a substantialist way – he goes to some length to make this clear.

It is important to realize that 'things' in this sense are not 'things' in the common-sense guise of physical objects. Durkheim rejected the metaphysical view that social facts had a material ontological status (or 'substance': this is represented in the quote below when Durkheim says, 'To treat the facts of a certain order as things thus is *not to place them in a particular category of reality*' (my emphasis). They are (materially) *real* only in their effects. Rules, for instance, are 'things' in this general sense, but are clearly not objects like stones or apples or cats. For Durkheim, the externality of the social is based in the fact that although it is 'within' us, it is not given to us in our immediate subjective experience – the relationship between subjectivity and the social is, as expressed in the previous chapter, 'tangential' or 'refracted', as in the relationship between the generative principle of *habitus* and its realization in social practice. Think of how we can be perfectly competent speakers without knowing the rules of grammar. An important implication of this is that 'the social' does not realize itself within subjectivity and behaviour in the *same form* as it exists at the level of the social (society) itself, in the same way that to describe the syntax of the sentence 'The cat sat on the mat' would not be merely to repeat it. Our speech is rule-governed, but the rules themselves exist outside immediate consciousness and have to be 'discovered' through a science of linguistics, rather than simply read off from natural speech. But when we discover them, the rules as written in the *theoretical* language of linguistics are *not* representations of 'things' that are real objects located materially in the world – we do not discover, and then describe, the laws of language deep in the middle of a jungle or hidden in a dark cave in the Atlas mountains. Things of this type have real properties and effects, but exist in time and not in space. Our theoretical accounts of such 'things' are not representations but homologues that model their constitutive possibilities and effects (as with Bernstein's principles of classification and framing).

In order to 'see' the social, we have, as it were, to go off at an angle. The social cannot be recovered from experience; neither is it reducible to it.

Just what is a 'thing'? A thing differs from an idea in the same way as that which we know from without differs from that which we know from within. A thing is any object of knowledge which is not naturally controlled by the intellect, which *cannot be adequately grasped by a simple process of mental activity*. It can only be understood by the mind on condition that the mind *goes outside itself* by means of observations and experiments, which move progressively from the more external and immediately accessible characteristics to the less visible and more deep-lying. To treat the facts of a certain order as things thus is not to place them in a particular category of reality, but to assume a certain mental attitude toward them; it is to approach the study of them on the principle that we are absolutely ignorant of their nature, and that of their characteristic properties, like the unknown causes on which they depend, cannot be discovered by *even the most careful introspection*. (Durkheim 1956: 58–9, my emphasis)

The mind 'goes outside itself' through theory and 'reflection' – the practice of science. Furthermore, this is a *collective* not an individual accomplishment. In these terms, social facts or things are *external* to the individual and independent of *immediate* awareness.

The Social Production of Knowledge

Approached from this point of view, knowledge as social is understood in terms of fields of intellectual production like those of material production: fields structured by distinctive social relations (generative principles) of production whereby existing symbolic materials are transformed into new ideas or artefacts (art objects, etc.): 'the social transformation of intellectually constructed objects' (Whitley 2000: 32). Following Popper, at one level these fields are 'problem fields': it is *problems* that form the focus of attention and activity. Following Randall Collins, problems have their sources in 'deep troubles':

> A deep trouble is a doctrine containing a self-propagating difficulty. Alternative paths open out, each of which contains further puzzles. Exploration of such conundrums becomes a chief dynamic on the medium to higher reaches of the philosophical abstraction-reflexivity sequence. Intellectual life gets its energy from oppositions. It thrives on deep troubles because these provide guaranteed topics for debate. Once a deep trouble is discovered, it tends to be recycled through successive levels of abstraction. The recognition of deep troubles enables us to reformulate with greater precision a basic principle of intellectual creativity: oppositions divide the attention space under the law of small numbers, not merely along the lines of greatest importance to the participants, but along the lines of the available deep troubles. (R. Collins 2000: 837)

There are three key points to be taken from Collins's statement and from his magnificent, seminal study *The Sociology of Philosophies*: (a) intellectual problem fields tend to be structured around three to five responses to a 'deep trouble' (the 'law of small numbers'); (b) they develop through a dynamic of differentiation and refinement of positions; (c) this dynamic of differentiation may be recapitulated at successively higher levels through 'abstraction-reflexivity' sequences – the elaboration of concepts over historical time. Fields are extended in time and space, based on networks amongst contemporaries structured around the set of contending positions just described and 'master–pupil' chains moving back and forwards in time and associated with canonical texts and debates. Collins's exhaustive and detailed work examines such fields in the major world civilizations and provides a foundational study and reference point for further work in this area.

Whitley argues that a distinctive feature of modern science is its concern with 'constant novelty production' (2000: 33). The pursuit of originality is the driving force of knowledge-producing systems, and this provides a distinctive value and motivation set for those working within them. Individuals, teams and institutions acquire reputations through innovation and originality. On the one hand, this entails a high level of individual autonomy in intellectual work, and on the other, Whitley argues, the field in itself provides the *collective* means and sources of validation. Knowledge is the product of the *field*, not of isolated individuals. Similarly, for Niiniluoto:

> [K]nowledge is a *social* product of a community of investigators. Peirce argued that 'logic is rooted in the social principle'. our interests should be identified 'with those of an unlimited community', since it is to be hoped that truth can be reached by a process of investigation that carries different minds 'by a force outside of themselves to one and the same conclusion'. Thus, the proper subject of knowledge is the *scientific community*. Popper expressed this idea by arguing that no conclusion of an individual scientist can be a result of science before it has gone through and passed a process of critical discussion within the scientific community.
>
> The social character of science is thus a consequence of the fallibility of individual scientists. But also any finite group of scientists can present only more or less conjectural knowledge claims. (Niiniluoto 2002: 94)

Whitley describes knowledge-producing fields as special forms of 'work organization' bearing similarities to professional and craft organizations, but differing as a result of the primary emphasis on constant innovation (what Collins terms 'rapid discovery'). In particular, although scholarship is continually pressured to be relevant to outside interests ('users'), in the first instance scholars produce for each other, because it is only *within* the field that innovation can be properly accessed and reputation conferred, withheld or fought over. As Schmaus (1994: 256–66) points out in his critique of interest theory, conditions such as these provide a distinctive and irreducible *cognitive* interest (and *habitus*) for knowledge producers qualitatively distinct from those invoked, reductively, by interest theory – an interest *internal* to knowledge itself.

Conclusion

The problems of knowledge are fundamental for both education and the sociology of education. For education there must be things *worth* teaching, and for the sociology of education there must be ways of producing knowledge that say something *worthwhile* about education. This chapter has addressed a crucial set of concerns that in education are represented in the conflict between progressivism and traditionalism, and in sociology between constructionism and foundationalism. It did so by taking two steps backwards, as it were, from the curriculum through the sociology of knowledge to the underpinning epistemological issues and debates, by examining three approaches to the relationship between knowledge and the social. These three approaches are foundationalism, constructionism and realism.

In different periods these basic positions were expressed in various secondary forms or schools: positivism, types of qualitative sociology, contemporary post-modernism, schools of Marxism and Durkheimian sociological realism, structuralism, post-structuralism, etc. Typically, foundationalism and constructionism (positivism and post-modernism) are presented as radical alternatives. However, on closer inspection, it appears that they have in common:

1 a commitment to the centrality of language,
2 the reduction of knowledge to knowing,
3 an infallibilist principle of certainty in knowledge (the 'grand' truth).

Their disagreement is over the possibilities of language and the realization of positivism's univocal, non-mediated language of description. Whereas positivism puts knowledge (language and experience grounded in sense data) outside history and society, constructionism reduces it to its particular local context of construction.

By contrast, the realist position agrees with constructionism that knowledge is social, but its model is non-reductive, paying attention, instead, to the collective conditions of knowledge production and their emergent properties. It agrees with positivism that knowledge is possible, but understands this in terms of its sociality rather than on the basis of a linguistic model, and as provisional rather than absolute. The realist position is supported by:

1 a fallibilist model of truth that accepts it as conjectural and provisional,
2 a reliabilist approach to evaluating truth claims,
3 an ontological realist acceptance of a mind-independent reality (the 'simple' truth).

In essence, the concern here is that the received default settings of the curriculum debate have made it virtually impossible to defend a *knowledge*-based model of education or an epistemologically strong version of sociology of education without that attempt being dismissed as inherently conservative and reactionary – as a defence of entrenched privilege and power relations. For a long time the sociology of education has been strongly influenced by epistemologically weak forms of relativistic constructionism. In both areas these two tendencies reinforce each other. It is strange that both these areas concerned with education want to *deny* its most fundamental category! The promise of critical realism lies in its capacity to support an anti-reductive position *vis-à-vis* the *autonomy* of knowledge.

Conclusion

This review of the sociology of education has stressed the complexities of education in society, and also of the ways in which sociology has attempted to understand them. Inevitably this leads to a somewhat inconclusive Conclusion, in that it recognizes that there are no simple solutions to the questions and issues raised and that there can be no simple checklist of results. It was stated in the Introduction that this book contains the thread of an argument and that it is against some things and for others. In part, the argument is reflected in the organization of the book. The first three chapters cover the key areas of educational differentiation, economy and class, state and status. In each case there is a *limitation* on explanation. We cannot adequately account for what we know to be the case about education in society and history by appeal to only one of those dimensions and the approaches to them. Each makes an important contribution, but in order for work in each of these areas to be complementary, there must be a 'device' that makes possible an exchange between them. It is here that there is a major problem. The last three chapters indicate possibilities for overcoming those limitations. The type of structural-dynamic model exemplified by Boudon's work, and the contextualization of decision-making processes that it offers, supplies, from this point of view, the best candidate for the systematic production of synthesizing explanatory accounts. However, this also requires a critical re-examination of epistemological debates in the field.

The problem alluded to above is that the field of sociology of education is characterized more by *discontinuities* than by complementarity (it is not unique in this). This is not simply a matter of the introspection of an array of specialized areas. It is underpinned by a certain epistemological stance that has informed the field for a long time. In essence, this stance is characterized by a tendency towards standpoint reductionism that, by default if not always explicitly, veers towards relativism. It is strange that the sociology of *education* should, from phenomenology to post-modernism, have such a predilection for sceptical, epistemologically weak perspectives. But then, this same predilection has also, in varieties of *progressivism*, been powerfully influential in educational discourse. The two field orientations, positivism/constructionism and traditionalism/progressivism, run parallel, and to a considerable extent the constructionist position in sociology has serviced (rather than problematized) the progressive position in education.

Constructionist approaches to the sociology of knowledge work through a kind of shaming by naming, in which knowledge that is held to be rationally objective and universal is revealed to be self-interested and partial. It is *named* in terms of the standpoint and interest of those whose perspective and position it is held to represent. The work of 'critical' sociology is to rewrite knowledge relations as power relations, as the relations between groups defined *experientially* as categories of knowers. On this basis the boundaries between perspectives and bodies of knowledge assume a strong classification. They represent the incommensurable standpoints and incompatible interests of competing power blocks engaged in zero-sum games. The field assumes the augmented form of what Bernstein calls a 'horizontal knowledge structure'. The standpoints are ideologized by being personalized in terms of categories that multiply through the fragmentation of post-structuralist hyphenation. The final chapter went to some length to demonstrate the incoherence and inadequacies of such reductionism, and presented a realist alternative that is concerned instead with *emergence*.

This condition reflects the absence of any alternative language through which to approach the problems of knowledge that supersedes the outmoded dichotomies and assumptions of an old debate over positivism. The position of positivism in the sociology of education (and elsewhere) is peculiar. As a credible philosophical project, it collapsed many years ago, yet its spectre continues to haunt us. It is long dead and gone, but it remains the touchstone for much contemporary thinking. As the final chapter attempts to demonstrate, the sceptical, relativistic logic of post-modernism makes sense and has force *only* in relation to positivism and in terms of the implicit acceptance of its foundationalist principles. Far from being a radical break with the past, post-modernism merely proliferates, in ever decreasing circles, the constructionist tautology. As Luntley observed, the real problem with post-modernism is that it is not *post-modern* enough! It is impervious to the considerable advances that have taken place in post-positivist philosophy of science, and to their implications for the sociology of knowledge.

What is at issue, here? The issues can be presented under three headings:

(1) **The sociology of education.** The point of the sociology of education must be to produce *knowledge*. It should produce (a) knowledge about education *in* society and (b) knowledge *about* society through education. Ideally these two should be complementary. As far as the former is concerned, much effort has been expended in examining the internal

processes of education, of schooling and the classroom. Undoubtedly this work has done much to sensitize us to the subtle dynamics of classroom interactions. But it contributes little to our understanding of the macro-dynamics of socio-educational regularities and changes. This is a sociology of *weak* effects – a sociology *for* education. Such accounts of the work-ings of educational processes require embedding within the dynamics of macro-structural models, so constituting a sociology of *strong* effects – a sociology *of* education (Moore 1996). The reductive logic of construction-ism renders this task difficult by ideologizing the distinction between mi-cro/qualitative and macro/quantitative approaches. In the earlier positivist debate of the early 1970s, structural and quantitative approaches came to be demonized as positivist and conservative. Today, post-modernism refines that caricature in terms of androcentrism and ethnocentrism. The need is for perspectives and approaches able to 'speak' to each other rather than assuming the incommensurability and exclusiveness of standpoint specificity.

(2) **Education.** The parallelism between the positivist/constructionist and traditionalist/progressive polarities of the sociological and educa-tional fields has effectively ceded, in a remarkable post-Enlightenment reversal, epistemologically powerful, strong forms of rational knowledge to conservatism. In education, there is no language whereby a knowledge-based curriculum can be supported for socially progressive purposes. The default settings of the field of educational discourse assume that the 'pro-gressive' position must be equated with epistemologically weak modes of curriculum and pedagogy. Or, the other way around, that epistemologi-cally weak forms of *progressive* education represent the best educational interests of working-class, ethnic-minority and female pupils. This asso-ciation has systematically encouraged teachers to approach such pupils in a therapeutic/compensatory rather than an academic mode, as *victims*, and has thereby preserved the privileged access of the social elite to epis-temologically powerful forms of knowledge. Basil Bernstein noted that the actual beneficiaries of 'progressive' education were the children of the professional middle class. Maureen Stone noted the consequences of this for black and working-class pupils in British schools. The gender revolu-tion was fuelled by middle- and upper-middle-class girls in 'traditional' schools accessing and, quite rightly, using to their advantage knowledge that confers not merely 'cultural capital' but *real* epistemic advantage. The category of knowledge is becoming increasingly crucial, because of the way in which the idea of a knowledge society is central to political and educational discourse. There is an urgent need to find a language that recovers knowledge for progressive purposes and opens it to all.

(3) **Knowledge.** The stance that underpins this book is one of a criti-cal emergent materialism that is concerned with the social *production* of knowledge rather than with anti-realist forms of constructionist idealism. Its concerns are historically produced and enduring collective relations of knowledge production and transformation, rather than experientially

based subjectivities of identity. To state this distinction is not to seek to establish one more form of an old tension within sociology. There is the recognition that the exploration of subjectivity is crucial, but that it must be located within its material conditions of existence, and that this can only be accomplished within a form of epistemological *realism* that properly acknowledges that those conditions are beyond us, yet can also become available to us through theory and scientific investigation. They can 'announce' themselves to us, and, crucially, in acknowledging them, we can adapt them. Constructionism is problematical only when inflated beyond a perspective and mode of social inquiry into an epistemology, where it collapses under the internal contradictions and incoherence of anti-realist relativism. Although in many key respects its criticisms of positivism are correct, it cannot in itself provide an epistemological alternative to positivism. Critical realism does, now, present such a rigorous and robust alternative, which might provide a framework within which constructionist insights can be reconstituted within material structures and their dynamics.

In essence, the basic argument here is that the sociology of education requires synthesizing frameworks and forms of general theory that can weld together into broader explanatory accounts what, currently, tend to stand as piecemeal and *ad hoc* fragments of knowledge. Crucially, this requires a return to realism in sociological inquiry and explanation – a return to *knowledge* in a strong form. Beyond that, this defence of knowledge supports the view that the intelligibility of teaching as a vocation resides in the conviction that there are things *worth* teaching – as Arnold said: 'the best that has been thought and known current everywhere' (1960: 70). And for sociology, that it can produce knowledge worth having.

References

Ahier, J. (1991) Explaining economic decline and teaching children about industry: some unintended continuities? In R. Moore and J. Ozga (eds), *Curriculum Policy* (Oxford: Pergamon Press/Open University Press).

Ahier, J. and Moore, R. (1999) Post-16 education, semi-dependent youth and the privatisation of inter-age transfers: re-theorising youth transitions. *British Journal of Sociology of Education*, 20 (4), 515–30.

Ahier, J., Beck, J. and Moore, R. (2003) *Graduate Citizens: Issues of Citizenship and Higher Education* (London: Routledge Falmer).

Alexander, J. C. (ed.) (1990) *Durkheimian Sociology: Cultural Studies* (Cambridge: Cambridge University Press).

Alexander, J. C. (1995) *Fin de Siècle Social Theory: Relativism, Reduction and the Problem of Reason* (London: Verso).

Althusser, L. (1972) Ideology and the ideological state apparatuses. In B. Cosin (ed.), *Education: Structure and Society* (Harmondsworth: Penguin Books).

Apple, M. (1997) What postmodernists forget: cultural capital and official knowledge. In Halsey et al. (1997).

Apple, M. (2000) Standards, markets and curriculum. In B. Franklin (ed.), *Curriculum and Consequence: Herbert M. Kliebard and the Promise of Schooling.* (New York: Teachers College Press, Columbia University).

Arnold, M. (1960) *Culture and Anarchy* (Cambridge: Cambridge University Press).

Arnot, M. (2002) *Reproducing Gender? Essays on Educational Theory and Feminist Politics* (London: Routledge Falmer).

Arnot, M. (2003a) A reconsideration of Paul Willis' 'Learning to Labour'. In C. Vincent (ed.), *Social Justice, Identity and Education* (London: Routledge Falmer Press).

Arnot, M. (2003b) Working class masculinities, schooling and social change: reconsidering the sociological significance of Paul Willis' 'Learning to Labour'. In G. Dimitriades and N. Dolby (eds), *Learning to Labour in New Times* (New York: Routledge).

Arnot, M. and Dillabough, J. (1999) Feminist politics and democratic values in education. *Curriculum Inquiry*, 29 (2), 159–90.

Arnot, M. and Whitty, G. (1982) From reproduction to transformation: recent radical perspectives on the curriculum from the USA. *British Journal of Sociology of Education*, 3 (1), 93–103.

Arnot, M., David, M. and Weiner, G. (1999) *Closing the Gender Gap: Post-War Education and Social Change* (Cambridge: Polity).

Ball, S. (ed.) (1992) *Foucault and Education* (London: Routledge).

Ball, S., Bowe, R. and Gerwirtz, S. (1997) Circuits of schooling: a sociological exploration of parental choice of school in social class contexts. In Halsey et al. (1997).

Barnett, C. (1986) *The Audit of War: The Illusion and Reality of Britain as a Great Nation* (London: Macmillan).

Beck, J. (1998) *Morality and Citizenship in Education* (London: Cassell).

Beck, J. (1999) Makeover or takeover? The strange death of educational autonomy in neo-liberal England. *British Journal of Sociology of Education*, 20 (2), 223–38.

Becker, H. (1971) Social class variations in the teacher–pupil relationship. In B. Cosin, R. Dale, G. Esland, D. Mackinnon and D. Swift (eds), *School and Society* (London: Routledge & Kegan Paul/Open University).

Bennett, N. (1976) *Teaching Styles and Pupil Progress* (London: Open Books).

Bernstein, B. (1973) *Class, Codes and Control*, vol. 1: *Theoretical Studies Towards a Sociology of Language* (St Albans: Paladin).

Bernstein, B. (1977) *Class, Codes and Control*, vol. 3: *Towards a Theory of Educational Transmission*, 2nd edn (London: Routledge & Kegan Paul).

Bernstein, B. (1990) *Class, Codes and Control*, vol. 4: *The Structuring of Pedagogic Discourse*: (London: Routledge).

Bernstein, B. (1996) *Pedagogy, Symbolic Control and Identity: Theory, Research, Critique*, 1st edn (London: Taylor Francis).

Bernstein, B. (2000) *Pedagogy, Symbolic Control and Identity: Theory, Research, Critique*, rev. edn (Oxford: Rowman & Littlefield).

Bernstein, B. (2001) Symbolic control: issues of empirical description of agencies and agents. *International Journal of Social Research, Methodology, Theory and Practice*, 4 (1), 21–34.

Bhaskar, R. (1975) *A Realist Theory of Science* (Leeds: Leeds Books).

Bilton, T. et al. (2002) *Introductory Sociology*, 4th edn (Basingstoke: Palgrave).

Blackburn, R. and Mann, M. (1979) *The Working Class in the Labour Market* (London: Macmillan).

Blanning, T. C. W. (2002) *The Culture of Power and the Power of Culture* (Oxford: Oxford University Press).

Bohman, J. (1991) *New Philosophy of Social Science* (Cambridge: Polity).

Bonnett, M. and Cuypers, S. (2001) Autonomy and authenticity in education. In N. Blake, P. Smeyers, R. Smith and P. Standish (eds), *The Blackwell Guide to Philosophy of Education* (Oxford: Blackwell).

Boudon, R. (1974) *Education, Opportunity and Social Inequality* (New York: John Wiley).

Boudon, R. (1977) Education and social mobility: a structural model. In J. Karabel and A. H. Halsey (eds), *Power and Ideology in Education* (New York: Oxford University Press).

Bourdieu, P. (1977) *Outline of a Theory of Practice* (Cambridge: Cambridge University Press).

Bourdieu, P. (1986) *Distinction* (London: Routledge).

Bourdieu, P. (1988) *Homo Academicus* (Cambridge: Polity).

Bourdieu, P. (1993) *The Field of Cultural Production: Essays on Art and Literature*, ed. R. Johnson (Cambridge: Polity).

Bourdieu, P. (1997) The forms of capital. In Halsey et al. (1997).

Bourdieu, P. and Passeron, J.-C. (1977) *Reproduction in Education, Society and Culture* (London: Sage).

Bowles, S. (1977) Unequal education and the reproduction of the social division of labour. In Karabel and Halsey (1977).

Bowles, S. and Gintis, H. (1976) *Schooling in Capitalist America* (London: Routledge & Kegan Paul).

Bradley, H. (1996) *Fractured Identities* (Cambridge: Polity).

British Journal of Sociology of Education (2002) Special issue: *Basil Bernstein's Theory of Class, Educational Codes and Social Control*, 23 (4).

Brown J. R. (2001) *Who Rules in Science* (Cambridge, MA: Harvard University Press).

Brown, P. (1987) *Schooling Ordinary Kids* (London: Tavistock).

Brown, P. and Lauder, A. H. (1997) Education, globalisation and economic development. In Halsey et al. (1997).

Brown, P. and Lauder, A. H. (2001) *Capitalism and Social Progress* (Basingstoke: Palgrave).

Calhoun, C., Li Puma, E. and Postone, M. (eds) (1993) *Bourdieu: Critical Perspectives* (Cambridge: Polity).

Chubb, J. and Moe, T. (1997) Politics, markets and the organisation of schools. In Halsey et al. (1997).

Cladis, M. (ed.) (1999) *Durkheim and Foucault: Perspectives on Education and Punishment* (Oxford: Durkheim Press Ltd).

Clark, T. (1973) *Prophets and Patrons* (Chicago: University of Chicago Press).

Cole, M. (ed.) (1988) *Bowles and Gintis Revisited: Correspondence and Contradiction in Educational Theory* (Lewes: Falmer).

Cole, M. (2003) Might it be in the practice that it fails to succeed? A Marxist critique of claims for postmodernism and poststructuralism as forces for social change and social justice. *British Journal of Sociology of Education*, 24 (4), 487–500.

Collier, A. (1994) *Critical Realism: An Introduction to Roy Bhaskar's Philosophy* (London: Verso).

Collins, C., Kenway, J. and McLeod, J. (2000) *Factors Influencing the Educational Performance of Males and Females in School and their Initial Destinations after Leaving School* (Deakin University).

Collins, R. (1977) Functional and conflict theories of educational stratification. In Karabel and Halsey (1977).

Collins, R. (1981) *The Credential Society* (New York: Academic Press).

Collins, R. (1990) The Durkheimian tradition in conflict sociology. In Alexander (1990).

Collins, R. (2000) *The Sociology of Philosophies: A Global Theory of Intellectual Change* (Cambridge, MA: Harvard University Press).

Dale, R. (1997) The state and the governance of education. In Halsey et al. (1997).

Dale, R. and Robertson, S. (2002) The varying effects of regional organisations as subjects of globalisation of education. *Comparative Education Review*, 46 (1), 10–36.

Dale, R., Esland, G. and MacDonald, M. (eds) (1976) *Schooling and Capitalism* (London: Routledge/Open University).

Daniels, H. (2001) Bernstein and activity theory. In Morais et al. (2001).

Davis, K. and Moore, W. E. (1953) Some principles of stratification. In R. Bendix and S. M. Lipset (eds), *Class, Status and Power* (London: Routledge).

Diaz, M. (2001) Subject, power and pedagogic discourse. In Morais et al. (2001).

Dummett, M. (1996) *Origins of Analytic Philosophy* (Cambridge, MA: Harvard University Press).

Durkheim, E. (1933) *The Division of Labour in Society* (London: Collier-Macmillan).

Durkheim, E. (1952) *Suicide* (London: Routledge & Kegan Paul).

Durkheim, E. (1956) *Education and Sociology* (Toronto: The Free Press).

Durkheim, E. (1961) *Moral Education* (New York: Free Press).

Durkheim, E. (1972) *Selected Writings*, ed. A. Giddens (Cambridge: Cambridge University Press).

Durkheim, E. (1973) *Emile Durkheim on Morality and Society*, ed. R. Bellah (Chicago: University of Chicago Press).

Durkheim, E. (1977) *The Evolution of Educational Thought* (London: Routledge).

Durkheim, E. (1995) *The Elementary Forms of Religious Life* (New York: Free Press).

Edgerton, D. (1996) *Science, Technology and the British Industrial 'Decline' 1870–1970* (Cambridge: Cambridge University Press).

Edmonds, D. and Eidinow, J. (2001) *Wittgenstein's Poker: The Story of a Ten-Minute Argument between Two Great Philosophers* (London: Faber).

Erikson, R. and Goldthorpe, J. (1993) *The Constant Flux: A Study of Class Mobility in Industrial Societies* (Oxford: Oxford University Press).

Fay, B. (1996) *Contemporary Philosophy of Social Science* (Oxford: Blackwell).

Floud, J. and Halsey, A. H. (1961) English secondary schools and the supply of labour. In Halsey et al. (1961).

Floud, M. and Hammer, M. (eds) (1990) *The Education Reform Act, 1988: Its Origins and Implications* (Lewes: Falmer).

Foster, P., Gomm, R. and Hammersley, M. (1996) *Constructing Educational Inequality* (Lewes: Falmer).

Freidson, E. (1994) *Professionalism Reborn: Theory, Prophecy and Policy* (Cambridge: Polity).

Gellner, E. (1992) *Reason and Culture* (Oxford: Blackwell).

Gephart, W. (1999) The realm of normativity in Durkheim and Foucault. In Cladis (1999).

Giddens, A. (1990) *The Consequences of Modernity* (Cambridge: Polity).

Gillborn, D. and Mirza, H. (2000) *Educational Inequality: Mapping Race, Class and Gender* (London: Commission for Racial Equality).

Gillborn, D. and Youdell, D. (2000) *Rationing Education: Policy, Practice, Reform and Equity* (Buckingham: Open University Press).

Gintis, S. and Bowles, H. (1988) Contradiction and reproduction in educational theory. In Cole (1988).

Giroux, H. (1997) Crossing the boundaries of educational discourse: modernism, postmodernism and feminism. In Halsey et al. (1997).

Goldthorpe, J. (1997) Problems of 'meritocracy'. In Halsey et al. (1997).

Goldthorpe, J. (2000) *On Sociology* (Oxford: Oxford University Press).

Gorard, S. (2000) One of us cannot be wrong: the paradox of achievement gaps. *British Journal of Sociology of Education*, 21 (3), 391–400.

Grace, G. (1997) Politics, markets and democratic schools: on the transformation of school leadership. In Halsey et al. (1997).

Grayling, A. C. (2001) *Wittgenstein: A Very Short Introduction* (Oxford: Oxford University Press.

Green, A. (1990) *Education and State Formation* (Basingstoke: Macmillan).

Haack, S. (1998) *Manifesto of a Passionate Moderate* (Chicago: University of Chicago Press).

Habermas, J. (1995) *Postmetaphysical Thinking* (Cambridge: Polity).

Hacking, I. (2000) *The Social Construction of What?* (Cambridge, MA: Harvard University Press).

Hakim, C. (2000) *Working-Lifestyle Choices in the 21st Century* (Oxford: Oxford University Press).

Halsey, A. H. (1971) Theoretical advance and empirical challenge. In Hopper (1971).

Halsey, A. H. (1997) Trends in Access and Equity in Higher Education: Britain in Internal Perspective. In Halsey et al. (1997).

Halsey, A. H., Floud, J. and Anderson, J. (eds) (1961) *Education, Economy and Society* (New York: Free Press).

Halsey, A. H., Heath, A. and Ridge, J. (1980) *Origins and Destinations* (Oxford: Clarendon Press).

Halsey, A. H., Lauder, H., Brown, P. and Wells, A. S. (eds) (1997) *Education, Culture, Economy, Society* (Oxford: Oxford University Press).

Harding, S. (ed.) (1987) *Feminism and Methodology* (Milton Keynes: Open University Press).

Hargreaves, A. (1989) *Curriculum and Assessment Reform* (Milton Keynes: Open University Press).

Hargreaves, D. (1967) *Social Relations in a Secondary School* (London: Routledge & Kegan Paul).

Harré, R. and Krausz, M. (1996) *Varieties of Relativism* (Oxford: Blackwell).

Hartley, D. (1997) *Re-Schooling Society* (London: Falmer).

Harvey, D. (1990) *The Condition of Postmodernity* (Oxford: Blackwell).

Hasan, R. (2001) The ontogenesis of decontextualised language: some achievements of classification and framing. In Morais et al. (2001).

Hatcher, R. (1998) Class differentiation: rational choices? *British Journal of Sociology of Education*, 19 (1), 5–24.

Heath, A. and McMahon, D. (1997) Education and occupational attainment: the impact of ethnic origins. In Halsey et al. (1997).

Hickox, M. (1982) The Marxist sociology of education: a critique. *British Journal of Sociology*, 33 (4), 563–78.

Hickox, M. (1986) Has there been a British intelligentsia? *British Journal of Sociology*, 37, 260–8.

Hickox, M. (1995) Situating vocationalism. *British Journal of Sociology*, 16 (2), 153–63.

Holmwood, J. (1995) Feminism and epistemology. *Sociology*, 29 (3), 411–28.

Hopper, E. (ed.) (1971) *Readings in the Theory of Educational Systems* (London: Hutchinson).

Hopper. E. (1977) A typology for the classification of education systems. In Karabel and Halsey (1977).

Horkheimer, M. and Adorno, T. (1979) *Dialectic of Enlightenment* (London: Verso).

Hough, J. R. (1987) *Education and the National Economy* (Lewes: Croom Helm).

Husén, T. (1979) *The School in Question* (Oxford: Oxford University Press).

Hymes, D. (1995) Bernstein and Poetics. In P. Atkinson, B. Davies and S. Delamont (eds) *Discourse and Reproduction: essays in honour of Basil Bernstein*, (Cresskill, NJ: Hampton Press).

Ignatieff, M. (1998) *The Warrior's Honour* (London: Chatto & Windus).

Israel, J. (2001) *Radical Enlightenment* (Oxford: Oxford University Press).

Jencks, C. (1972) *Inequality* (New York: Basic Books).

Jessop, B. (1993) From social democracy to Thatcherism: twenty-five years of British politics. In N. Abercrombie and A. Warde (eds), *Social Change in Contemporary Britain* (Basingstoke: Macmillan).

Jones, L. and Moore, R. (1996) Equal opportunities, the curriculum and the subject. In J. Ahier, B. Cosin and M. Hales (eds), *Diversity and Change: Education, Policy and Selection* (London: Routledge).

Jordan, B. (1996) *A Theory of Poverty and Social Exclusion* (Cambridge: Polity).

Karabel, J. and Halsey, A. H. (eds) (1977) *Power and Ideology in Education* (New York: Oxford University Press).

Keddie, N. (1971) Classroom knowledge In Young (1971).

Kitcher, P. (2001) *Science, Truth and Democracy* (Oxford: Oxford University Press).

Klee, R. (1997) *Introduction to the Philosophy of Science* (Oxford: Oxford University Press).

Kuhn, T. S. (1970) *The Structure of Scientific Revolutions* (Chicago: Chicago University Press).

Lopez, J. and Potter, G. (2001) *After Postmodernism: An Introduction to Critical Realism* (London: Athlone).

Lopez, J. and Scott, J. (2000) *Social Structure* (Buckingham: Open University Press).

Lukes, S. (1973) *Emile Durkheim, His Life and Works: A Historical and Critical Study* (London: Allen Lane).

Luntley, M. (1995) *Reason, Truth and Self: The Postmodern Reconditioned* (London: Routledge).

Mac an Ghaill, M. (1988) *Young Gifted and Black: Student Teacher Relations in the Schooling of Black Youth* (Milton Keynes: Open University Press).

Mannheim, K. (1952) *Essays on the Sociology of Knowledge* (London: Routledge & Kegan Paul).

Marx, K. (1976) *Capital*, vol. 1 (Harmondsworth: Penguin Books).

Mathieson, M. and Bernbaum, G. (1991) The British disease: a British tradition? In R. Moore and J. Ozga (eds), *Curriculum Policy* (Oxford: Pergamon Press/Open University Press).

Maton, K. (2000) Languages of legitimation: the structuring significance for intellectual fields of strategic knowledge claims. *British Journal of Sociology of Education*, 21 (2), 147–67.

Measor, L. and Sikes, P. (1997) Feminist theories. In B. Cosin and M. Hales (eds), *Families, Education and Social Differences* (London: Routledge).

Merton, R. (1959) *Social Theory and Social Structure* (New York: Free Press).

Mills, C. (1998) Alternative epistemologies. In L. A. Alcoff (ed.), *Epistemology: The Big Questions* (Oxford: Blackwell).

Mills, S. (1997) *Discourse* (London: Routledge).

Mirza, Heidi Safia (1992) *Young, Female and Black* (London: Routledge).

Moore, R. (1987) Education and the ideology of production. *British Journal of Sociology of Education*, 8 (2), 227–42.

Moore, R. (1988) The correspondence principle and the Marxist sociology of education. In Cole (1988).

Moore, R. (1996) Back to the future: the problem of change and the possibilities of advance in the sociology of education. *British Journal of Sociology of Education*, 17 (2), 145–62.

Moore, R. (2000) For knowledge: tradition, progressivism and progress in education – reconstructing the curriculum debate. *Cambridge Journal of Education*, 30 (1), 17–36.

Moore, R. and Maton, K. (2001) Founding the sociology of knowledge: Basil Bernstein, intellectual fields and the epistemic device. In Morais et al. (2001).

Moore, R. and Muller, J. (1999) The discourse of 'voice' and the problem of knowledge and identity in the sociology of education. *British Journal of Sociology of Education*, 20 (2), 189–206.

Moore, R. and Muller, J. (2002) The growth of knowledge and the discursive gap. *British Journal of Sociology of Education*, special issue: *Basil Bernstein's Theory of Class, Educational Codes and Social Control*, 23 (4), 627–38.

Moore, R. and Young, M. (2001) Knowledge and the curriculum in the sociology of education: towards a reconceptualisation. *British Journal of Sociology of Education*, 22 (4), 445–61.

Morais, A., Neves, I., Davies, B. and Daniels, H. (eds) (2001) *Towards a Sociology of Pedagogy: The Contribution of Basil Bernstein to Research* (New York: Peter Lang).

Mortimore, P. (1997) Can effective schools compensate for society? In Halsey et al. (1997).

Müller, W. and Karle, W. (1996) Social selection in educational systems in Europe. In J. Ahier, B. Cosin and M. Hales (eds), *Diversity and Change: Education, Policy and Selection* (London: Routledge).

Muller, J. (2000) *Reclaiming Knowledge* (London: Falmer).

Nash, R. (1999) Bourdieu, 'habitus' and educational research: is it all worth the candle? *British Journal of Sociology of Education*, 20 (2), 175–88.

Niiniluoto, I. (2002) *Critical Scientific Realism* (Oxford: Oxford University Press).

Noden, P. (2000) Rediscovering the impact of marketisation: dimensions of social segregation in England's secondary schools, 1994–99. *British Journal of Sociology of Education*, 21 (3), 371–90.

Ogbu, J. (1997) Racial Stratification and Education in the United States: why inequality persists, in Halsey et al. (1997).

Papineau, D. (ed.) (1996) *The Philosophy of Science* (Oxford: Oxford University Press).

Parsons, T. (1961) The school class as a social system: some of its functions in American society. In Halsey et al. (1961).

Poggi, G. (1972) *Images of Society: Essays on the Sociological Theories of Tocqueville, Marx, and Durkheim* (Stanford, CA: Stanford University Press).

Pollard, A. (ed.) (1994) *Look Before You Leap* (London: Tuffnell Press).

Popper, K. (1972) *Objective Knowledge: An Evolutionary Approach* (Oxford: Clarendon Press).

Popper, K. (1994) *The Myth of the Framework* (London: Routledge).

Power, S., Aggleton, P., Brannen, J., Brown, A., Chisholm, L. and Mace, J. (eds) (2001) *A Tribute to Basil Bernstein* (London: Institute of Education).

Power, S., Edwards, T., Whitty, G. and Wigfall, V. (2003) *Education and the Middle Class* (Buckingham: Open University Press).

Ramp, W. (1999) Durkheim and Foucault on the genesis of disciplinary society. In Cladis (1999).

Ranson, S. (1990) From 1944 to 1988: education, citizenship and democracy. In Floud and Hammer (1990).

Reay, D. (1998) Engendering social reproduction. *British Journal of Sociology of Education*, 19 (2), 195–210.

Reeves, F. and Chevannes, M. (1988) The ideological construction of black underachievement. In M. Woodhead and A. McGraph (eds), *Family, School and Society* (London: Hodder & Stoughton).

Rikowski, G. (1996) Left alone: end time for Marxist education theory? *British Journal of Sociology of Education*, 17 (4), 415–52.

Ringer, F. (1969) *Decline of the German Mandarins: German Academic Community, 1890–1933* (Cambridge, MA: Harvard University Press).

Ringer, F. (1977) Cultural transmission in German higher education in the nineteenth century. In Karabel and Halsey (1977).

Rutter, M., Maughan, B., Mortimore, P. and Ouston, J. (1979) *Fifteen Thousand Hours: Secondary Schools and their Effects on Children* (London: Open Books).

Sarup, M. (1977) *Marxism and Education* (London: Routledge & Kegan Paul).

Savage, M. and Egerton, M. (1997) Social mobility, individual ability and the inheritance of class inequality. *Sociology*, 31 (4), 645–72.

Savage, M., Barlow, J., Dickens, P. and Fielding, T. (1992) *Property, Bureaucracy and Culture: Middle-Class Formation in Contemporary Britain* (London: Routledge).

Schmaus, W. (1994) *Durkheim's Philosophy of Science and the Sociology of Knowledge* (Chicago: University of Chicago Press).

Scott, J. (1996) *Stratification and Power* (Cambridge: Polity).

Scruton, R. (1997) Kant. In *Oxford Past Masters. German Philosophers* (Oxford: Oxford University Press).

Scruton, R. (1999) *Spinoza* (London: Routledge).

Sewell, T. (1997) *Black Masculinities and Schooling: How Black Boys Survive Modern Schooling* (Stoke on Trent: Trentham Books).

Singh, P. (2001) Pedagogic discourses and student resistance in Australian secondary schools. In Morais et al. (2001).

Smith, D. and Tomlinson, S. (1989) *The School Effect: A Study of Multi-Racial Comprehensives* (London: Policy Studies Institute).

Stone, M. (1981) *The Education of the Black Child in Britain* (London: Fontana).

Turner, B. (ed.) (1993) *Citizenship and Social Theory* (London: Sage).

Turner, B. (1999) *Classical Social Theory* (London: Sage).

Turner, R. (1961) Modes of ascent through education: sponsored and contest mobility. In Halsey et al. (1961).

Usher, R. and Edwards, R. (1994) *Postmodernism and Education* (London: Routledge).

Walkerdine, V. (1984) Developmental psychology and the child-centred pedagogy: the insertion of Piaget into early education. In J. Henriques, W. Holloway, C. Urwin, C. Venn and V. Walkerdine, *Changing the Subject* (London: Methuen).

Ward, S. (1996) *Reconfiguring Truth: Post-Modernism, Science Studies and the Search for a New Model of Knowledge* (New York: Rowman & Littlefield).

Weber, M. (1930) *The Protestant Ethic and the Spirit of Capitalism* (London: George Allen & Unwin).

Weber, M. (1966) *The Sociology of Religion* (London: Methuen).

Weber, M. (1967) *The Religion of China* (London: Collier–Macmillan).

Weiner, G. (1994) *Feminisms in Education* (Buckingham: Open University Press).

Weiner, G., Arnot, M. and David, M. (1997) Is the future female? Female success, male disadvantage and changing gender patterns in education. In Halsey et al. (1997).

Weiss, L. and Hobson, J. (1995) *States and Economic Development* (Cambridge: Polity).

Wells, A. S. and Serna, I. (1997) The politics of culture: understanding local political resistance to detracking in racially mixed schools. In Halsey et al. (1997).

Westergaard, J. (1995) *Who Gets What: The Hardening of Class Inequality in the Late Twentieth Century* (Cambridge: Polity).

Whitley, R. (2000) *The Intellectual and Social Organisation of the Sciences* (Oxford: Oxford University Press).

Whitty, G. (1991) The New Right and the national curriculum: state control or market forces? In R. Moore and J. Ozga (eds), *Curriculum Policy* (Oxford: Pergamon Press).

Whitty, G. (1997) Marketisation, the state, and the re-formation of the teaching profession. In Halsey et al. (1997).

Wiener, M. (1981) *English Culture and the Decline of the Industrial Spirit 1850–1980* (Cambridge: Cambridge University Press).

Willis, P. (1977) *Learning to Labour* (Farnborough: Saxon House).

Woodhall, M. (1997) Human capital concepts. In Halsey et al. (1997).

Wright, C., Weekes, D., McGlaughlin, A. and Webb, D. (1998) Masculinised discourses within education and the construction of black male identities amongst African Caribbean youth. *British Journal of Sociology of Education*, 19 (1), 75–88.

Youdell, D. (2003) Identity traps or how black students fail: the interactions between biographical, sub-cultural, and learner identities. *British Journal of Sociology of Education*, 24 (1), 3–20.

Young, M. F. D. (ed.) (1971) *Knowledge and Control* (London: Collier–Macmillan).

Young, M. F. D. (1998) *The Curriculum of the Future* (London: Falmer).

Index